Missing
411

• WESTERN U.S. & CANADA •

Unexplained Disappearances of
North Americans that have never been solved

DAVID PAULIDES

ISBN: 1466216298
ISBN 13: 9781466216297
Library of Congress Control Number: 2011914493
North Charleston, South Carolina

CONTENTS

ABBREVIATIONS

BCI	Bureau of Criminal Investigation
BIA	Bureau of Indian Affairs
CCC	California Conservation Corp
DOI	Department of the Interior
FBI	Federal Bureau of Investigation
FLIR	Forward Looking Infrared Radar
NPS	National Park Service
RCMP	Royal Canadian Mounted Police
SAR	Search and rescue
USFS	United States Forest Service
WMA	White Male Adult

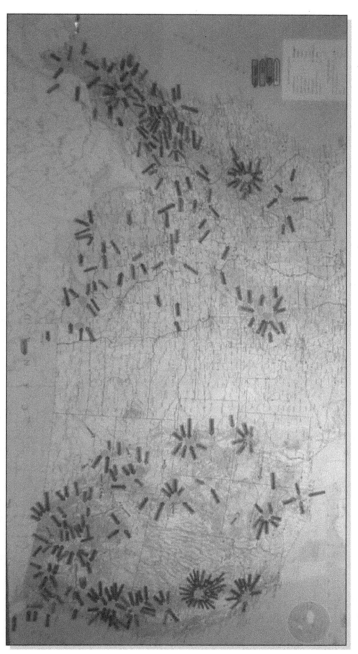

This map identifies the missing people included in both versions of this book, covering the eastern and western United States. The twenty-eight large dots on the map represent clusters of missing people. When you study the map, you can clearly see a defined area in the middle of the United States where there are no missing people fitting the book's criteria. This made it easy to decide where to split the versions of this book—I could easily write an entire book on the many disappearances in these states—thus no marks on the map. The light-colored tabs represent females; the dark tabs represent males.

INTRODUCTION

Several years ago I was visiting a national park in the United States and asking a series of questions to a law enforcement supervisor. It soon got around the park that I was making inquiries into specific topics that caused a great deal of conversation among the park's employees. The park was at its tourist capacity, so I was staying at a lodge outside the park's perimeter. The night after I made the inquiry at the park, an off-duty ranger in street clothing knocked at my door. The conversation I had with this ranger dictated my investigative course for the following three years.

The ranger introduced himself and stated that he had read my books. He said that he knew of my law enforcement and investigative background and felt that I was the perfect individual to research an issue that he had known concerned him for many years.

I sat in my room at the lodge and listened to the ranger tell me about a series of missing people inside our national parks. The ranger stated that the events were very unusual, many people were never found, and the park service was doing everything possible to keep a lid on the publicity surrounding the missing. He explained that non–law enforcement employees weren't privy to all the information, but that the upper-echelon law enforcement supervisors inside the park service were concerned about the numbers and certain facts surrounding specific cases. I asked the ranger if this was exclusively at the park where they were employed, or if it occurred at other parks as well. The ranger stated that it appeared to be happening at others parks, but the totality of the issue wasn't completely understood by the personnel communicating the information.

I am purposely excluding the gender and park where the ranger was working in an effort to conceal the ranger's identity. We never had another conversation after that, but I did leave my e-mail address in case the ranger wanted to forward any further information. I never heard from the ranger again.

Driving home the following morning, my mind was racing. I had phoned a few friends in law enforcement and told them of my discussion. I asked them for contacts they may have inside the NPS (National Park Service). When I eventually got home, I immediately started to work on my computer and was shocked by what I found. Yes, there were several people missing from many national parks. Yes, the stories behind these people disappearing were quite unusual and bothersome. I was hooked on the investigation.

Information

Documents to support the stories in this book were found through exhaustive searches of various periodicals' archives. I also made numerous FOIA (Freedom of Information Act) inquiries through the United States federal government; sometimes my requests were granted, and sometimes they were denied.

Clusters

After spending months, and eventually years, working on the missing person project, I started to realize that many of the missing people in rural areas of North America were in "clusters." When I realized they were in clusters, meaning their disappearances could be loosely grouped together by location, time, and type of occurrence, I started to have a different perspective on this issue. Understand that clusters can also include people who went missing hundreds of miles apart if the facts of the disappearances are similar.

There was a point in my law enforcement career when I worked as a detective attached to a special team investigating high-profile cases. One of the cases we participated in was a series of missing girls from California. The FBI had made a presentation showing that several girls were missing in a corridor close to a major interstate that bisects the state. Similarities in age, appearance, facts of the actual incidents, and proximity to the highway showed a consistency that linked the girls' disappearances. The large geographical spread on these cases made investigations cumbersome and difficult. The circumstances I have just described apply—in much smaller geographical regions—to clusters of missing people across North America.

Four national parks in the United States have clusters of missing people with highly unusual stories. The missing people issue is not a recent development in these areas; in some regions it has been occurring for as long as centuries and is still happening. Each National Park on this list has their own group of missing people.

The four parks are:

1. Yosemite National Park
2. Great Smoky Mountains National Park (This area is discussed in book #2 (Missing 411, Eastern United States), which includes disappearances in the eastern United States.)
3. Glacier National Park
4. Crater Lake National Park

The FOIA was signed into law to give citizens the right to access reports and information held by the government. I have requested case files on many of the missing people in the parks listed above via the FOIA process. Only in a few cases were the documents withheld. Why the reports were not released by the NPS is the million-dollar question. When someone has been missing for thirty years (Stacy Arras, Yosemite, for example), and the case has been classified as a missing person with no suspects (like many others that were released), why would they withhold the case report?

Here is a list of the clusters in the western United States:

Northern California/	Northern California/
Mount Shasta	Sierra Nevada
Meru	Suden
Knowles	Cooper
Kuntz	Manial
Kantonen	Luchessi
Zaccolini	Burmer
Sparks	
McKoen	
Landers	
Fullmer	

Southern California
Barkley
Mitchell
Hatch
Gonzales
Bowers
Baumgarten
Zweig

Washington Coast
Bratcher
Inman
Herda
Baum
Flink
Matlock

Washington, Mid–North Cascades)
Piatote
Duffy
Klein
Brown
Goodwin
Panknin

Southern Idaho
Bendele
Felix
Lobears

Montana
Prange
Jordan
Marshall
Ginevicz
Curtis

Washington-Oregon-Idaho Border
Woollett
Davis
Boatman
McDonald

Washington-Idaho Border
Weflen
Swanson
Finley
Schaper

Western Montana
Prange
Jordan
Marshall
Curtis

Wyoming
Norris
Crouch
Olson
mean
Pehringer
Bechtel

Southern Montana
Little Light
Springfield
Bent
Koza
Mason

Rocky Mountains National Park, CO
Polley
Atadero
Devitt
Gerling
Baldeshwiler
Vanek

New Mexico
Cross
McGee
McGee
Nadel
Riffin
Tresp

Utah
Edmonds
Ewer
Bardsley
Hawkins
Daines
Jaramillo/Reese

Southern Arizona
Hays
Kalaf
Fugate
McDonald

Central Arizona
McGee
Shelton
Shellenberger
Parscale
Sisco
Riggs
Betts

Glacier National Park, MT
Hwa
Lumley
Whalen
Whitehead/Whitehead

The lists for Yosemite and Crater Lake are too lengthy to post here.

Clusters of missing people are not exclusive to the United States. Such clusters exist in Vancouver Island, British Columbia, and the area between Jasper, Banff, and Calgary, Alberta, Canada, and Timmins, Ontario. However, the largest cluster of missing people in the western United States is in Yosemite National Park; no other location in the West comes close. I have made the state of Pennsylvania a cluster in itself, although it is not included in the twenty-eight specific clusters on the map of the United States. The amount of young children that have disappeared in the Keystone State is baffling.

This study had to be split into two books because it became extremely long, and some stories had to be redacted. One section that suffered removal was British Columbia. An area near the center of the province is named The Highway of Tears. Dozens of women have been reported missing—and never found—along this stretch of roadway between Prince George and Prince Rupert. A special RCMP (Royal Canadian Mounted Police) task force has been working these cases for a number of years. Another major investigation focuses on a series of tennis shoes that have washed onto beaches in British Columbia with a human foot inside. As of December 2010, seven feet have been found in Canada, three in Washington, and one on a beach outside Crescent City, California. One foot has been identified as an individual who was depressed and thought (but not confirmed) to have committed suicide. An RCMP task force is still actively investigating these cases.

Two U.S. states had to be removed from the book because of the large number of missing in each location. I could write volumes about the missing people in Florida and Texas, each equally unusual and unique. Also, I only include two stories about disappearances in Alaska, even though chapters could be written about the many unusual missing person cases in that state.

Unique Factors of Disappearances

The factors I describe here relate to the entire study of missing people and not solely to this book. Many of these factors are quite evident in the eastern United States, while others just are in the West.

As you read the story behind each missing person, you will start to hear a consistent theme that includes facts found in other disappearances. The criteria I used to select specific cases for this book include a number of factors that are common among the disappearances:

Rural setting. All of the missing people outlined in this project disappeared from a rural setting, not a city or downtown location. There were usually no witnesses, significant cover, and difficult terrain.

Dogs. Dogs play a major role in many of the disappearances. Sometimes the dogs disappear with the victim and are found later with the person; other times the dogs disappear and return home without the person; sometimes the dogs disappear and are never found.

Bloodhounds/canines can't track scent. A very unusual trend I found in many of these cases is that expert tracking dogs were brought to the scene of the disappearance but were not successful at doing their job. The dogs were given the person's scent via a worn shoe or shirt; they were brought to the location where the person was last seen; but they either refuse to track or can't pick up a scent. This behavior has occurred too many times to ignore, though it's not understood why this occurs.

Storms. Soon after a person has gone missing, reports of storms hitting the area of the disappearance seem to occur more than would be normal. This has happened in all four seasons, even when a storm would seem unusual. The storms have caused delays in starting the SAR (search and rescue) and have eliminated tracks and scents for tracking.

Afternoon disappearance. From the information gleaned from the project, the most common time for a disappearance to occur is between 2:00 p.m. and 5:00 p.m.

Swamps and briar patches. Many of the missing are found in the middle or on the perimeter of a swamp and/or briar patch. Some rescuers commented on the unusual locations where children, in particular, were found: they simply don't understand how they got there.

Conscious or semiconscious state. I believe this is one of the most unusual conditions found in many missing person cases: being found in a conscious or semiconscious state. I understand that when a person goes missing for an extended period of time without food or water, hallucinations can occur; however, these conditions were prevalent even when those factors did not exist. You will read about cases where the missing were found unconscious, lying on the ground, and when questioned later, have no recollection of how they went missing. In some cases the missing do recall the facts surrounding their disappearance, and those facts make for fascinating reading.

Berries. The fact that berries and berry bushes play a common role in many disappearances is quite intriguing. People disappear and are found in the middle of berry bushes; they go missing while picking berries; and some are found while eating berries. The connection between some disappearances and berries cannot be denied.

Clothing removed. In numerous cited cases, the missing person is found and at least one major piece of clothing has disappeared, or they are inexplicably completely naked. While this may sound like a minor issue, it isn't once that you will read the facts surrounding these cases and understand why these details are common in each incident. While searchers scour every inch of the quadrant (from the point last seen to where the missing was found), the clothing is often never found. Some search manuals indicate that children remove their clothing when it is extremely detrimental to their survival; however, the facts surrounding these cases do not seem to support that assertion.

The missing is found in an area previously searched. Another common factor found in several SARs: the missing person is found in a previously-searched area. Searchers are often adamant that the area where the person was found had been thoroughly searched numerous times in the past. The missing are also sometimes found on a major trail that searchers had used daily. SAR commanders are often mystified by the location the missing is discovered.

Cases to Study

We will always learn more by studying a missing person case in which the person was found than if the person was never located. Many of the cases in this book are of people who disappeared and were later found. Many of them were found significantly outside the bounds of where traditional SAR commanders would believe a person would travel. SAR teams use guidelines based on the age of the missing, the terrain, the weather, and other variables, such as charts and tables that have been successfully utilized in the past. The SAR commander will set perimeters to search based on the information they have available.

SAR Teams

The vast majority of SAR teams in the United States comprise of committed volunteers. These people are not monetarily compensated but do the job merely for the love of helping others. They train on their own time, with their own equipment, at their own expense. There are few rewards for being a SAR member until you are able to find someone in serious need of your services. SAR members are also on-call for service on weekends, holidays, and nights, and their agency expects them to respond to every event. These are the people who actually go into the field, pound the trails, and do the difficult work. Anytime you have the opportunity to meet a SAR team member, tell them how much you appreciate their service.

The individuals placed in charge of setting search guidelines are usually specialists inside the NPS, the state parks, the USFS (United States Forest Service), or the county sheriff's office. The amount of experience these people have, or how many SAR classes they have taken, is always questionable. The SAR commander could be an experienced veteran or a newbie. It's really a crapshoot, and therein lies one of the problems of SAR: You definitely do not want a newbie learning the trade while they are searching for *you*.

Chapters

This book is divided into chapters based on regions of the United States and Canada. The missing are listed in the state/province where they disappeared, and then in the clusters where they would be grouped. I also developed three subcategories for missing people throughout North America: Farmers, Sheepherders, and Berry Pickers. Each represents people who were lost in the wild and, in most instances, were alone. These three groups are included in the eastern United States edition of this book.

Every story in this book is 100 percent factual. As you read, attempt to keep an open mind and attitude regarding its contents. Understand that I didn't set out to locate stories that supported a hypothesis; the hypothesis was developed after I finished investigating the cases. I also didn't search for stories that mimicked each other. There was already an overwhelming amount of data that seemed to be cut from the same mold. Stories were not selected based on their location; instead, they were chosen because they fit my criteria.

Some areas in North America are extremely rural, have significant vegetation, and do not have clusters of missing people. However, there seems to be something unique about the areas where the clusters occur, and what causes that uniqueness is part of the intrigue of this book.

CHAPTER ONE

Yukon Territory

While the Yukon Territory does not have a cluster of disappearances, I have included the Bart Schleyer story because his disappearance closely mimics others identified in this book.

Missing Person	Date, Missing	Age•Sex
Bart Schleyer	09/14/04	49•M

**If no time is listed then the time is unknow.

Bart Schleyer
Missing 09/14/04, Reid Lakes, Yukon Territory, Canada
Age at disappearance: 49

If there ever was an outdoorsman who would be considered a man's man, it was Bart Schleyer. Bart was born in Cheyenne, Wyoming, in 1954. Due to the location of his birth and the fact that his father, a physician named Otis, was an avid hunter, Bart's life was destined to be lived outdoors. His father took him around the world on hunting adventures, and this had the boy hooked on the hunt, but not the kill.

Bart graduated in 1979 from Montana State University (MSU) with a master's degree in wildlife biology. He wrote his thesis on bear activity in Yellowstone National Park and attempted to understand how the bear reacted when confronted by humans. Bart later worked for the Interagency Grizzly Bear Study at MSU and learned live bear trapping skills. Later in life he became the world master of luring bears into traps. Many professionals stated that Bart knew more about bear behavior, tracking, and luring than anyone in the world.

Bart worked for a variety of groups after he graduated from college. At one point he was employed by the Montana Fish and

Game Department, where he would set bear trap lines in some of the toughest terrain in the Bob Marshall Wilderness. Once the bears were trapped, Bart would install collars and follow the bears throughout the summer to study their behavior.

One of the many stories about Bart's athletic prowess tells of days he spent hiking the mountains, tracking and walking for some twelve hours—where there were no trails—before heading back to his cabin. Once home, Bart would start an exercise regime of push-ups, squats (using logs he had crafted for the task), and a variety of other exercises that would cripple the average man. Remember, Bart was doing these exercises after a full day in the mountains!

He moved to Alaska for a short period and studied taxidermy while enjoying the Alaskan outdoors. For Bart's next adventure, he was recruited by a friend to travel to the Russian Far East to study and trap Siberian tigers. Bart was again the optimum expert for trapping, collaring, and studying the tigers. It was also in Russia that he developed a relationship with a beautiful Russian woman, Tatiana. Bart and Tatiana had a son, Artyom. This was the first time he had dedicated time to a relationship and family.

In 2002 Bart moved to the Yukon Territory and called White-horse home. He developed a keen interest in the Yukon wildlife and was specifically interested in bowhunting sheep and moose. As a hunter, Bart had conquered almost every continent and most big game with his bow. He felt it offered a bigger challenge than hunting with a rifle. It should be clear to all readers that bowhunting is a skill that can take years to perfect. You must be stealthy, patient, and committed to be a successful bowhunter. Bowhunting is much more dangerous than using a firearm because you must get very close to your game. You will read about bowhunters in this book that disappeared and were never found.

On September 14, 2004, Bart arranged for a floatplane to fly him to Reid Lakes. The lakes sit approximately 110 miles east of the Alaska border, five miles west of the Klondike Highway, and ten miles south of McQuesten, Yukon. There are four major lakes in the Reid Lakes chain, with the largest being 1¼ miles long and about the same distance wide. The lakes are isolated from the highway by a river, and travelers cannot get to the lakes unless they fly in.

Bart's plane successfully landed at the largest of the Reid Lakes and dropped him and his gear on the shoreline. Bart not only took a tent and supplies but also an inflatable raft to meander around the lake.

I have spent many weeks in the Yukon and developed a few contacts. Warren Lafave is the owner of Inconnu Lodge in the eastern side of the province. When I asked Warren for a provincial wildlife contact to discuss the region around Reid Lakes, he sent me to Rick Fernel.

Rick spent twenty-five years as a wildlife biologist for the Yukon Territory before retiring in 2008. I asked Rick about the Reid Lakes area because I wanted to understand what type of wildlife and habitat it offers. Rick immediately stated that he knew about the Bart Schleyer incident and could never understand why he went to Reid Lakes. He said the fishing wasn't good at the lakes, and there wasn't much wildlife in the area. Rick made it clear that there were many other locations with better fishing and outstanding wildlife opportunities that put Reid Lakes to shame.

Bart had scheduled his floatplane to pick him up at Reid Lakes on September 28. The pilot arrived at the lake, pulled up to Bart's camp, and was confused by what he found.

Bart's tent was found knocked down, but the pilot was not sure by what. Near the tent, he found Bart's backpack with bear spray, along with his VHF radio and a knife. The pilot yelled for Bart but did not get a response. He imagined that if Bart had left, he would have taken his backpack and supplies. The pilot left the area and contacted RCMP, who later contacted friends.

The RCMP initially had a very limited role in the search for Bart. After he was reported missing, the RCMP did a flyby over Reid Lakes. That was it. Bart's friends arrived at the area and immediately went across the lake from his tent. Here they found his inflatable boat. Sixty feet inland from the boat, the team found a bag full of gear. Leaning next to the bag on an adjacent tree was Bart's bow and arrows. The bag of supplies had not been touched, and it was obvious to his friends that he had been sitting on it. They said it appeared as though Bart had been calling moose from the location, so they continued to scour the area. A short distance away, they found a camouflage facemask with a small amount of blood on it. They then decided to call the RCMP back to the scene.

On October 3, 2004, Yukon RCMP and conservation officers went to Reid Lakes in mass and set a grid search pattern in an attempt to find Bart Schleyer. Sixty yards from the bow, searchers found a skull and a few teeth. They also found a pair of camouflage pants, a camera, and a few small bones. The teeth were later positively identified as Bart's. Most investigators would stop the investigation at this point and claim a grizzly killed the wildlife biologist. But there were too many strange circumstances to claim a grizzly had killed a man who lured grizzly bears for a living.

For starters, there was significant bear and wolf scat at the scene. Many samples of scat were recovered and sent to a lab for testing. One issue that completely baffled investigators: there was no clothing found in any of the bear scat. When bears eat people, they eat everything—clothing, jewelry, anything you are wearing goes in and eventually comes out. It was also odd that Bart's pants were lying on the ground near the scene, almost as though he had removed them, or they had somehow come off. Most of the clothing that Bart would have been wearing was never found, even after a wide and comprehensive search of the area.

Conservation officers at the scene knew that bears usually cache their kills, burying them for a later meal. A thorough search of the Reid Lakes area didn't produce any evidence of a cache or any bloody ground from a body being dragged or wounded. The other troubling issue is that there was no sign of a struggle anywhere in the Reid Lakes camp where Bart was staying or near his bow. No moss, tundra, or branches were disturbed; it was a very calm site.

Several investigators made statements that his death is a mystery, and the idea that a bear killed him does not make any sense. People who worked with Bart all claimed that he would have gone down with a struggle. His friends said Bart was in outstanding shape and would have fought for his life. They do not believe a bear could have attacked Bart by surprise.

One of the last items that investigators found sixty yards from the bow was Bart's cap and a balaclava he was wearing. There was no damage to the cap or the balaclava, no blood, nothing to indicate something dreadful had happened. Investigators also found it very strange that Bart's balaclava was found with no punctures or bite marks in it, which is unusual because bears normally bite the head and neck. The coroner would later make a supporting statement that the skull did not have punctures or bite marks that would be associated with a bear attack.

Investigators find it difficult to believe that animals would have killed Bart and then left his bag completely undisturbed. Investigators also don't understand why a predator would kill and consume Bart and not travel the half mile to his camp to consume his food. Based on what they found at Bart's campsite, investigators believe that he had been alive at Reid Lakes just one night.

Coroner Sharon Hanley examined the little remains of Bart Schleyer and stated that with no tissue to examine it was difficult to draw conclusions. The coroner also stated that the bones that were recovered were "gnawed on by an animal." She did not specify what type of animal.

I asked Rick Fernel to share his thoughts about the scene where Bart was found. He said if I were to ask him about the strangest case in almost thirty years in the Yukon, it would be the Bart Schleyer disappearance. Rick stated that in all his years in the Yukon, it was his expert belief that "bears don't consume people up here." He stated that the largest of the Reid Lakes is shallow, with lots of bugs. It's a place where people don't travel. He said it appeared that Bart had taken his inflatable boat across the lake to hunt. Maybe he heard or saw something, but it was obvious from the scene that he was sitting and calling moose when something terrible happened.

One of the last statements Rick made about the disappearance of Bart was in regard to bears. He said it did appear that a bear had eaten a portion of Bart, but he didn't believe it killed or consumed all of him because there was no clothing in the scat and his pants were found in the bush. Rick stated that if Yukon Conservation Officers find any carnivorous bear in the area, they form a team to hunt and kill the bear. They never did this in Bart's case, and there was never any follow-up. Rick's closing statement on the Bert Schleyer case: "This was really, really an odd case."

Case Summary

Bart was a man that was very much in touch with the environment. He knew how to stalk and hunt game and how to attract, trap, and collar bears. The man even made his own bow and arrows with which he hunted—he was that in touch with nature. Everyone who made a statement about Bart called the man extremely humble, not your typical wildlife biologist.

Bart was sixty feet from the lake, sitting on a bag and calling for moose. He was keenly aware of every sound around the lakes. He felt he was not in any imminent danger, as his bow was found leaning against a tree (unless, of course, someone put that bow in that position after his death).

Bart was attacked and killed. His pants were off his body but not torn to shreds, although they did sustain some damage. The idea that Bart removed his own pants in an area known for significant bug activity and clouds of mosquitoes is quite doubtful. Whatever took Bart was very fast, very powerful, and had no interest in any of his food or tools. It does appear that something took Bart's clothes but left his pants. Something felt that Bart was a threat, but why?

Investigators believe that Bart had spent one complete night at his camp (based on the supplies used and garbage found at the scene). If Bart had been there one night, the odors that emanate from cooking would have been apparent miles away in a desolate region like Reid Lakes. It might have been these smells that brought Bart's predator to his location.

Bart Schleyer was the optimum man to be bowhunting in the Yukon Territory. If Bart could become a victim, any of us could be a victim. A recurring theme in this book is that many of these stories have never had significant press coverage and the vast majority of North Americans have never heard of these victims. I would hope that making the reader aware of the dangers that exist in the wilds of North America would elevate their senses and take additional precautionary measures when enjoying the wild.

Cases Similar to the Schleyer Disappearance

Bart's strange disappearance shares similarities with others, including the cases of Charles McCullar and Robert Winters from Crater Lake (OR), Atadero, Colorado, and Geraldine Huggan in Minaki, Ontario. Three men, one boy, and one girl disappeared into a very desolate region. When their remains were found, only their skulls and small pieces of bone were located.

In the Charles McCullar case, they found his pants and socks. That's it. Just like in Bart's case, they never found the majority of his other supplies, his shirt, or his coat. Also, one major item was missing in both cases: boots. Both of these men's boots were missing from the scene, yet in both cases their pants were left. There are no grizzly bears in Oregon, and yet Charles was completely consumed.

In the Geraldine Huggan case, investigators found one of her pant legs pulled inside out. American Indian trackers found human footprints in the area, although RCMP discounted their statements. They also found threads and bits of cloth from Geraldine's shirt. The physician who examined the clothing and the few remnants of Geraldine stated there was no blood on any clothing found, same as the other two incidents. There were a few tufts of hair found in the area where it is believed Geraldine died.

What happened to Bart Schleyer, Geraldine Huggan, and Charles McCullar?

Vancouver Island

Vancouver Island sits just west of Vancouver, British Columbia, and is a very large island—290 miles in length and fifty miles at its widest point. There are small settlements with cabins throughout the island, but much of it is wide-open forest with significant wildlife, and it has areas where man may never have walked.

Vancouver Island has a very rich and long history of logging, hunting, and fishing, and it is home to many Canadian First Nations People. The 2001 Canadian census listed the population on the island at 656,312.

Vancouver Island Missing People by Date

Missing Person	Date Missing•Age•Sex,
Alma Hall	06/09/51•28•F
Raymond Hall	06/09/51•6•M
Annie Puglas	04/19/67•43•F
Kenneth Coon	04/28/67•5•M
Yehudi Prior	09/23/74•2•M
Lynn Marie Hillier	07/24/86•2•F
William Pilkenton	02/15/08•7•M

Alma Hall, 28 years old
Raymond Hall, 6 years old
Missing: 06/09/51, Woss Logging, Englewood, Vancouver Island, BC

Alma Hall and her son, Raymond, left their Saskatoon residence to visit Thomas Glen Hall, the boy's father and Alma's husband. Glen worked for Woss Logging at "W" Camp in Englewood, outside of Alert Bay. This is a rural camp near the Nimpkish River.

On June 9, 1951, Alma took Raymond for a hike in the woods to a waterfall on the Nimpkish River. Loggers saw the boy and the woman near the falls, but this was the last time anyone ever saw the pair.

Glen was quickly made aware of the disappearance. He notified the RCMP and gathered a group of the best loggers and woodsmen in the area to search for his family. The RCMP dragged the river while the others focused on the land. A search of over a week failed to find the two people, and neither body ever floated up in the river. It was as if the mother and son had vanished.

Annie Puglas
Missing: 04/19/67, Alert Bay, Vancouver Island, BC
Age at disappearance: 43

Kenneth Coon
Missing: 04/28/67, Alert Bay, Vancouver Island, BC
Age at disappearance: 5
    The Puglas and Coon cases are combined for a few reasons. Annie Puglas is the great-aunt of Kenneth Coon and both resided in Alert Bay. They disappeared within ten days of each other. I only found one article describing each event, and each article had minimal information.
    Annie resided across the bay from Kenneth on Gilford Island, a very short distance across the water. There were no details about Annie's disappearance other than the date and where she went missing.
    One article stated that fifty RCMP officers searched for Kenneth. It states that four separate searches were made in the bush for the small boy, but he still wasn't found. When the RCMP couldn't find the boy on land, they turned to the water and beaches.
    I could not find an article that indicated either person was ever found.

Lynn Marie Hillier
Missing: 07/24/86, Horne Lake, Parksville, BC
Age at disappearance: 2
    Colleen Hillier and her parents took Colleen's daughter, Lynn Marie, for a short vacation to the Hilliers' cabin at Horne Lake on Vancouver Island. The lake sits approximately four miles from the eastern shore of the island, just west of Spider Lake Provincial Park and Horne Lake Caves Provincial Park. Horne Lake has a ridgeline

coming down to it that terminates to the north and sits in a bowl with a large opening on the eastern side of the lake. A steep, rocky road runs in front of the cabin, which sits in an isolated location downhill from the main road.

On July 24, 1986, Lynn Marie went outside the cabin and vanished. The grandparents and parents searched and found no evidence of her. They contacted the RCMP and a massive search was immediately started. People were yelling her name and driving the roads, all looking for the young girl. Four hundred people volunteered to search for Lynn Marie; they found nothing. The RCMP brought in canines to pick up a scent; they could not locate a scent, or refused to track. The RCMP brought in airplanes with infrared scanning equipment to look for body heat, but they didn't find anything on their air-to-ground search.

After a week of searching for the girl, Lynn Marie's great-grandfather, Ernie Miner, posted a $25,000 reward for her return. Ernie was interviewed by the *Toronto Star* and stated, "I don't think she is here." He later stated, "She doesn't like water, and she doesn't wander." I believe the implication of Ernie's statements was that Lynn Marie was nowhere near the family cabin.

The formal search for Lynn Marie was terminated after almost ten days.

On August 19, 1986, almost four weeks later, two men were scouting for hunting locations on a steep hillside 3½ miles from the Hillier cabin. They thought they saw something under a fallen log. They looked closer and found the body of Lynn Marie Hillier. The RCMP was notified and recovered the body. Formal notifications were made to the Hilliers. An RCMP officer had stated that they felt it might be possible that the girl walked to the location where she was found.

On August 21, 1986, Colleen Hillier responded to the RCMP statements about their daughter being found. The *Windsor Star* ran the following article on the same day: "Colleen Hillier, 25, mother of the little girl, refused to believe her daughter walked up a mountain to her death. 'There's no way,' she stated in an interview Wednesday night. 'It just doesn't seem possible. It's so hard to imagine her making it there on her own.' ... Relatives couldn't explain how the little girl climbed up the rocky road behind their cabin. Les Hiller stated, 'I don't believe she could have walked there herself.'"

The coroner stated that Lynn Marie Hillier died of exposure on her second or third day away from her home.

Case Summary

Readers need to remember that Lynn Marie Hillier was two years old. Children who go missing almost always walk downhill, not uphill, as Lynn Marie had done for 3½ miles. Parents are generally a good judge of their children's stamina and abilities. If parents state that a child would not walk into the woods or couldn't climb a hill at two years old, I tend to believe them. It's hard to imagine a two-year-old girl leaving a cabin, not her home, and immediately walking up a steep, rocky road. Considering searchers were looking for the girl within three hours, all yelling for Lynne Marie, why wouldn't or couldn't she respond?

I think it's an amazing coincidence (if you believe in coincidences) that the RCMP put up aircraft equipped with FLIR (forward-looking infrared radar) to look for heat signatures on the ground, did not find her, and then Lynn Marie was found by hunters underneath an old log. In all of the searches I have ever read about, this is one of the rare times that FLIR was used, and one of the only times a child was found under something as penetrable by FLIR as a log.

William Pilkenton
Missing: 02/15/08, 10:00 a.m., Tofino, Vancouver Island
Age at disappearance: 7

David and Camilla Pilkenton left their home in Bellingham, Washington, for a leisurely vacation at a bed-and-breakfast on the west coast of Vancouver Island. The couple chose the city of Tofino to bring their sons, Timothy and William.

Tofino is a somewhat isolated community at the end of a long peninsula sitting to the south of Vargas Island Provincial Park and to the west of the giant Strathcona Provincial Park. The small city is surrounded by dozens of small islands and is known as a city where many First Nations People reside.

Cable Cove Inn, the bed-and-breakfast, is near Duffin Cove, which is at the far western side of the city. It sits just to the north of the cove and has a commanding view of the water and nearby islands.

On February 15, 2008, David awoke early and decided to take a walk on the beach. His son William asked to join him. The boys walked to the street and then down a set of steep stairs to the rocks and beach area of the cove. The two were in the area of Tonquin Beach. William stayed at the bottom of the stairs as David walked the rocky beach area. William wanted to get a little closer to his dad. David was approximately thirty-six feet from his son when he took his eyes off of him for just a few minutes. William vanished. David frantically searched the beach area and the steps. He found nothing. He went back to the inn and notified his wife and the inn operators, who notified the RCMP.

The RCMP supplied a huge response to the disappearance of William. Land, sea, and air units responded. Canine units also responded the first day and tried to pick up a scent. A very lush and thick forest borders the beach, and that was searched as well.

On the second day of the search, a steady rain hit the area and hampered efforts. The search lasted three days and involved scuba divers, helicopters, and two hundred volunteers that included people from a local First Nation tribe. Nothing was ever found of William Pilkenton. RCMP forces believed the body and parts of clothing and shoes would wash onto nearby beaches in the following days, but nothing appeared.

There are no more than twenty streets in the tiny city of Tofino; everyone knows everyone else. When people come to town, there are only a few places to stay. There were only two places for William to be: the ocean or the forest. Neither location offered any clues. William and his clothes have never surfaced.

Yehudi Prior
Missing: 09/23/74, Wild Duck Lake, Vancouver Island
Age at disappearance: 2

William Prior took his son Yehudi berry picking at an old tribal area four miles north of Wild Duck Lake, which is located in the southern area of Vancouver Island. As the father was picking the berries, the boy suddenly disappeared. William immediately started to call out the boy's name, but there was no answer. He frantically searched the entire area but couldn't find the boy. It was at this time that William contacted authorities.

At the height of the search, multiple tracking dogs, helicopters, and over fifty trained searchers scoured the mountains looking for Yehudi. The searchers found no evidence of the boy anywhere in the area.

Six days later, there was one last big push to find Yehudi. Late on September 29, searchers found Yehudi in rugged brushland four miles north of Wild Duck Lake. The boy had died. A September 30 article in the *Edmonton Journal* had some very enlightening statements by the search leader, Hal Orrick: "The boy's body was found near Hope Creek in the next valley north of Wild Duck Valley where he had spent most of his life. It was a fantastic long distance ... It seemed so impossible that he could go that far." It appeared the boy had died of exposure. There was no inquiry into the death of Yehudi, and the case was closed.

Chapter Summary

Vancouver Island is known for its great fishing, hunting, hiking, and general outdoors activities. The statistical oddity of Vancouver Island missing people is that there are no adult men listed as missing, even though men are the predominant sex enjoying the outdoors. There are five children and two female adults listed in this chapter. The predominant category of missing are juvenile males. Another reason this statistic is so odd is that the island is known as a major location for First Nations People, and they have lived in very remote locations.

Washington

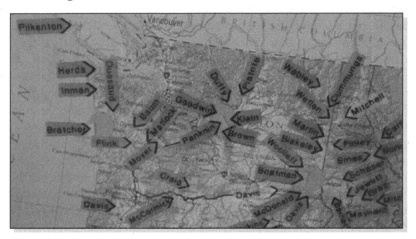

Missing People in Washington by Date

Missing Person	Date Missing•Age•Sex
Wesley Piatote*	08/04/32•7•M
Daryl Webley**	04/30/49•2•M
Keith Parkins	04/10/52•2•M
Richard Craig*	08/15/57•5•M
John Davis*	08/26/57•72•M
Richard "Dicky" Herman	08/30/59•6•M
James McCormick	12/05/61•16•M
Claude Goodwin	06/16/63•8•M
Bobby Panknin	08/03/63•4•M
Laura Flink	02/21/69•21•F
Marcelene Cummungs*	07/14/69•54•F
Jimmy Duffy	10/19/73•2•M
Jeffrey Bratcher	06/15/74•7•M
Steve Martin	08/16/75•15•M
Tyler Inman	12/21/82•3•M
Tom Klein	09/08/86•27•M
Corey Fay	11/23/91•17•M
Bryce Herda	04/09/95•4•M

Raymond Matlock	09/07/98•28•M
Jennifer Dussaud	05/01/03•22•F
Gregory Brown	07/05/05•49•M
Nancy Moyer	03/06/09•36•F
Lindsey Baum	06/22/09•10•F

For more information about these individuals, refer to the second book of this series, which includes the information on Sheepherders and farmers..

Daryl Webley
Missing: 04/30/49, 4:00 p.m., Colville, WA
Age at disappearance: 2
      The Webley family lived in a small house on the far outskirts of Colville, Washington. The city sits just twenty miles west of the Idaho border and has an American Indian reservation as its neighbor.
      On April 30, 1949, Daryl Webley was playing in the yard outside his home at approximately 4:00 p.m. Somehow his parents lost track of him and he disappeared. The parents initially searched the yard and surrounding area, yelling the boy's name and asking neighbors for help. He wasn't found.
      The Webleys contacted local law enforcement, who then requested federal assistance. The Washington Highway Patrol responded along with local sheriffs. The Stevens County sheriff took command of the situation and placed a call to Spokane for canines from the Coast Guard.
      Throughout the first night, searchers scoured everything within two miles of the residence, finding nothing of value. At 5:30 the following morning, the canines arrived and were given a whiff of Daryl's scent from his clothing. The dogs took off at a slow run and led searchers to a ravine approximately one mile from the residence. At this first location, they found the boy's cap, his pants, and one of his shoes, but he was alive. Approximately thirty minutes later, and further up the canyon, the searchers found the boy. A May 2, 1949, article in the *Lewiston Tribune* reported: "The boy, Daryl Webley, was almost nude and badly scratched when the dog led rescuers to him. He was cold and wet after his 14-hour experience,

during which rain fell and the temperature dropped to 35 degrees." Daryl was taken to a local doctor and found to have a case of mild exposure.

Case Summary

This is an unusual case for several reasons:

(1) Many cases in this book reveal that canines usually do not work in these situations, but they did in this case. I can't explain why they tracked the scent this time. Maybe it was that the dogs were not from the area or were trained differently.

(2) It was a cold night with bad weather; *nobody* removes clothing when it's moderately cold.

(3) Small children take the path of least resistance. The fact that this little boy had severe scratches on his body doesn't make sense. A child of two years isn't running at high speed through the brush; he is moving slowly to ensure he won't get hurt.

(4) Before the dogs arrived, over two hundred people unsuccessfully searched the area where Daryl was later found. It doesn't make sense.

Keith Parkins
Missing: 04/10/52, noon, Ritter, OR
Age at disappearance: 2
Note: This case occurred in northern Oregon but appears here because of its proximity to the southeast Washington cases.

At age two, Keith Parkins visited his grandparents' farm outside of Ritter, Oregon. Ritter is located in the far northeast corner of the state, on the fringe of the Umatilla National Forest and the Bridge Creek Wildlife Area. His grandparents' residence is located in very rugged country close to the North Fork of the John Day River.

The story of Keith Parkins is one of the most unusual you will read in this book. The exact cause of his disappearance is unclear from the newspaper clippings, but it is a fact that he wandered away from his grandparents' home. A call was made to law enforcement agencies, and there was a large response. Keith went missing at noon on a Wednesday, and the search went through Wednesday night. This is where the story gets murky.

A search for a lost two-year-old in the mountains would normally be confined to a one- or two-mile radius of the residence. This search wasn't. In cold temperatures, 95 percent of all missing children between one and three years old are found within two miles in a rural location (Lost Person Behavior, by Robert Koester, pg 130). For some unknown reason, searchers knew something about where this boy would end up, and it was an unbelievable distance even for a mature man to cover.

An April 10, 1952, article in the *Lewiston Daily Record* reported the following: "A little boy who ran and stumbled over a dozen miles in 19 hours was found unconscious this Thursday morning and is expected to recover." Yes, a searcher was twelve miles from the grandparents' home when he found the boy lying unconscious in a creek bed. Keith had many scratches over his entire body and was taken to a hospital. He suffered from exposure but lived. On April 12, the same newspaper printed an article stating the following: "His mother said the boy has apparently forgotten his night of horror. His pants, she said, were torn to shreds, and he climbed through fences and brush in the mountains."

News clippings state that Keith Parkins had to climb numerous fences, cross icy creeks, and climb at least two mountains to get to the location where he was eventually found—all of this in just nineteen hours. Keith's father stated that the boy must have been running almost continuously to cover that amount of ground.

Case Summary

I have shown this case to several SAR coordinators, and none have ever heard of a two-year-old that could cover that much ground—over mountains, ravines, and creeks—in nineteen hours. One of the best questions they asked was, Why was a searcher looking for the boy twelve miles from the point last seen? There is no way a SAR coordinator would send a searcher twelve miles out inside of twenty-four hours. It would never happen. It's almost as though the searcher knew something that nobody else knew. Something about the disappearance of Keith Parkins is highly unusual.

Authors Note: The Keith Parkins disappearance is highlighted in our movie, "Missing 411" and the excursion that Keith took was re-enacted by Survivorman, Les Stroud. It is a very compelling part of the movie. Please go to our website for more details, www.canammissing.com

Richard "Dicky" Herman
Missing: 08/30/59, noon, Emigrant State Park, OR
Age at disappearance: 6
Note: This case appears in the Washington section because of its proximity to Washington and the disappearance of Keith Parkins.

Mr. and Mrs. Richard Herman of Sunnyside, Washington, took their family to Emigrant State Park in northeastern Oregon for a weekend in the woods. On August 30, at approximately noon, the Hermans' six-year-old son, Dicky, went missing while playing hide-and-seek with other children (circumstances very similar to the disappearance of Dennis Martin from the Great Smoky Mountains, story located in the eastern United States version of Missing411.). The family immediately started to search the area but could not find the boy. A call was soon made to the local sheriff's department.

At eight o'clock the morning after Dicky went missing, a deputy on horseback found him. Dicky was remarkably nine miles from where he was last seen. He was walking a trail when the deputy happened to spot him. He had wandered through miles of brush and timber before being found near Meacham, Oregon. Searchers described Dicky as tired and hungry, but despite his tear-stained face, doctors said he was in remarkably good condition.

James McCormick
Missing: 12/05/61, Larch Mountain, Multnomah Falls, OR
Age at disappearance: 16
Note: This case appears here because of its proximity to cases in Washington; it occurred within two miles of the Washington-Oregon border.

Multnomah Falls is approximately thirty miles east of downtown Portland. It sits adjacent to the Columbia River and is one of the most beautiful waterfalls you will ever see. The area to the south of the falls is Larch Mountain; this area is very rugged and wild.

On December 4, 1961, James McCormick Sr., his son, and their hunting dog left their Portland residence for a bobcat shoot at Larch Mountain. Mr. McCormick was on vacation from his job as a fire inspector for the City of Portland and enjoyed the outdoors. Even though Larch Mountain was only thirty miles from a metropolitan setting, don't let that fool you; it gets very wild very quickly in this region of the Northwest.

The first day they were hunting, the weather started to turn bad. The first indicator of cold striking the area was a heavy rain, which was soon followed by snow that blanketed Larch Mountain. The three were temporarily lost and spent the night huddled in a tree for protection. The next morning they started back out but were again lost. And for some unknown reason, James Jr. became "delirious," according to a December 4, 1961, article in the *Eugene Register*. James Sr. carried his 215-pound son for three hours before he became exhausted and laid him down. He told the boy to stay put while he went to investigate what he thought were car lights. He returned to the area in just minutes and found the boy had disappeared. James Sr. searched for his son for almost an hour and then left to get help. Many hours later James Sr. stumbled into the Multnomah Falls Lodge.

Two hundred off-duty firefighters from Portland responded to assist in the search for James Jr. Sheriff's department searchers used canines and planes to search the mountain. Searchers found the case for the boy's glasses, and his socks and boots were found somewhat near where his father had lost the boy. Later in the day, searchers found James's body at the bottom of a slight cliff three hundred yards from where they had found his clothing. He was dead.

The appearance of the body made searchers believe that he didn't die from a fall. Several articles stated that James Jr. may have died from exposure, but there was no definitive statement.

Case Summary

Many questions arise from this case, and many of the facts mimic those found throughout this book: People are out in the woods with a dog; the weather turns bad; one person becomes dazed or delirious, gets lost, and later loses articles of clothing. The lost person is later found: sometimes they are alive, sometimes not. I am interested in the statement made by Mr. McCormick about seeing lights and going to search for them. What kind of lights would he see in the middle of the wilderness that could be mistaken for headlights?

Claude Goodwin
Missing: 06/16/63, thirty miles upstream from Entiat, WA
Age at disappearance: 8
The Goodwin family drove from their home in Seattle to a camping spot on the Entiat River thirty miles north of Entiat, Washington.

On June 16, 1963, the family was taking a hike in the area of the campsite when they momentarily lost sight of their eight-year-old boy, Claude. The family looked for the boy for several hours and then called the Chelan County Sheriff's Office for assistance.

Sheriff Dick Nickell responded with a large contingent of SAR members and deputies. The teams scoured the hillside where the boy had disappeared but could not locate him. Some feared that maybe the boy had wandered to the river and drowned. Two bloodhounds tracked the boy's scent to the river and stopped. Dive teams from the county sheriff's Office searched the river for two days but never found the boy. It should be noted that there are stories in this book where other bloodhounds tracked children's scents to a river but the kids were later found nowhere near the river. In the months after Claude disappeared, his body never surfaced in the river and Claude was never found.

Bobby Panknin
Missing: 08/03/63, Deep Lake (Kettle Falls), WA
Age at disappearance: 4
Note: If there is one case in this book that exemplifies how quickly a child can become lost in the forest, this is case. Read this thoroughly and understand how quickly things can go horribly wrong in the wilds of North America.

The Panknin family lived just south of Deep Lake in Spokane. The family moved to the eastern Washington city in 1962 after Mr. Panknin had moved the family from Turkey where he had served for the U.S. Air Force. He had just retired and decided to take the family to the Big Lake resort for a weekend of camping. They found a camping location at the northeast section of the lake near a small stream.

The first day of camping was uneventful. On Saturday, Mr. Panknin and his son Ted went fishing while Mrs. Panknin took their other sons, Bobby (4), Jimmy (6), and Billy (10), on a hike behind their campsite to look at a small waterfall just off an old logging road. The group reached the area of the falls, and Mrs. Panknin told Bobby to sit on the ground on the old road and wait a few minutes while she and the brothers walked ten feet to look at the falls. Mrs. Panknin knew that Bobby couldn't walk through the brush to see the falls because he was only wearing a swimsuit, and no shoes, and the ground was very rough.

Mrs. Panknin and the two boys walked ten feet to look at the falls, and in less than two minutes, were back on the logging road. Bobby was gone (Spokesman Review, August 6, 1963). The group knew a car hadn't driven down the road, as they would have heard it. Besides, the road was too rotten for cars to travel. The group hadn't heard any people. The boys and their mother immediately started to yell out for Bobby, but there was no answer. The group started to spread out and yell. Still, there was no answer. They ran back to the resort to get more assistance, and immediately a search was initiated.

The Deep Lake Resort is located in the far northern section of Stevens County, only five miles from the Canadian border. The local sheriff sent men to aid in the search and also requested bloodhounds. At midnight on August 6, the sheriff gave a bloodhound Bobby's scent from the boy's shoe, and the dog took off on a dead run. He ran for almost two miles until it came to a fork in the logging road, where it then came to a screeching halt and didn't move. Why the dog stopped and what may have happened to Bobby at this point are confusing. The road wasn't drivable; there were no cars. What happened here? On August 6, 1963, Stevens County Sheriff

A. E. "Dutch" Holter gave an interview to the *Spokesman Review* admitting he could not understand the strange disappearance of the child.

The search for Bobby Panknin lasted one week, with over one thousand searchers on horseback and foot. The sheriff was at a complete loss for an adequate explanation. There were some theories that a bear may have grabbed Bobby, but bear dogs were brought into the area and didn't find a bear or a scene with blood, clothing, etc., that would indicate a bear attack. Searchers could not find any drag marks on the ground, causing some to believe a giant eagle carried Bobby away; however, the majority of the searchers discounted that.

On August 12, 1963, Mr. Panknin gave an interview to the *Tri-City Herald* and summed up his thoughts about his lost son: "It's as if Bobby climbed to the top of a tree and then kept on going." The sheriff made several statements to the effect that Bobby could not have walked very far because the ground area was quite rugged and the boy was not wearing shoes, which is the reason his mother didn't take him to the waterfall.

Case Summary

In the thousands of missing persons cases I have reviewed, this is one case that indicates someone was watching the Panknins as they walked that logging road. As unusual and odd as this sounds, there really is no other explanation. Someone waited for the opportunity and then grabbed Bobby. This person must have had tremendous strength and dexterity, and must have known the region like their own backyard, to muzzle Bobby so he wouldn't scream and carry him a very long distance to get out of the area. No, it wasn't a wild animal; there was no scene of violence, blood, or drag marks. Someone was very stealthy, very smart, and very quick to grab Bobby and flee the entire area in less than two minutes—an amazing feat.

The lack of identifiable footprints in this area is not unusual. The ground in many forests is very hard and covered with leaves and twigs. To escape without leaving any prints, the abductor must have walked up the creek and on rocks, never leaving behind any evidence.

One thousand people combed every foot of the mountainside where Bobby disappeared; they found no evidence that he was ever in the area. The facts surrounding Bobby's disappearance are indisputable and were validated by the boy's brothers.

About eighty miles southeast of Deep Lake is Lake Wenatchee, the approximate location of the disappearance of another boy, Jimmy Duffy, under very similar circumstances. And, almost exactly halfway between Wenatchee and Deep Lake is Nespelem, the town where yet another boy, Wesley Piatote, disappeared almost exactly twenty-nine years to the day from the date Bobby Panknin disappeared. As someone who does not believe in coincidences, this strikes me as an overwhelming connection. Piatote and Duffy were two years old and Panknin was four at the time each disappeared. None of these boys were ever found.

Jimmy Duffy
Missing: 10/19/73, 2:15 p.m., Little Wenatchee Ridge, Wenatchee Lake, Wenatchee, WA
Age at disappearance: 2

On October 19, 1973, James and Carol Duffy parked their camper and truck in a clear-cut seven miles northeast of Lake Wenatchee in a location known as Little Wenatchee Ridge. While the entire family took a walk around the area of the camper, Little Jimmy Duffy was misbehaving on the hike and Carol Duffy hit her son for not keeping up with the group, per her own statement in sheriff's department reports. The family then headed back to the camper to put the kids down for a nap. Thirty-two-month-old Jimmy and eighteen-month-old Natalie were left in the back of the camper sleeping while James went hunting in the area and Carol took a walk.

After fifteen minutes of hunting the nearby clear-cut, James returned to the camper to check on the children and found them still asleep; Carol was still out on her walk but saw James check on the kids. He then circled the clear-cut where they were parked and joined his wife. When James and Carol were approximately 150 yards from their children, they heard a scream or screech come from the camper. They ran to a spot where they could see the camper and saw the camper door open. The parents ran to their vehicle and found the back door opened. Natalie and their two cats were still asleep inside, but Jimmy was nowhere in sight. James immediately checked the Caterpillar tracks beside the clear-cut, and Carol checked the road. They found nothing. The time at this point was approximately 2:15 p.m.

By 3:15 p.m. deputies from the Chelan County Sheriff's Office had arrived and already notified SAR personnel. The deputies and forest service employees searched the soft ground near the camper but could not find any prints in the dirt roads that matched the boy's. At 4:20 p.m. James arrived back at the camper from searching and stated that he had not found the boy. At 4:25 p.m. deputies re-interviewed Carol and asked her again to explain the circumstances of the disappearance. She did. At 5:00 p.m. deputies interviewed James again, and he repeated the circumstances of the boy's disappearance. He stated that the sound he heard coming from the area of the camper could have been something similar to a baby's cry.

The following day canines were brought to the location and thoroughly searched the area. They found nothing.

For five days following Jimmy's disappearance, searchers performed a massive grid layout involving more than 150 men, including rescue units, SAR teams, and the sheriff's posse. Helicopters were also brought to the area to search cliffs and small valleys. The search produced no evidence of Jimmy Duffy's location. At 8:30 p.m. on October 24, the lead deputy from Chelan County called James aside. He told James that he didn't believe his story about his son's disappearance and thought the child had never been in the area. He also told James that he thought the child had been accidentally or intentionally killed and disposed of and that his story was a cover-up. James insisted his story was true and there was no cover-up. The deputy then asked him if his wife had a boyfriend, to which he replied, "Not that I know of."

At 11:30 the following morning, the formal search operations were terminated.

During the extensive follow-up conducted by the Chelan County Sheriff's Office, one witness described Jimmy Duffy as "retarded" and with a very frail build. Most of the witnesses stated that they rarely saw the boy outside of the Duffys' home. It's obvious from the reports that Chelan County did a very extensive follow-up by contacting the Duffys' neighbors, friends, and child protective services. They also attempted to locate evidence of violence against Jimmy, but nothing was found. At one point investigators requested that Carol and James Duffy take a polygraph test. They agreed.

Twelve days after their son went missing in the mountains of Washington, James and Carol Duffy were seated in a police interview room taking a polygraph in an effort to clear their names. Polygraph experts from the Seattle Police Department were brought in to question the Duffys and administer the polygraph. Both parents took the polygraph simultaneously in different rooms. In a report written by N. Matzke and D. Gillespie of Seattle PD's polygraph unit, they stated the following after interviewing both parents: "Each subject was given a polygraph examination and it is the opinion that Mr. and Mrs. Duffy do not know the whereabouts of their son Jimmy nor did they conspire with each other to cause the disappearance." The passing of the polygraph hopefully focused the Chelan County Sheriff's Office on finding Jimmy rather than building a case against his parents.

Case Summary

I was fortunate to get the Chelan County Sheriff's Office to expend significant resources to get the case file on Jimmy Duffy. A records supervisor took an interest in my request and spent hours looking through microfiche attempting to build a case file. Nobody had one inside the detective division; nobody even knew of the case. After more than a month, I was sent the complete case file of over 150 pages.

This is a truly fascinating case. Jimmy Duffy was only slightly older than two. He was frail and could barely get into and out of the camper without assistance. The scream that the parents heard definitely came from the camper and was related to the disappearance. It's very odd that the scream heard by the parents 150 yards away didn't wake Natalie, who was sleeping in the camper or their cats.

I am comfortable in saying that I'm 99 percent certain Jimmy was abducted. The parents were at the camper in a matter of minutes. They searched immediately but never found their boy. He had to have been abducted. The unusual part of this abduction is that the family was on a hunting trip; everyone in that area at that time of the year was most likely a hunter and was armed. Whoever took Jimmy Duffy was watching when the family took their walk and when James came back to check on the children. The perpetrator(s) waited for James and his wife to be at a safe enough distance and out of view to open the closed camper door, take Jimmy, and make a getaway. Where were they taking Jimmy, and how did they know they could successfully make their escape? How did they know that his parents wouldn't catch up to them?

None of the reports mentioned animal tracks in the area. All people and all vehicles that were in the area were later accounted for through follow-up by the sheriff's department. There is no way a thirty-two-month-old boy could escape the search efforts of professional trackers in the area where Jimmy was lost.

I thought it was a highly risky assertion by the lead Chelan County deputy to accuse James of fabricating facts about his son's disappearance, especially without documented and elaborated facts he could put in his report. I saw none. The frustration among the searchers and deputies was understandable after six days without finding any evidence of Jimmy. I don't blame the deputies for being frustrated, and without knowing that other cases very similar in nature have occurred consistently throughout the U.S. in the last seventy-five years, maybe that frustration and allegation against James could be excused. If that comment were made today, especially now knowing that the Duffys played no part in the disappearance, that deputy would be severely reprimanded for his conduct.

SAR reports on this incident indicated that personnel searched two miles out from the camper. That was not enough. Even considering Jimmy's age and frail build, hundreds of reports similar in nature indicate that a search of two miles out from the location of the event isn't sufficient. The distance to search on an event such as this shouldn't be dictated by how far the child could walk, it should be dictated by how far an abductor could carry the victim.

Laura Flink
Missing: 02/21/69, Pacific Beach, WA
5'2", 115 lb.
Age at disappearance: 21

At the time of her disappearance, Laura Flink was the mother of a sixteen-month-old, and there were also reports that she was two-months pregnant. She driving her live-in boyfriend's 1967 Ford Ranchero toward the area of Moclips and Pacific Beach to pick up furniture and children's clothing. As best as law enforcement can determine, she disappeared somewhere in this area on February 21, 1969.

The Ranchero was later found abandoned near J Street in Hoquiam. Her wallet was also found there lying on a sidewalk. This was mailed to law enforcement. The Aberdeen Police Department headed the investigation into her case but had few leads.

Laura's disappearance occurred in proximity to that of Jennifer Dussaud, who was lost near Humptulips. Jennifer disappeared thirty-four years after Laura was reported missing. Jennifer and Laura have the exact same height and weight (5'2", 115 lb.). Jennifer was twenty-two years old and Laura twenty-one at the time each disappeared.

Jeffrey Michael Bratcher
Missing: 06/15/74, Ocean City State Park, WA
3'9", 45 lb.
Age at disappearance: 7

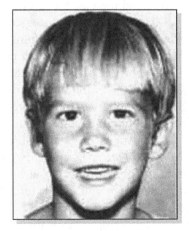

The Bratchers lived in Mesquite, Texas. Gayle, Jeffrey's mother, decided to take him and his siblings to the Washington coast for an early summer vacation.

On June 15, 1974, Jeffrey was playing with five other children in a section of Ocean City State Park. The kids knew they needed to be back in the area of the adults at 7:00 p.m. for dinner. As dinnertime got close, the kids started to take a trail back to their parents. Jeffrey decided to take a different path. He never arrived for dinner and was never seen again.

A segment of the law enforcement community believes Jeffrey got too close to the ocean and was swept out to sea; others believe he may have been abducted. It was determined that Jeffrey was last seen near the ranger station inside Ocean City State Park. In 1974 there was a $1,500 reward for information leading to Jeffrey's return.

Steve Martin
Missing: 08/16/75, noon, Petit Lake, Washington
Age at disappearance: 15

The North Central High School cross country team from Spokane, Washington, spent a week camping at Petit Lake, two miles from the Washington-Idaho border and five miles from Priest Lake, Idaho. The team was there to train by running the logging roads in the area.

At approximately noon on August 16, Steve Martin ran off—wearing his cross-country shoes, shorts, and shirt—and was never seen again. At approximately 4:30 p.m., the group realized Steve had not returned, and a search was initiated. The local sheriff was called and the USFS responded.

The night Steve disappeared, a rain and fog hit the area around Petit Lake, making searching very difficult. Air searches were halted for two days because of the bad weather.

A portion of Steve's teammates told searchers that Steve may have left the trail momentarily to pick huckleberries that were in the hills. Searchers combed logging roads and trails in an effort to find tracks, but none were found.

On August 19, 1975, Steve's mother, Lindy Martin, stated in the *Spokane Daily*, "If anybody took him from those roads and trails up there, I'm sure they did it by force." There were some rumors that maybe Steve voluntarily left the road or trails, but his mother didn't believe that.

The formal search for Steve lasted a week and failed to find a clue as to where the boy may be. There were many rumors that he ran off to California or Idaho, but all appeared to be untrue.

On July 14, 1976, two USFS employees were conducting a survey approximately two miles northeast of Petit Lake, and three hundred yards from the nearest trail, when they stumbled onto bones and clothing in extremely dense brush and heavy timber. The team found shorts, a shirt, and tennis shoes. They had found Steve Martin.

The Pend Oreille sheriff stated that the bones were scattered across a forty-foot area, and his glasses were found twenty feet from his skull. The sheriff stated that it appeared that Steve had gotten lost, panicked, and died of exposure. The location of the body was in Sema Meadows, an area that had one of the main logging roads in the area, a road that would be hard to miss in the middle of the meadow. The road in Sema Meadows is the main road that runs to Petit Lake, the road that Steve had probably run.

Case Summary

There are many cases of young men disappearing in this area of the Washington and Idaho mountains. Steve's disappearance is definitely suspicious. If you read his mother's statements, she does not believe that her son would have voluntarily left the trails or roads. There is a possibility that Steve was picking huckleberries when he disappeared. If this was the case, Steve is yet another person who disappeared under suspicious circumstances related to berries.

Tyler Jennings Inman
Missing: 12/21/82, Aberdeen, WA
2'8", 32 lb.
Age at disappearance: 3

Tyler Inman lived in Aberdeen, Washington, with his mother, Sherrie, and her boyfriend, Jeff Green. On December 21, 1982, Sherrie Inman went to a local bingo game, and Tyler stayed home with Jeff and his dog, Shepherd. Sometime while Sherrie was gone, Tyler ran out the front door of the apartment and disappeared. There was a severe storm in the area at the time of his disappearance that included winds over sixty miles per hour that killed two local residents.

On May 17, 1984, an article ran in the *Spokane Chronicle* about Tyler's disappearance. A female psychic named Shirley Anderson called law enforcement authorities and stated that she had been having ongoing visions of Tyler and wanted to help find him. She stated that she had the following visions: "plastic bag, a river, a German shepherd, abandoned property, two fruit trees, a sewage station, saw blade, a lock, and a For Sale sign."

The information the psychic supplied prompted law enforcement officials to search the Wishkah River a second time. Divers were sent in and conducted an extensive search but could not find Tyler. The lead officer on Tyler's case, Detective Jerry Cole, stated, "We believe he's in the river."

I believe a few select psychics can aid law enforcement in their search. I've interviewed several in an attempt to understand exactly what they see (envision) and how difficult it can be to interpret those visions. Some claim they are seeing what the victim observes just before they go unconscious. Those brief glimpses can be very complicated to unwind and understand.

Tom Klein
Missing: 09/08/86, Entiat Drainage, Phelps Creek Trailhead, Chelan County, WA
Age at disappearance: 27

The disappearance of Tom Klein was not immediately reported. Klein was on a three-day hike in the Phelps Creek area of Chelan County. Friends in Seattle were not exactly sure where he was going and thus couldn't give searchers accurate information. The county sheriff was not notified until September 11, 1986, that Tom was even missing. The SAR teams had spent three days searching and were about to give up when they found his vehicle at the Phelps Creek Trailhead.

Once searchers found Tom's car, the efforts to find him were upgraded. Chelan County utilized their helicopter, along with helicopters from Fairchild Air Force Base, to search for Tom. Searchers looked around Mount Maude, Entiat Drainage, and the Leavenworth area south of Phelps Creek. After almost one week, search parties pulled out of the area and gave up looking for the missing man. Tom Klein has not been found.

Corey Fay
Missing: 11/23/91, 6:30 p.m., west of Tygh Valley, OR
Age at disappearance: 17

The disappearance of Corey Fay, a student at Jesuit High School in Beaverton, Oregon, ranks in my list of the top ten most unusual cases I describe in the two books.

Corey was a junior in high school when he asked Mark Maupin if he could accompany him and his friend elk hunting in a region west of Tygh Valley on the fringe of the Badger Creek Wilderness. Mark was a good friend and agreed to bring Corey along. Corey had training in outdoor survival and had hunted in the past. He knew what to do in case of emergency or if he was ever lost. He carried an emergency solar blanket, a compass, extra food, ammunition, a small backpack, and a rifle.

The three young men arrived at their hunting spot and decided to split up until 6:30 p.m., when they had agreed to arrive back at the vehicle. That was the last time anyone saw Corey.

The afternoon was cold and the hunting fruitless. Maupin later told investigators that they were in the correct spot—a spot he knew there were elk—yet inexplicably they didn't see any. When they arrived back at their vehicle, Corey wasn't there. He never arrived, so they called the sheriff.

The Wasco County Sheriff's Office was the lead agency in the search for Corey. The SAR included helicopters with special search capabilities, equestrians, hikers, and seven of the best-trained search dogs in the world from the Rocky Mountain Search and Rescue in Salt Lake City. A total of 250 searchers scoured twelve square miles for ten days and did not find one trace of Corey Fay.

There were many theories about what happened to Corey. The one that got the most press supposed that he may have been accidentally killed by another hunter and buried; however, cadaver dogs never found a gravesite. There were also theories that Cory may have survived for a long time, and one searcher thought they may have found a campsite with an old fire, but this was never confirmed. With so many searchers and substantial air support on this SAR, it is doubtful that Corey lived long after he initially disappeared; otherwise, I believe they would have found him.

The official search was terminated on December 1, but many volunteers kept the effort going for many weeks. The Wasco County sheriff was so perplexed by Corey's disappearance and the lack of evidence, he called the FBI and asked for their assistance in unraveling what happened.

There wasn't much activity on Corey's case until September 1992, when two hunters were hunting a ridge ten miles from the point where Corey was last seen. They found his backpack and his rifle. Another searcher found Corey's jacket more than a mile away from his other belongings. The hunters notified authorities.

Corey's items were located at an elevation of 6,500 feet and ten miles from where he was last seen. A quarter mile from his backpack, searchers found small bone fragments and one tooth. The sheriff stated that Corey would have been in snow up to his waist for more than five miles at the point the discovery was made. An article in the *Eugene Register* on September 18, 1992, reported the following: "Authorities know the snow was deep there because a helicopter had spotted tracks during an intensive search for Fay last November. The tracks turned out to be animals' but the snow was almost waist deep, and that was a good three miles from where the items were discovered yesterday." The article later states that searchers didn't believe Fay could have gone as far as he apparently did. An interesting sidelight to this finding is that a September 19, 1992, article in the *Eugene Register* clearly states that Corey's grandparents told the press that the boy was trained to follow a stream downhill if he ever became lost. This is odd because the article makes you believe that Cory did just the opposite.

The sheriff makes it clear that back in November 1991 his helicopter crews did see tracks on the ridgeline near where Corey was found. He makes it sound as though they landed and determined they were animal tracks. However, if the snow in the area was new and four feet deep, no helicopter would land there because it would blow the snow—and evidence—away. This assertion by the sheriff sounds like he really didn't know but was instead guessing.

Corey was found three thousand feet higher in elevation than where he was last seen and ten miles from the point he should have been hunting. Could he have covered this distance and elevation in less than a day in waist-deep snow? Remember, the sheriff stated that he didn't believe Corey could have made it that far, and that's why the search didn't focus on this location. Was the sheriff correct?

You may need to go back and again read what was found on the ridgeline. They did not find Corey's pants, boots, or socks. In Charles McCullar's story (Crater Lake), the interview with the ranger who discovered his body states that McCullar's boots were never found. The ranger stated he had always found boots with the bodies he recovered. Boots are heavy. They don't disappear. What is equally unusual about the discovery of remnants of Corey's body is that no skull was found and only one tooth could be located. This is all that was recovered, even though the sheriff sent in thirty people to do grid searches of the ridgeline across a 1¼-mile area. Searchers did not find large bones normally associated with finding a skeleton, femur, ribs, hip, vertebrae, etc.

This case disturbs me greatly. There are many similarities in other cases in this book, including those of Springfield (Montana), Schleyer (Yukon), Huggan (Ontario), and McCullar (Crater Lake). The fact that searchers could only find bone fragments—no skull and only one tooth—is highly unusual. The fact that Corey's gun, backpack, and other personal belongings were strewn along a ridgeline strikes me as bizarre—nothing any hunter would voluntarily do. Corey's disappearance and the sheriff's lack of initially found evidence was deemed unusual when the search was nearing completion. Corey was a smart boy. He was well trained and knew not to walk uphill. Anyone who has spent time outdoors in the winter knows that it gets colder the higher you go. Rain turns to snow and that leads to hypothermia. Corey was trained to follow creeks and rivers downhill, which will eventually lead you to a roadway and civilization.

You will read about several hunters in Oregon, Washington, and Idaho that disappeared while elk hunting. Many of the facts of their

disappearances do not make sense. As you read about these incidents, think about these facts and ask yourself: Could these things
have voluntarily occurred, or was there something else at play? I
believe that the Wasco County sheriff believed something highly
unusual happened to Corey, something so unusual and so beyond
his investigative ability that he got the FBI involved. Remember,
the FBI does not get involved in any missing person cases unless
there is some evidence of a crime, abduction, kidnapping, etc. Here
is another case where the FBI gets involved in a rural disappearance,
yet law enforcement does not tell the press any facts justifying the
FBI's involvement.

Questions to consider in this disappearance:
Where are Corey's boots, socks, and pants?
Why would Corey remove his coat?
Why would Corey drop his firearm?
Why would Corey do everything contrary to his survival
training?
Could Corey have walked three miles in waist-deep snow
on a cold ridgeline, and why would he if he looked below
and saw there was no snow?
Why would he even be on a ridgeline in cold weather?
Why would he be ten miles from the point he needs to be
at in a one-day hunting trip?
Why would the sheriff summon the FBI unless there was
evidence of a crime?
Where are the rest of Corey's bones?

Bryce Florian Herda
Missing: 04/09/95, Neah Bay, WA
Age at disappearance: 6
4', 60 lb.

Neah Bay is located in the far western section of Washington,
adjacent to Olympic National Park. This community is quite isolated because it's at the end of a long point of land. The community
of Neah Bay has approximately twelve streets and sits on a beautiful harbor that two hundred commercial and sport-fishing vessels

call home. The city of Neah Bay is the center point of the Makah Indian Reservation. The population of Neah Bay is listed at 794.

On April 9, 1995, Bryce Herda and his family were walking on the Shi Shi trail inside the reservation. Bryce was a Native American, and his grandfather was the reservation police chief. Bryce and his family were walking adjacent to the beach when the trail became too steep for him to keep up. The family told him they would meet him at the beach after they walked the loop. Bryce never arrived at the  meeting location and was never seen again.

Bryce's grandfather orchestrated a major search that included the Clallam County Sheriff's Office. The Shi Shi trail is in a very isolated area, especially in April, without significant vehicular traffic or beachcombers. The Pacific Coast in this region is very rugged, with large rocks and rough water. There are numerous small lakes, creeks, and rivers in this area, and heavy forests and woods are quite close. Directly south of this location is the Quinault Indian Reservation and more isolated and desolate areas.

Raymond Lee Matlock
Missing: 09/07/98, Raymond, WA
5'9", 165 lb.
Age at disappearance: 28

Raymond Matlock enjoyed the outdoors and, specifically, hunting. On September 7, 1998, Raymond went to the area of State Route 101 at the Bone River to go elk hunting. It was a remote area just five miles from his hometown, Raymond, Washington.

Raymond got separated from his hunting companions and was never seen again. His companions had performed an extensive search for Raymond before they notified law enforcement. No clues of Raymond's disappearance were ever found.

The Pacific County Sheriff's Office is the lead law enforcement agency on this case.

Jennifer Danielle Dussaud
Missing: 05/01/03, Humptulips, WA
5'2", 115 lb.
Age at disappearance: 22

This case has very, very little information. The Grays Harbor Sheriff's Office is the lead investigative agency. The only information that has been released to the public is that Jennifer disappeared near Humptulips, Washington. An extensive archival search could find no articles on this case. However, the age and physical similarities between Jennifer Dussaud and Laura Flink, coupled with the proximity of where they disappeared, cannot be overlooked. There are several disappearances within a 60 mile radius of where Jennifer went missing.

Gregory R. Brown
Missing: 07/05/05, Rachel Lake Trailhead, Lake Kachess, WA
5'7", 145 lb.
Age at disappearance: 49

Lake Kachess is approximately forty miles east of Bellevue, Washington, and just north of Snoqualmie Pass. Rachel Lake is just northeast of Lake Kachess on the fringe of the Alpine Lake Wilderness, a very rugged and desolate area.

On July 5, 2005, Gregory Brown was reported missing. He had borrowed a friend's vehicle and driven it to the end of Forest Service Road 4930. Gregory had a one-mile hike from where he parked the car until he reached the lake. Box Canyon Lake was approximately halfway between the car and Rachel Lake.

The Kittitas County Sheriff's Office did the original search before the county SAR teams took over with the assistance of USFS personnel. Helicopters and canines were brought in to search for Gregory. The canines did not pick up a scent, and the helicopters did not find any indicators of the missing person.

On July 11, 2005, Sergeant Fred Slyfield of the Kittitas County Sheriff's Office gave an interview recorded by the *Ellensburg Daily Record*. Slyfield stated, "Brown was in good health and was not suicidal." The article stated that Brown "disappeared without a trace," and searchers from five Washington counties searched for 3½ days without any success. The search was terminated when inclement weather hit the area.

Nancy Moyer
Missing: 03/06/09, Tenino, WA
4'11", 120 lb.
Age at disappearance: 36

Nancy Moyer was the mother of two girls, ages nine and eleven. She was employed by the Fiscal Office of the Washington State Department of Ecology in Lacey. On Friday, March 6, 2009, Nancy left work and gave a fellow employee a ride home. Nancy dropped her off and continued on to her home in rural Tenino.

Nancy was still married to Bill Moyer, but the two had been separated for two years with dual custody of their daughters. Bill had custody of the girls that weekend and came to Nancy's residence to drop them off on Sunday night. The three found her front door unlocked, her car in the driveway, the heater and television on, and a glass of wine sitting on the table. Her purse and keys were sitting near the kitchen table. Nancy was gone.

Detectives from the Thurston County Sheriff's Office have stated that all signs indicate Nancy should have been at the house. They have turned the case into a homicide investigation so it gets the highest priority.

The city of Tenino is approximately three miles east of Interstate 5 and ten miles south of Olympia. It is a rural community at an elevation of four hundred feet. There are dozens of small lakes, creeks, and rivers in the area, and the mountains and hills are covered by dense woods and forests. Nancy's residence sits in a rural area that does not have fences, so there is open space between each of the homes.

Lindsey Baum
Missing: 06/26/09, 9:15 p.m.,
Grays Harbor, WA
4'9", 80 lb.
Age at disappearance: 10

At approximately 9:15 p.m. on June 26, 2009, ten-year-old Lindsey Baum was making the four-block walk from her friend's home on Maple Street in McCleary to her house on Mommsen Road. Mommsen Road is on the perimeter of McCleary, and a portion of the road goes deep into the woods. Several small lakes, a river, and many small creeks surround McCleary, and it's in an area known for its bear, elk, deer, and general abundance of wildlife.

At 10:50 p.m. Lindsey had still not arrived home. Her mother, Melissa, called the McCleary Police Department. An intensive search around McCleary was conducted without any clues as to Lindsey's whereabouts. At 4:00 a.m. McCleary PD asked for the assistance of the Grays Harbor Sheriff's Office in the search for Lindsey, but the girl was never found.

At the time of her disappearance, Lindsey was wearing a hooded sweatshirt and sneakers. Melissa Baum stated that she disappeared without extra clothes, her cell phone, or any money. She said her daughter had a good relationship with the family and would not have run away.

Chief George Crumb of the McCleary Police Department stated he had been with his department for five years and had never dealt with an abduction or instituted an Amber Alert. The police department had a 2010 budget of $476,000, with $36,000 allocated for overtime. They are a small department with limited manpower and extremely limited experience dealing with child abductions. This is not to imply that the officers did not do a great job. It is a reality that working in a small town gives officers little exposure to working major crimes.

Lindsey disappeared almost in the physical midpoint of three other female disappearances: to the east, Nancy Moyer (Tenino) and Jennifer Dussaud (Humptulips); and to the west, Laura Flink (Pacific Beach). All four of these females were very short (4'9" to 5'2"), and all were between 80 and 120 pounds. All three had dark hair.

Chapter Summary

Washington is a very unique state in regards to the number of missing people. Of the twenty-two people listed as missing, eleven are boys under age ten. There are no girls under ten listed. The ratio of adult males to females missing is close: six to five.

The cluster of missing over the Washington Cascades includes four boys under the age of ten: Duffy, Piatote, Goodwin, and Panknin (eastern edge of the Cascades). I would now like you to refer to the chapter on Crater Lake and notice the number of missing boys in the Oregon Cascades under the age of ten.

Here is the timeline of missing boys under age ten in the Cascades:

Age/Missing Person	Location•Date
7/W. Piatote	WA•08/04/32
8/M. Ryan	OR•06/30/60
8/C. Goodwin	WA•06/16/63
4/B. Panknin	WA•08/03/63
9/N. Madsen	OR•10/22/89
8/D. Engbretson	OR•12/05/98
8/S. Boehlke	OR•10/04/06

Here are six boys between seven and nine years old who disappeared under highly unusual circumstances in the forests of the Pacific Northwest. Goodwin and Panknin disappeared in the same state only forty-three days apart, and the locations of their disappearances were a mere seventy-five miles apart.

Another case I discovered involves a missing eight-year-old boy from Tiger Mountain, four miles southeast of Issaquah. David Adams was walking home from a friend's house to his new home of two weeks when he disappeared. A five-day search failed to find any trace of the young lad. The age fits with other missing boys in northern Washington, and the location is in a wooded area (though fairly close to Issaquah, a suburb of Seattle). I didn't include David's case in the primary study group, but I did want to mention the specifics of his disappearance and acknowledge there are some similarities with other missing boys in Washington who were never found.

If you look just to the northwest of the Washington Cascades to Vancouver Island, the proliferation of missing boys under ten continues. The disappearances of these boys are just far enough apart not to alert law enforcement, or the media, of the commonality among these cases.

Oregon

Crater Lake

Crater Lake sits in a gorgeous setting, but there is a very dark story associated with this alpine spot. Early American Indians knew the lake as a place that they would not roam. There were stories of bad things occurring to travelers who ventured into the area, and the natives knew to stay away. Many people in North America, however, tend to travel where and when they want, and occurrences of missing people have been a part of Crater Lake's history since the beginning of the 1900s. I don't believe there is anywhere in North America where such a desolate and beautiful spot is associated with the disappearances of so many good men and boys.

Missing People near Crater Lake by Date

Missing Person	Date Missing•Age•Sex
B. B. Bakowski	02/22/1911•30•M
Herbert Brown	1935•Unknow•M
Betty McCullough	06/21/41•10•F
Jess Davis	05/08/55•2•M
Martin Ryan	06/30/60•8•M
Robert Winters	10/08/69•78•M
Charles McCullar	10/14/76•19•M

Two Years Between Incidents

Edward Nye	06/22/78•14•M
Daniel Hilkey	01/22/85•29•M

Four Years Between Incidents

Nathan Madsen	10/22/89•9•M

Five Years Between Incidents

Wayne Powell	06/18/94•39•M

Four Years Between Incidents

Robert Bobo   10/2/98•36•M
Derrick Engebretson   12/5/98•8•M

Three Years Between Incidents

Corwin Osborn   06/17/01•45•M
Jason Franks   08/09/01•21•M

Three Years Between Incidents

Celia Barnes   09/01/02•53•M
Roy Stephens   11/16/05•48•M
Samuel Boehlke   10/04/06•8•M

The Crater Lake missing people are featured below in alphabetical order.

B. B. Bakowski
Missing: 02/22/1911, Crater Lake National Park
Age at disappearance: 30

B. B. Bakowski broke new ground in photography. He made Burns, Oregon, his home. He was thirty years old, had a girlfriend, and truly enjoyed the pristine beauty that Oregon affords its residents.

While making a name for himself in landscape photography, he temporarily lived in a rooming house in Klamath Falls, Oregon, 150 miles southwest of Burns. Bakowski chose to photograph Crater Lake in the summer months of 1910. He made the trip on the rough and winding road from Klamath Falls. The road winds through heavy forests and mountains that eventually lead to the lake. He was greatly rewarded upon arrival. He was astounded by the beauty of the lake and was enthralled with the idea of photographing the region on a future trip during the winter, something that had never been done.

On or near February 1, 1911, Bakowski left his boarding house with two months' worth of supplies and took his snow sled to the trailhead to start his one-man excursion to the lake. The snow was very high in February 1911, but he told people the route he would take and the exact place he would be staying. He advised his friends to start looking for him if he wasn't back in a month.

According to articles published in the *Mail Tribune* between February 2 and March 3, 1911, a search party was sent to the lake to search for Bakowski when he hadn't returned.

Frank Burns and Albert Gipson were the first two searchers that left for Crater Lake to look for Bakowski. They returned to report that they had found his sled and shovels. They found these items covered in snow approximately 1½ miles east of the lake. They indicated that there were no supplies on the sled and believed he had arrived safely and had stored the supplies elsewhere.

A later article indicated that searchers from Medford had gone to look for Bakowski. They found his camera cases at the park's hotel building on the lake rim, but they failed to find any of his other supplies.

A final article was published days after the previous one, stating that searchers believed Bakowski had died. They had gone back to the location near the sled and found wood that had been chopped. They dug in the deep snow until they found a large canvas covering a ten-foot-deep tunnel where Bakowski's supplies were located. At the very entrance to the tunnel, searchers found a pencil stuck in the snow. Inside the tunnel, searchers found three cases of exposed film and sixty cases of unexposed film. They also found his telescope, provisions, shoes, socks, underwear, extra clothing, and other supplies. Searchers believed that Bakowski was in the tunnel for up to three nights based on what they observed. The searchers made one very interesting notation: no cooking utensils were ever found. Searchers did find two of Bakowski's cameras at the lodge building on the rim of the lake, a logical place to leave them since that was his primary position to take photos.

Case Summary

Bakowski was the first case in the modern era of someone disappearing at Crater Lake. His disappearance is quite interesting for a multitude of reasons. Six people have disappeared in the Crater Lake region during the winter months—an odd statistic considering 90 percent of the visitation to the area occurs during the summer.

It's obvious that Bakowski made it to his destination. He was able to set up a nice shelter in a snow tunnel. He brought sixty-three rolls of unexposed film for a three- to four-week excursion. If he had planned to be at the lake for twenty-one days, he would have used approximately three rolls of film per day. Three rolls of exposed film were found. Bakowski was obviously making noise while at his campsite: he was chopping wood. If anyone had been in the area, they would have heard the chopping. If he had started a fire and cooked food, the odors would have permeated the area around his camp, letting anyone in the region know he was there.

Bakowski had stretched the canvas cover over his tunnel prior to the last time he left it. It seems quite odd that searchers did not find cooking utensils at the site. Was Bakowski cooking at the site when he heard something, went outside, and was taken? Maybe he casually went out with his plate of food and was taken. It's possible. It's also possible that he was at the hotel building and something drastic happened. Two of his cameras were found at the building near the edge of the lake, and this is the exact location where Charles McCullar would later disappear (1976). Some people may easily explain the disappearance of Bakowski as an accident—he slipped into the lake and drowned. I don't think so. I've always believed that people are much more careful when they are alone in the wild with no possibility of rescue—the exact situation that Bakowski was in. Bakowski knew the risks associated with his excursion; he would have been extremely careful.

One last item not mentioned in area reports is that no firearms were ever found with his supplies. If Bakowski was outside the tunnel, and there was a threat, he would have had a firearm. Where is it?

Celia Barnes
Missing: 09/01/02, Gold Hill, OR
5'2", 110 lb.
Age at disappearance: 53

Celia Barnes is a former marine. She is 5'2" and weighs 110 pounds, a small woman. On September 1, 2002, Celia got separated from her sister while hiking along the 6000 block of Sardine Creek Road in Gold Hill, approximately fifty miles southwest of Crater Lake near the "House of Mystery." The House of Mystery is a tourist location that supposedly has an unusual vortex. The American Indians claimed that this area was forbidden ground, and all were told to stay away. The area of Celia's disappearance is among steep mountains at an elevation of 1,200 feet.

Celia is one of only two women on the list of missing from the Crater Lake region. The only photo of Celia that I could find shows a very small woman with very short hair, someone who at a distance could be mistaken for a small man. When reviewing disappearances from this region, a missing woman is quite unusual. If there was a predator in the area looking for a man, it's possible that Celia was taken by mistake.

Robert Michael Bobo
Missing: 10/02/98, Union Creek, OR
Age at disappearance: 36

On October 2, 1998, Robert Michael Bobo set up camp in Woodruff Meadows just south of the Union Creek Resort and just west of the highway 62. Robert was at that location for hunting season, which started the following morning. He was dropped at his campsite by a female friend and later seen at the site by two other hunters.

On the morning of the opening of deer-hunting season, a friend of Robert's arrived at his campsite but couldn't find him. A search of the site showed that Robert had left behind all of his firearms, supplies, and clothes. Robert was known to wear a distinctive hat that he never went anywhere without; this was located on the ground at his campsite. Law enforcement believes that he went in search of another campsite when he was injured and became unable to move. This doesn't sound plausible to me. According to his family, Robert would not travel anywhere without that hat.

Before his disappearance, Robert was at his campsite planning for an early morning. He was last seen at 9:00 p.m.—bedtime for many hunters. In October in Oregon at 9:00 p.m., it is dark, making it doubtful anyone is going to be searching for a new campsite. If his relatives and friends say that Robert wouldn't go anywhere without his cap, we need to respect that opinion. It would appear that some type of disturbance or hostility had occurred, and Robert suddenly left the campsite or was taken against his will. This site is not far from a church camp and the Union Creek Resort.

Samuel Boehlke
Missing: 10/14/06, Crater Lake National Park
4'8", 85 lb.
Age at disappearance: 8

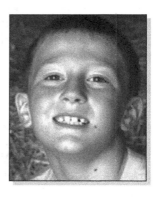

I received the Boehlke file through an FOIA request I filed with the NPS. The file is thick and shows a huge effort on the part of regional law enforcement to find this boy.

Samuel Boehlke is the son of Kenneth Boehlke and Kirsten Becker. Kenneth and Kirsten were married and later divorced in 2005. Kenneth and Kirsten lived in the area of Portland, Oregon.

The weekend of October 14, 2006, was a special father-and-son weekend for eight-year-old Sammy and his dad. Sammy had been diagnosed with a mild form of autism, and this was a chance for the two to head to the mountains for some bonding time.

Kenneth and Sammy made the drive from Portland to rented cabin #62 at Diamond Lake resort, ten miles north of Crater

Lake and just outside the northern border of the national park. Diamond Lake is a year-round resort on a beautiful reservoir in the heart of the Oregon Cascades. The boys spent the first night in their cabin watching television and then decided to take a trip to Crater Lake.

Kenneth and Sammy headed south on Highway 138 to the northern entrance to the park. They eventually made their way around the lake to the Crater Lake Lodge, where they had lunch and played a card game called Yugio. Sammy had a grilled cheese sandwich and then drank a sprite. They departed the lodge and started to slowly make their way along the eastern side of the lake, driving north.

At approximately 4:00 p.m., they stopped in a parking lot on the west side of the road near Cleetwood Cove, a location that would become etched into the mind of Kenneth Boehlke for eternity.

The two exited the car, and Sammy ran across the road to look at a large rock formation. Sammy had a lot of energy and liked to have his dad chase him when they were out of the car. He ran around the mound, over a small crest, and disappeared over the small hill. Kenneth followed as fast as he could. Once over the hill, he faced directly into a large wooded area and couldn't see Sammy. Kenneth yelled for his son and ran in half circles around the area attempting to catch a glimpse of him. He found nothing. Kenneth started to get frantic and tried to call 911 on his cell phone, but there was no reception. He ran to the roadway and flagged down two separate vehicles asking them to call 911 for assistance.

Inside of thirty minutes, the first park representative arrived at the scene and immediately called for additional rangers. Within hours, there were dozens of searchers scouring the area looking for Sammy. Later in the day, a storm hit the Crater Lake area and significantly hampered any rescue attempts. The NPS and nearby agencies searched for Sammy Boehlke for almost a month.

Kirsten and Kenneth had been staying at an NPS cabin during the search period and had monitored the activity. Kenneth had been questioned numerous times about his activity with Sammy and continued to tell a believable story about what happened to his son. On November 11, 2006, Ranger David Brennan wrote a report (CRLA#0600000542), and in it outlined that $540,000 had been expended for the search of Samuel Boehlke. In that search, two helicopters, two hundred searchers, canines, fourteen agencies, and the FBI participated. The ranger estimated that there was an 88 percent probability of detection in the primary search area based on the SAR efforts.

The only evidence they found were footprints of a young person with a small stride found October 20, 2006, going downhill in an area of Grouse Hill. The area was searched extensively and nothing else was found.

On November 7, 2006, the Jackson County Sheriff's Office produced a report addressed to the Crater Lake National Park. The report outlined the search conducted by a canine and its handler. On pages 6–7 of that report, they outlined a peculiar response from the canine. The dog was placed next to the location adjacent to Crater Lake where the victim's vehicle was parked. From that location the dog was to pick up the scent, track it across the road, down the trail, and presumably into the woods. The dog moved along the rock wall adjacent to the parking lot and the lake, never going anywhere near the other side of the road. It looked toward the lake, put its front paws on the wall and barked while looking at the lake. It did this twice. The handler terminated the tracking, believing that the dog could not pick up a scent in the area. It would almost appear from the dog's response that it had no interest in the area across the road where Sammy disappeared.

David Brennan's report also stated that it was the opinion of the NPS and the FBI that there is no evidence that Samuel Boehlke was the victim of a crime.

Case Summary

The search for Sammy Boehlke changed from an SAR to a recovery over many months. In the *Herald and News* on September 11, 2009, an article appeared about the Samuel Boehlke case and additional training occurring at Crater Lake National Park. On column three of the article, Crater Lake National Park Chief

Ranger Marshall Neeck stated, "We have had a lot of turnover in staff in the last few years, and this is an opportunity to train with local partners and build a strong and efficient search and rescue cooperative here at the park." What is interesting about this statement is the amount of turnover they had experienced at the park just prior to the Boehlke disappearance. If the NPS relies on the institutional memory of their rangers to assist in missing people and criminal matters, Crater Lake National Park staff does not possess that knowledge.

Authors Note: The Samuel Boehlke disappearance is one of the cases we covered in our movie, "Missing 411." Please refer to our website for additional details, www.canammissing.com.

I received a bulk of information about many NPS cases from an ongoing series of FOIA requests that I had submitted over many months. In several of these requests, I was advised that the NPS had lost reports (such as the Charles McCullar case) or, in numerous cases, didn't have any information.

All FOIA requests for the western U.S. go through the western regional office of the NPS in Denver. Specifically, they are addressed to Charis Wilson, the NPS FOIA officer. When I asked Ms. Wilson for a list of all missing people from the NPS in the western United States, she stated that they didn't maintain a list of that information. When I asked for a list of all missing people inside their parks for the entire U.S., she stated they didn't maintain that information. When I asked for a park-by-park list of missing people inside their system, she stated they did not maintain lists of that type. I asked Ms. Wilson if there was any way to get a list of missing people in Crater Lake National Park. She stated that it would probably cost me thousands of dollars because they would have to search boxes and boxes, year by year, looking at reports one by one. I asked if there was a year-by-year ledger of reports indicating the type of report and the report number. I was told that there was not. When I asked if all missing person reports were kept in one file, I was told they were not.

On October 21, 2010, I sent Ms. Wilson an e-mail asking the same questions in a different way, hoping for a different response. This time I asked specifically about one of the biggest parks in the system, Yosemite. I wanted to ensure that there wasn't some mistake in the way the NPS was interpreting my questions. Here is her response: "I have also re-verified with the park that they do not maintain any such list. Instead they rely on the institutional memory of employees who have worked at the park for years." Ms. Wilson also stated, "There is not any kind of master list that is maintained, on an NPS-wide basis, of missing persons or even persons who have died on National Park Service Lands."

The lunacy of the statement will not be lost on the Boehlke family. If the NPS is relying on the "institutional memory of employees," Samuel Boehlke was a victim of the lack of longtime experience at Crater Lake. It might have been appropriate to read the reports of other young men who had disappeared on the road around the lake to see where their bodies were located. Perhaps that would have been a good place to look for Sammy. Based on the statement from the chief park ranger at Crater Lake regarding the high turnover they experienced, this may be an issue when it comes to remembering the specifics about disappearances.

On October 29, 2010, Ms. Wilson sent me another e-mail explaining the NPS position and their lack of lists on missing people. She stated, "I understand that while Yosemite and other National Park sites do not maintain a list such as what you have requested, you may be able to piece together one based on what other authors have compiled." The NPS still does not maintain a list of people missing on their property, anywhere. When I asked how much they would charge me for developing a list of missing people in Yosemite, the quote was $37,848. I have discussed this with some of the most experienced law enforcement directors in the U.S., and they are astounded that the NPS doesn't keep this information readily available. I personally believe they have the information but don't want you to know the statistics as it may affect visitations to parks and, thus, revenue.

Herbert Brown
Missing: 1935, Silver Creek Falls State Park, OR
Very little information is available about this incident other than Brown disappeared in the Silver Falls State Park in 1935.

Jess Davis
Missing: 05/08/55, a.m., Gopher Valley, McMinnville, OR
Age at disappearance: 2
Note: This disappearance occurred to the west of the Cascades yet is included in this chapter because it fits the profile of other young boys who have gone missing in the Cascades.

The Davis family left their home in The Dalles to visit the ranch of Mr. and Mrs. William Fagan, the parents of Mrs. Davis, on the outskirts of McMinnville, Oregon.

On Sunday morning, May 8, 1955, Jess Davis was in the backyard of the ranch house, and his three sisters were playing in the front yard. Jess was alone for only ten minutes when the family realized he was missing. The search for Jess was started immediately with hollering, walking the grounds, etc., but they couldn't find the boy. A call was made to the local sheriff and a formal search was initiated.

The sheriff called for three teams of bloodhounds to report to the Fagan ranch. The bloodhounds could not pick up a scent. Over one hundred professional and volunteer searchers scoured the hillsides in an effort to find the young boy. The teams continued to search through the night without any success.

In the morning hours of May 9, loggers were walking through a valley in Panther Creek and heard someone crying. The men walked toward the sound and found Jess Davis. Jess had been missing for twenty-four hours in forty-degree temperatures but appeared to be in satisfactory condition. A doctor examined the boy and found deep scratches on his legs. The loggers stated that it appeared as though the boy had been wading in the creek even though the water and outside temperature were cold.

The idea that a two-year-old boy survived twenty-four hours in the woods of Oregon is an interesting story in itself. An article in the *Daily Chronicle* on May 9, 1955, reported the following: "It appeared that the child had covered about six miles, part by road and part over a hill, in a circuitous journey ... Searchers were puzzled about how [Jess Davis] got so far in the brush covered country." I referenced a terrain map to understand the topography of this area. Jess Davis had to cross at least two sets of mountains with an average elevation of one thousand feet in order to reach Panther Creek. The map does show a distance of six miles—six *air* miles. The idea that a two-year-old boy could cover that distance in twenty-four hours makes me as puzzled as the searchers were in 1955.

Derrick Engebretson
Missing: 12/05/98, Winema National Forest, Rocky Point, OR
Age at disappearance: 8

Rocky Point is located adjacent to Highway 140 on the banks of Upper Klamath Lake. It sits just on the east side of the Sky Lakes Wilderness Area, a very desolate and wild region of Oregon. This is the area Robert Engebretson picked for a Christmas tree–cutting excursion for his dad and son, Derrick. The three made the fifty-mile drive from their home in Bonanza through beautiful forests and a gorgeous setting next to the lake.

It was in the late afternoon that the boys reached the area near Rocky Point to look for their Christmas tree. Derrick was bundled in winter clothes and carried a small hatchet. There was snow on the ground, and the boys walked around the area trying to find the right tree. Both Robert and his father thought they were watching Derrick, but it turned out neither was. Soon they forgot the tree and needed to find Derrick.

Just west of the location where Derrick disappeared is a very steep mountain leading into a wilderness area; to the east is a small highway and then the lake. There were not a lot of places for Derrick to hide. The men realized they hadn't heard Derrick for a while and started to call his name. Soon, they were frantically looking for the boy. The men flagged down a passing car and asked the driver to contact the sheriff for assistance.

A storm had just arrived in the area and a light snowfall was starting. This light snowfall would soon turn into a major storm that crippled the search effort.

The ledger of response activity to Rocky Point follows:

4:38 p.m. The temperature in the area was 23 degrees and the snow was falling heavy.

5:01 p.m. Still no deputy on site, claimed he was caught in the storm, asked for assistance from State police.

5:04 p.m. Sheriff sergeant requests a SAR response. The search is being conducted between Rocky Point and mile marker 12.

5:36 p.m. 911 calls SAR team again and requests response. 911 is told that it is a whiteout, and the SAR team is having their annual Christmas party.

5:39 p.m. State police say they are sending snowmobiles.

6:30 p.m. USFS Law Enforcement Officer Doug Corrigan arrives at Rocky Point.

6:45 p.m. Sheriff Burkhardt gets on the radio and requests update.

7:00 p.m. Five State troopers arrive at the search location, Sgt. Bill Floyd, Lt. Mediger, Sgt. Chris Kabe, Trooper Randall, and Trooper Nork.

7:31 p.m. Snow stops falling.

8:25 p.m. Four hours and twelve minutes after original 911 call, dispatch calls Sheriff Burkhardt asking when SAR is going to respond. He states that there is no ETA because of weather and snow conditions.

8:44 p.m. Klamath Falls PD offers snowmobiles from a local shop owner.

9:00 p.m. First SAR units arrive, including trackers Larry Hawkins and Dan Anderson.

9:30 p.m. Five hours and seventeen minutes after original 911 call, seventeen Klamath County SAR units arrive at the scene.

When the weather did clear, the Air Force sent a FLIR-equipped helicopter into the area to scan the mountainside for heat, but nothing was found. Searchers poured into the area the following days and trudged through deep snow looking for Derrick.

The search effort did find some interesting items. On the hillside far above the location where Derrick disappeared, searchers found a crude shelter that was made out of several fallen fir trees. The shelter probably could not have been penetrated by FLIR as there were large logs utilized in the construction. Canines were at this location but didn't hit on Derrick's scent at the shelter. On the same mountainside, they also found shoestrings, a torn T-shirt, and eyeglasses—that's how complete this search was.

During the course of the last several years, investigators have interviewed dozens of people, from rapists to pedophiles, all with interesting results but all without finding Derrick or concrete clues of his whereabouts. Some investigators believe that Derrick made it back to the highway, where someone picked him up. Other private trackers believe Derrick fell through ice at the lake and drowned. The problem with the drowning theory is that Derrick's body never surfaced. I also don't believe that Derrick would have crossed the road knowing that his dad and grandfather were on the side of the road he was on.

Robert Engebretson spent weeks at the site searching for his son. Derrick's mom, Lori, also spent weeks searching and supporting other SAR members in their efforts. The Engebretson's left a Christmas tree up in their house for three years hoping Derrick would return home. Derrick's grandfather, Bob, beat himself up badly after the disappearance, taking blame for Derrick vanishing.

Case Summary

I went to the spot where Derrick disappeared. It is a lonely spot in the winter, and there was very little vehicular traffic the day I was there. The idea that Derrick made it back to the road and a vehicle happened to come by and pick him up with a pedophile in it seems highly unlikely. However, I am very concerned about the fact that three eight- to nine-year-old boys have disappeared in a forty-mile radius of Crater Lake National Park in a very remote area of the woods. The fact that there is not significant press coverage on this issue is even more disturbing.

Commonalities: Nathan Madsen, Derrick Engebretson, Samuel Boehlke

Missing in the woods near Crater Lake National Park.
Missing while in or very near the presence of their fathers or authority figures.
All missing near large bodies of water.
Two missing in October; one missing in December.
Two boys eight years old; one boy nine years old.
Storms hit the area immediately after their disappearances.
Massive searches for each boy.
No evidence of the boys being in the area.

The commonalities amongst these boys' disappearances are facts. The public should demand answers and policy changes inside the National Park Service. It costs nothing to keep lists of missing people, yet it may create an atmosphere where people want to understand the circumstances of some disappearances, and it may heighten the awareness of park personnel to these issues in the region. I have no doubt that local rangers have no clue of the number of missing in and around their parks, but, I believe administrators within NPS fully understand the situation.

Jason Franks
Missing: 08/09/2001, Winema National Forest, Chiloquin, OR
Age at disappearance: 21

In August 2001, Jason Franks was camping with five longtime friends in the Beaver Marsh area east of Chiloquin. The friends state that they left Jason alone when they went to run errands. When the friends returned to the camp, Jason was gone and his dog was tied to a nearby tree. The campers had been at this site for two days when Jason vanished. Jason's family stated that he is a very reliable person and would not have left without telling them where he was going.

Jason disappeared approximately thirty-five miles southeast of Crater Lake National Park and twenty miles east of the location of the Derrick Engebretson disappearance. The campsite where Jason disappeared is on federal land that was previously owned by American Indians. It is ten miles east of Highway 197 on Silver Lake Road.

There are many similarities between the Franks and Bobo disappearances: both at remote campsites, both alone, and nothing was missing from either location.

Law enforcement officials have said they believe foul play was involved in Jason's disappearance.

Daniel Hilkey
Missing: 01/22/85, Gold Hill, OR
Age at disappearance: 29

Daniel Hilkey was at his residence on Holcomb Springs Road in Gold Hill, Oregon, when he disappeared. This is a road in a wooded area at an elevation of 1,200–1,400 feet. There is a cemetery on the road and a small lake in the area. This is only two air miles from the location that Celia Barnes disappeared.

Law enforcement officials have said they believe foul play was involved in Hilkey's disappearance.

Nathan Madsen
Missing: 10/22/89, Little Deschutes River Valley, Deschutes National Forest, OR
Age at disappearance: 9

In late October 1989, family and friends of the Madsens' were in the Little Deschutes River canyon near the Mount Thielsen Wilderness Area doing an annual herding of family cattle prior to the onset of winter. The Madsens' lived in Veneta, Oregon, and made the trip east to herd their cattle every fall. It was a family event that everyone looked forward to. The team was on horseback herding range cattle when, at approximately 2:00 p.m., nine-year-old Nathan Madsen rode up to his father, Jerry, and said he was cold and would head back to camp. Nathan was riding his sorrel pony, Tony. His father later reported that he had told his son to go back and assumed that he'd follow the dirt road back to camp. Later that evening Jerry made it back to camp and was told by his wife, Sarah, that Nathan had not returned. Jerry and all others on hand headed back into the canyon and searched throughout the night for Nathan. They found nothing.

As Jerry and his crew were searching for Nathan, a call was made to law enforcement officials and a formal search was mobilized.

The fall of 1989 was not a season that anyone would want to remember. The weather immediately started to turn bad once Nathan went missing. The temperature dropped into the twenties, and snow flurries began to fall. U.S. Air Force reserves, the Klamath County Sheriff's Office, USFS, U.S. Smoke Jumpers, Civil Air Patrol, Oregon National Guard, Douglass County Sheriff's Office, tracking dogs, and citizen volunteers were all searching for Nathan. The search was initially confined to a thirteen-square-mile canyon, but it was later expanded to cover over sixty square miles.

On October 26, Klamath County Sheriff Carl Burkhardt stated, "Right now it seems like he disappeared off the face of the earth."

On October 29, the sheriff called in a homicide detective to monitor the Madsen case. The sheriff ordered Detective Mark Hannigan to interview everyone who was on the cattle drive. Burkhardt made no mention of possible suspects or any reason to suspect foul play.

During the first ten days of the search, as many as 350 people scoured the mountains for Nathan Madsen. After one of the largest ten-day searches in the history of Oregon, Sheriff Burkhardt called off the primary search for the boy, stating, "We ran out of places to search."

Even after the vast majority of law enforcement had left the area, Jerry Madsen kept searching for his son. Jerry rode out every morning to look for signs of the pony or Nathan. The temperature was in the low twenties; snow was deep; and sometimes the snow was still falling. On November 19, 1989, at 2:00 p.m., a glimmer of hope rewarded Jerry Madsen. In a large meadow at the headwater of the Little Deschutes River, Jerry found Nathan's pony. The pony had lost weight and did not have its tack, saddle, or blanket.

Four days after Jerry found Nathan's pony, someone donated four hours of flight time in a helicopter to fly over the area where the pony was found. The helicopter flew out of Eugene and quickly made its way to the region of the Mount Thielsen Wilderness Area.

The four hours passed quickly and nothing was found. Winter started to reach central Oregon and all searches for Nathan stopped. The Madsen's returned to their home in Veneta.

The *Spokane Review* ran an article on November 30, 1989, on Nathan's disappearance. It included an interview with Klamath County District Attorney Edwin Caleb. He stated, "The state police are approaching it [the disappearance of Nathan] from the point of view that there was foul play." In the same article, State Police Major John Collins was questioned about the rationale of believing a crime may have occurred. He stated, "It seems far fetched that someone bent on abducting a child would find the area, much less be in the area at the exact time Nathan was separated from his family." This statement does show that law enforcement investigators were entertaining the idea that something other than Nathan being lost was coming into play. This thinking starts to occur when officers believe that they've searched all possible locations and can't find any clues. In the same article, Caleb stated, "It's the strangest case I've ever been involved in."

U.S. Forest Service investigators actually pulled all wilderness permits issued for the time when Nathan went missing. They proactively went out and interviewed each of these individuals—a great angle and attempt to locate witnesses.

Through early July 1990, the Madsen family continued their search for Nathan. In an article printed on July 23, 1990, in the *Seattle Times*, the Oregon State Police stated that they were notified on July 21 that human remains had been found by the Madsen family in the Mount Thielsen Wilderness Area. Oregon State Police detectives hiked into the area on Sunday and confirmed that the remains appear to be those of a nine-year-old. The police confirmed that the saddle and clothing at the scene belonged to Nathan Madsen. The finding was made at 1:00 p.m. Saturday in the Mule Mountain drainage, approximately a half mile from where Nathan's pony was located and three miles from where Nathan disappeared. Jerry Madsen said he believed that the area might not have been searched.

An article from July 23, 1990, on the *Spokesman Review* Web site, column four, reported: "State police investigators were closed-mouthed Sunday night about their findings at the site. Sgt. Richard Stroup of the state police office in Klamath Falls said that 'clothing and tack identified as belonging to Nathan Madsen were found at the scene. Numerous small bone fragments were also located.'"

Nathan's remains were sent to the Oregon State Medical Examiner's office in Portland. Dr. Karen Gunson stated she examined bones, clothing, and other material, and none of the evidence showed any violence. Gunson stated, "Even though the bones are so scanty that we cannot tell exactly that they came from Nathan, we call them Nathan's because of the whole of the case." She stated that the remains included a skull and some long arm bones. She did not detect any signs of injury to the skull. Gunson also stated, "In looking at the scene, the possibility of foul play is very remote." She based her ruling for the cause of death—hypothermia—on the circumstances at the time Nathan disappeared. The jaw and teeth were later sent to forensics and positively identified as Nathan Madsen's.

Case Summary

I hope readers key in on several statements made by investigators on this case. The first flashing yellow light is that the sheriff assigned a homicide detective to this case at an early stage. He recognized that something wasn't right; something didn't feel right. Law enforcement officers get these feelings and sometimes act on them.

The second flashing yellow light is the state police making a statement about someone abducting Nathan. How could anyone possibly be in the area and just happen to see Nathan? Odd. It shows that the state police were thinking abduction on this case at an early stage. I believe that police investigators had always thought abduction on the case and handled it as such all the way through to the body recovery.

It's difficult for me to believe that searchers didn't thoroughly comb the area within a one-mile radius from where Nathan's pony was recovered. Knowing the diligence of Jerry Madsen's search, it's hard to imagine that he and other searchers didn't scour every inch of dirt in the area the horse was found. Jerry did not adamantly state that the area where Nathan's remains were found had been searched.

But, again, if they were found in a box canyon, as all indications show, why wouldn't searchers have gone all the way to the end to completely search the canyon?

It's disturbing that Nathan ended up where he did: the opposite direction from where he was headed. He was going out of the canyon to camp, but he ended up back at the head of the canyon. How did that happen? The river in the area flows out of the canyon. Anyone can determine the proper direction to leave based on just the river and creeks and the downhill path. It's very difficult to imagine how Nathan got turned around and then stayed in an area he knew was not close to their camp.

Gunson made an interesting statement when she said, "The possibility of foul play is very remote." Her statement indicates that foul play is still a possibility. Why does she think this? What was it about the remains that couldn't exclude foul play as a possibility? The more disturbing question is, Where were Nathan's large bones—hip, femur, spine? Why were there small bone fragments at the scene, and why were the bones fragmented?

Please read the section below about the body recovery of Charles McCullar from the Bybee Creek drainage at Crater Lake: the exact description was given for his body recovery. In the McCullar case, NPS law enforcement rangers on scene were so concerned about what they found, they called for an FBI evidence-response team to assist in the recovery and investigation. The location of Nathan's remains was about twenty air miles north of Crater Lake.

My prayers and my heart go out to the Madsen family over the loss of Nathan. Jerry Madsen made many heroic attempts to locate his son. I hope the misery that he suffers from losing his boy can somehow be minimized, though I couldn't understand how.

Charles McCullar
Missing: 10/14/76, Crater Lake National Park (Body Found)
Age at disappearance: 19

The disappearance of Charles McCullar is as unnerving as the finding of his skeletal remains. Official documents and facts surrounding this case were extremely difficult to find. I submitted a series of FOIA requests to the NPS over several months. The official response from Charis Wilson of NPS in Denver states that they have lost all reports related to this incident. They claim that the park did not have the space to maintain these files, so they were destroyed. I asked if the regional office or NPS headquarters in Washington DC had copies: No, those were missing as well.

An organization called the Crater Lake Institute maintains a Web site that highlights the unusual incidents that have happened in and around the lake. It was through this site that I learned about McCullar. It was also through this site that I learned the names of park rangers who responded to this incident.

An FOIA request submitted to the FBI did produce fifty pages of documents that were forwarded to me. Inside the box of papers was a series of letters written by Charles McCullar's father requesting that the FBI become involved in his son's disappearance. When the FBI stated that they couldn't join the investigation, Mr. McCullar wrote letters to Harry Byrd requesting that the congress intervene. Mr. McCullar was convinced beyond any doubt that his son had been abducted and taken against his will, and he may have been correct.

The story you are about to read was gleaned from reviewing FOIA documents, newspaper clippings, and interviews with NPS personnel.

Charles Wesley McCullar left his Virginia home on January 8, 1975, on the trip of a lifetime. He was going to travel the NPS system and photograph the splendor of our national parks. He was a very reliable and punctual son: he would routinely call his parents to explain where he was and the itinerary he would follow. He made calls to his parents on January 16 and 22 from Yuma, Arizona. The last call his parents would receive was on January 27, 1975, while Charles was at a friend's residence in Eugene, Oregon.

On January 29, Charles told his friend that he was going to travel to Crater Lake to photograph the park in its winter element. He said he would return by the thirty-first, and that if he wasn't back by February 1, call the police. This was the last time his friend ever saw Charles.

On February 1, 1975, Charles's friend called law enforcement and filed a missing person report. The NPS, in conjunction with state police, worked the McCullar case. The area around the lake and nearby cities were blanketed with flyers of Charles's face. The bulletins were not out long before a logger reported to police that he had given Charles a ride to the park entrance. He believed the date was January 30, 1975.

Per reports in the FOIA file, snow depths at Crater Lake were 24"–90" with drifts up to twenty feet. On January 31, four inches of snow fell at the park, with more in the outlying higher elevations.

On February 10, 1975, Charles's parents were notified that he was officially a missing person. It's hard to understand why it took so long to notify the family, but that is the fact.

The state police did confirm that Charles had traveled east and then south on Highway 138 to enter the park along the northern perimeter. This route would have taken Charles by Diamond Lake Resort, the closest resort to the northern entry of Crater Lake. The police gathered this information from interviewing witnesses who had responded to their request for assistance. This is where the story gets very cloudy. There seems to be little information beyond the fact that Charles was in this location on January 30, 1975.

His father made at least two trips to the park searching for his son. The father's letters indicate complete frustration with the Oregon State Police and their investigation, and complete admiration for the NPS investigators.

On the first trip that Mr. McCullar made to the park, he left a list of items that Charles would have been carrying should someone find them in the park. One item that was quite peculiar was an odd-shaped Volkswagen car key that would probably have been in Charles's backpack, which he would have been carrying. Several rangers were in the administration building and heard what Mr. McCullar was describing; one of those law enforcement rangers was Marion Jack.

Marion was a seasonal law enforcement ranger at Crater Lake, usually working from late May to early September. This seasonal employment was a perfect fit for Marion and his family, as he was a full-time science teacher at McLaughlin Junior High School in

Medford, OR. Each May, Marion would pack up and move his family to the seasonal housing area at Crater Lake in a region called Sleepy Hollow, where they spent twenty-four summers—1962 to 1986. Marion was a graduate of the Federal Law Enforcement Training Center in Harpers Ferry, West Virginia. The law enforcement academy training was a nice addition to his bachelor's degree from Southern Oregon University.

In early October of 1976, a group of hikers were well off the normal trails on the west side of the park, near Bybee Creek. This creek drains water from the western high perimeter of Crater Lake. The flow travels west toward one of the main highways surrounding the park. This is a very, very desolate area where most people would never travel. The hikers found a backpack and a scarf. They thought this was unusual. They searched the backpack, removed a few items, and then hiked to the main law enforcement office at Crater Lake. Once they arrived at the office, they removed an unusual key and other items. Just as the hikers placed the key on the table, Marion Jack remembered that this was the key that Charles McCullar's dad had stated would be in his possession.

Marion just happened to be at Crater Lake Park in October because the park superintendent had asked him to bring up his horses so they could ride the range to look for trespassing cows that were grazing on NPS land. Marion asked the hikers where they found the backpack; they stated that it was in the Bybee Creek drainage. The hikers drew a map of the location, and a decision was made that Marion and Ranger Dave Lange would ride Marion's horses into Bybee Creek and see if they could locate Charles McCullar.

I knew at this point that I needed to locate and interview one of the rangers identified on the Crater Lake Institute site that had found Charles McCullar. Through an exhaustive effort, I found Marion and drove to his residence in southern Oregon to meet him.

Marion is one of those people whom all of us are lucky to have had protecting us while in the National Park System. He was warm, gracious, and happy to be retired. We had a great talk about the general job he had every summer for twenty-four years and then started to discuss the specifics of the McCullar case. He immediately stated that he would always remember that day because of the many unusual aspects of the scene.

Marion confirmed that he and Dave Lange rode to the Bybee Creek area together. He said they found the scene fairly quickly because the hikers had hung clothing from a tree branch in an effort to make it easy to find. Marion said they walked down into a bowl-type area with a small creek running in one end and out the other. A tree with a four-foot diameter crossed the area and, partially, the creek. Dave and Marion searched the small canyon and did not find much until Marion stepped over the large tree and saw a pair of pants immediately on the other side. He explained that if you were standing straight up and melted straight down into your pants, that is what it looked like. The first thing about the scene that struck him as very unusual was that the belt buckle and the pants' snap were undone. He reached down and found one broken tibia or fibula in the right leg of the pants. It was broken in the middle and had blood on each end. There were no other bones in the pants or in the area. They found the elastic from underwear, but the underwear had deteriorated away. The 1¼-inch-wide brown leather belt was still in good condition. Marion looked under the pants and found socks with small bones inside but no boots, which McCullar had definitely been wearing when he disappeared in the middle of winter.

Dave and Marion then started to walk in circles from the pants to locate other evidence. On the other side of the fallen tree, approximately five feet away, they found a skull upside down and a lower jawbone. They also found an area that was scattered with very small bone fragments. The rangers did not find any large bones, such as hips, shoulders, femurs, or vertebrae. They continued to search for other evidence, such as Charles's coat, camera, and knife. After conducting a thorough search of the immediate area, they decided they needed to leave with the skull and other evidence they had recovered and return later with an FBI evidence response team (ERT).

Dave Lange took numerous photos of the scene, and Marion remembers writing three separate reports on the recovery and evidence collection. The reports were submitted through normal NPS channels. He specifically remembers the father (Mr. McCullar) telling them that they would find a camera and a specific type of folding knife—two items that were never recovered.

I asked Marion if there was anything about the scene on Bybee Creek that caused him concern or suspicion. He stated that he could never understand what happened to the young man's boots. They would have been heavier than the pants, so the pants would have washed away before the boots (if that is what occurred). He felt that the pants had not been moved since Charles died. I asked him to explain why the pants and belt were unbuckled. Marion said that was another very unusual part of the scene that couldn't be explained. The camera, knife, and coat were never found at the Bybee Creek location, but those were all with Charles when he disappeared. Other questions I asked Marion included, Why were no large bones found, and why was there only one bone in one pant leg? He said these were all really good questions, but he didn't have any answers. It made no sense to him either. He asked me why there wouldn't have been bones in the other pant leg. It appeared to him that the pants hadn't been disturbed since the time of death. The last question I asked Ranger Marion Jack was, Why were bone chips and pieces at the scene when most animals would have taken the bones and left with them? Marion said this is another aspect of the scene that has confused him over the years. He knows that bears would take a piece of the body and walk with it, but these pieces were all consumed directly on scene—something he had never seen before.

After Marion and Dave returned to the park headquarters, Oregon State Police and the FBI were notified of the evidence and requested to respond and assist with further recovery efforts.

On October 18, 1976, FBI special agents and state police detectives delivered the skull and jaw to a Klamath Falls pathologist. It was the expert opinion of the pathologist that the skull belonged to Charles Wesley McCullar. It had not been damaged.

Case Summary

There are many questions surrounding the disappearance of Charles McCullar. One of the best descriptions of the complexities of this case appears on the Crater Lake Institute Web site under the year 1976:

> McCullar's cause of death is ruled by natural causes, but the mystery remains how it was possible for McCullar to have walked from the North Entrance, on top of 105 inches of new snow, 14 miles into Bybee Creek, especially considering that the young man was not prepared for winter survival. One theory is that McCullar may have followed snowmobile tracks, but the machines are not allowed into remote areas of the park, and secondly, the new snow was so fresh and deep, it would

have been impossible for snowmobiles to have traveled the distance.

So, just how McCullar was able to get into the Bybee Creek drainage remains conjecture, as does his exact cause of death. The boy's father remains convinced that his son was the victim of foul play because none of McCullar's expensive camera equipment was ever found.

I don't profess to be a conspiracy theorist, but I do find it almost unbelievable that both Charles McCullar and B. B. Bakowski simply disappeared from the Crater Lake perimeter. Both were photographers; storms hit the area immediately after each went missing; and the NPS has lost all reports for Charles's disappearance.

Yes, the pathologist did make a determination that Charles died of natural causes, but that is only an educated guess based on no visible injuries to the skull.

Here are the questions I want you to ponder:

1. Where are Charles's boots? Boots are heavy. They don't blow away in the wind.
2. Where is the camera and knife (carried on his hip) that were supposed to be with Charles?
3. Where is the coat that Charles was supposed to be wearing?
4. Why would Charles's pants and belt buckle be undone?
5. If Charles did die at the spot where his pants were recovered, why was there only one broken bone in the right pant leg?
6. Where were the left leg bones, the femur of the right leg, and the hip bones?
7. The pants weren't ripped to shreds as if a bear had gone for the meat of the leg; as Marion said, it was like he melted into those pants. The pants were found intact. How could an animal have consumed Charles without tearing the pants to shreds to get to the meat?
8. Charles's father was adamant with law enforcement that he felt his son was taken against his will and, because of those feelings, wanted the FBI to investigate the case. Do you think Charles's dad may have been correct?

Below is an excerpt from the letter Charles's dad wrote to Congressman Harry Byrd requesting FBI assistance: "With no evidence being found in the extensive winter and summer searching, and knowing him to be a responsible young adult, we can find no other presumption to explain his disappearance other than that he was involuntarily detained and killed."

I requested a complete case file from the FBI on the McCullar's disappearance. I was given a few papers and letters but was refused the Evidence Response Team's report and refused the case file report based on what they claimed were "privacy concerns." The NPS claims they have lost all of their reports on this incident.

Betty McCullough
Missing: 6/21/41, Silver Creek Falls State Park, OR
Age at disappearance: 10
**Disability

After spending many hours searching for information on the Betty McCullough disappearance there is really very little information available. We do know that Betty was staying at the Silver Creek Falls State Park in a cabin with her family. She woke earlier than her parents and other family members and put on a man's shirt and her sister's shoes and took a water bucket to the well. Nobody ever saw Betty again and she left no clues as to what happened.

An article in the *Salem News* stated that a man disappeared under "mysterious" circumstances in the same area earlier in the century. Herbert Brown is the other confirmed man that disappeared from the park and was never seen again.

It's worth noting that Betty's parents were at the park staying for the weekend and picking berries. Betty had a disability in which she couldn't hear or speak and it's unknown if that played into the disappearance.

Every photo of Betty that I have seen she is wearing a very short style haircut where if she was dressed as a boy, she easily could've been mistaken for a boy.

Case Summary

Every individual I have documented in this chapter is a male or could be mistaken as a male based on dress or hairstyle. I think this is a significant detail in all of the disappearances and something that cannot be overlooked by investigators.

The other detail in Betty's disappearance that's important is why her parents were in that area, they were berry picking. Berries bring people and animals to the area for picking and eating where they may not otherwise be there. Maybe berries play some role in how and why Betty disappeared.

Edward Chester Nye
Missing 6/22/78, Rogue River, Sky Lakes Wilderness, OR
Age at disappearance: 14
Fishing on River.

The disappearance of Edward Nye fits the profile of young missing boys in the greater Crater Lake region. On June 22, 1978 Edward was with a church group in an area near the Sky Lakes Wilderness adjacent to the Rogue River. Many reports state that he disappeared from Prospect, Oregon, this would be incorrect, he was between Butte Falls and Prospect.

The church group was camping in the region when Edward told his brother he was going to walk downstream to fish, this was the last time anyone saw him. A massive search was conducted by law enforcement without finding any evidence Edward was even in the Rogue River area. They were able to confirm everything to the point where his brother said goodbye but nothing after that.

Jackson County Sheriff's are handling the case and they believe that Edward somehow got lost in the woods.

The unusual part of this case is that it is difficult for people to become lost when there is a large river for them to follow. The Rogue River in this area is fairly large and Edward was old enough to understand directions, especially at what point he walked to the river to fish. None of the fishing equipment that Edward was carrying was ever recovered.

The location that Edward vanished is remote and sits near a wilderness area. There is significant game in the area and if you walk away from the river you can quickly get into a very desolate area.

Corwin Osborn
Missing: 06/17/01, Devils Lake trailhead, Three Sisters Wilderness, OR
Age at disappearance: 45

Corwin was in excellent shape for a 45-year-old when he left his Bellevue, Washington, home for a hiking excursion. He was going into the Three Sisters Wilderness, thirty miles west of Bend. He entered the wilderness from the Devils Lake trailhead on the morning of June 17, 2001. Corwin was last seen at 7:00 a.m., approximately one hour into the hike, by a fellow hiker on the trail to the South Sister. Based on what he had previously purchased, he was carrying a one-day supply of food and water.

Corwin was scheduled to meet his father at the Lava Camp trailhead on Highway 242 at 9:00 p.m. on June 17; he never arrived and was never seen again. An extensive air and ground search in a 150-square-mile area failed to uncover any clues regarding Corwin's disappearance. Corwin is listed as a missing person in the State of Oregon's law enforcement database.

Wayne David Powell
Missing: 06/18/94, Brushy Butte Mountain, Umpqua National Forest, OR
Age at disappearance: 39

There is very little information available about the Wayne David Powell disappearance. I do know that Powell's F-250 pickup was found in the Brushy Butte area near Dixonville. He enjoyed hunting and the outdoors. Authorities found the pickup on the western side of the Cascade Range. The truck was found at an elevation of approximately 2,600 feet.

Martin Jerome Ryan
Missing: 05/30/60, Silver Falls State Park, OR
Age at disappearance: 8

On May 30, 1960, Martin Jerome Ryan was with family and friends for a picnic at Silver Falls State Park. Several of the kids left the immediate area of the picnic to look at a squirrel. They watched the squirrel for a short time, and then all of the kids, except Martin, returned to the picnic. Family members soon realized that Martin wasn't in the group and started to search for him. Martin's parents couldn't find the boy and notified park personnel for assistance.

The Marion County Sheriff's Office responded to the park's call for assistance and started a grid search upon their arrival. Sheriff Denver Young took charge of the SAR and supervised the on-scene deputies. During the first night, deputies and other law enforcement officials covered a full square mile of the area without finding a trace of the boy.

On June 1, 1960, deputies found Martin's body at the bottom of a cliff approximately one mile from where he disappeared.

Here is the statement Sheriff Young gave the press at the time: "Wandering aimlessly through the dense forest, [Martin] walked at least a half mile through the woods and stumbled upon a trail. He followed it to a footbridge that spans a creek. By then it apparently was dark. There was safety at the bridge. The search parties used it frequently. But Martin darted across it. Panic must have seized him. He ran through another picnic area and into the woods. His flight ended a mile from where he disappeared. He plunged off a 100-foot cliff."

The statement is perplexing at best and disturbing at worst. Trackers may well have been able to determine that Martin was running through the dirt, and thus, the sheriff believed he panicked. If Martin did walk through the picnic grounds and across the bridge, he must have known he was very near people. What would have caused him to panic? Why would the boy have ran so fast to pass through a picnic area and cross a well-marked trail to eventually run off a cliff?

As I have consistently stated throughout this book, we can learn a lot about missing people by understanding what happened to the victims whose bodies were recovered. If they don't study these cases thoroughly, then law enforcement is not doing their job to thwart the next disappearance. In Martin's case, I believe there is much more to the story than the sheriff explained. At least two other people have disappeared from this park and were never found. What caused their disappearances? Did they panic in the same way Martin did? What is in the woods of the Cascades that would cause such extreme panic—panic so thorough and so penetrating that an eight-year-old would run for what he probably believed was his life?

It would appear that eight- to nine-year-olds have a higher incidence of going missing in the Oregon Cascades than any other age group.

Roy Stephens
Missing: 11/16/05, Waldo Lake, OR
Age at disappearance: 48

On November 23, 2007, Krista Dolby gave a radio interview about the disappearance of her father, Roy Stephens. Krista was living in Reno, Nevada, at the time of the interview. She is the adopted daughter of Roy. Her interview and other articles are the basis of the information in this story.

Roy was employed at Odell Lake Resort as a chef. He lived in Crescent, Oregon, with his wife and had a fifteen-minute commute to work. Crescent, Oregon, is approximately twenty miles north of Crater Lake, and Odell Lake is ten miles west of Crescent. Roy's wife had a serious heart condition and relied on Roy's care. Roy was a reliable man and enjoyed his work at the resort.

On the night Roy went missing, he called his wife and asked if she wanted to join him for dinner. She said she would rather stay home. Roy went to dinner and then to a local pub. Roy wasn't the type that went drinking and stayed out all night. He always came home after seeing friends or after working. On November 13, 2005, Roy did exactly as he had told his wife: he ate and went to the pub. He then called his wife again, stating that he was going to see some friends at their house and would be home in a few hours. She never heard from him again. The police agreed to take a missing person report five days later on November 18, 2005.

On Thanksgiving Day 2005 (November 25) Roy's gray 1991 Ford Taurus station wagon was found ten miles in the opposite direction of his friend's house. The vehicle was found 4.2 miles up Waldo Lake Road, north of Highway 58. Waldo Lake is approximately three miles farther west from Odell Lake and is in a very desolate region.

Krista stated that the police searched for four hours for her dad—that was all. The people who found the car said there was vomit next to the vehicle when they found it. Roy's wallet and his paycheck were sitting on the front seat of the car.

Krista went to Crescent after her dad went missing to rally support for a search. She was told by law enforcement that she should not go into the mountains to search for her dad because it was too dangerous. No other explanation was given to Krista about the associated dangers of traveling in the woods.

Krista stated that since Roy went missing, law enforcement agencies have passed the case around without anyone taking responsibility for the investigation. She claims that her dad's car was found in Lane County, but he went missing in the Willamette National Forest. Also, her dad lived in Klamath County, so all three agencies could possibly be involved.

Roy's body was never found. Krista is back living in Reno, and Roy's wife no longer lives in Crescent. Krista didn't know the status of the case or which law enforcement agency had responsibility.

Robert Winters
Missing: 10/08/69, Sparks Lake, OR
Age at disappearance: 78

Robert Winters was a retired logger, a family man, and an ardent hunter who enjoyed the outdoors. He and his sons, Charles, George, and Alvin, had hunted the area of Sparks Lake for twenty years. Sparks Lake is twenty miles east of Bend and just a quarter mile southeast of Devils Lake. It sits at an elevation of 5,400 feet.

In early October of 1969, the Winters men headed for Sparks Lake to make camp for their annual deer-hunting trip. At approximately 11:00 a.m. on October 8, the boys last saw their dad. The boys thought their dad would be hunting in the same general area they were—bounded by Soda Creek, Broken Top, Fall Creek, and their campsite at Sparks Lake. When Robert failed to return to camp at dark, the boys became concerned and started to search. Just as the night started to set in, snow started to fall, and it fell heavily throughout the night. Almost eighteen inches of snow fell during the first twenty-four hours that Robert was missing.

The Winters contacted the Deschutes County Sheriff's Office, and a search was immediately started. Robert's sons explained that they usually hunted at a higher altitude, but the amount of snow on the ground forced them down to Sparks Lake. They all had agreed to stay lower to hunt.

Sixty people were utilized for the search, according to the sheriff's office. At one point a helicopter was utilized in the SAR. Those on board thought they saw some type of tracks at nearly 7100 feet near Soda Creek. The tracks were discounted because nobody thought Robert would walk that high in snow that deep; it was too difficult and dangerous. The search was terminated after the fifth day without finding a trace of Robert.

Nothing happened in the Robert Winter case until nine months later when a physician on vacation found a peculiar site near Soda Creek. Dr. Jack Crosby of Bend was looking for a campsite when he found a deer rifle, glasses, clothing, and other items just off the creek. Crosby notified the sheriff's department, and Deputies Mel Newhouse and Norman Thrasher responded.

I was able to interview Thrasher, who is now retired. He spent twenty-eight years with the Deschutes County Sheriff's Office and stated that he would not ever forget the scene just off Soda Creek. Thrasher stated that it was just below timberline in an area of large trees. Tree coverage in the region was spotty, but in this location there were trees. The rifle was leaning against a tree, and clothes were at the base of the tree, along with glasses, one boot, one glove, and other items. He and Deputy Newhouse spent three days on site searching for evidence of what happened to Robert. One of their first jobs was to methodically search the area around the tree to ensure they didn't miss any evidence—bones, other personal effects, etc. Everything they had found was near the base of the tree. For three days they looked for bones, but they found nothing to confirm that Robert had died. There was no blood visible on the clothes, and it appeared as though the clothes were possibly removed from the body, not torn off.

When I asked Thrasher if he thought the scene looked odd, he stated, "Very odd." He clarified that this was one of the weirdest cases he had ever investigated. I asked him if there were any animals that would totally consume a human body (and the bones) and leave nothing behind. He said no. I asked him if he had an explanation of why Robert's body was gone but his clothes and personal effects were left behind. He stated, "I have no idea. This is one of the major peculiarities about this case." When I asked him how convinced he was that he and Newhouse adequately searched the entire area for other evidence, he stated that there was nothing else to recover; there were no bones anywhere in that area. He said that for three days they did nothing but scan the ground for bits of evidence to indicate that Robert Winters had died.

Thrasher also stated that the family needed a death certificate to finalize personal issues, but the local coroner refused it for almost a year. The coroner wanted a skull or other evidence to indicate a confirmation of death, but they didn't have it. He did state that there was no way that Robert was alive: he had no clothes, and there was almost six feet of snow in the area his personal effects were found.

Case Summary

A July 21, 1970, article in the *Bulletin Newspaper* stated that searchers did find Robert Winters' dentures and personal effects near Soda Creek. There was an old cabin in the area, but it was not utilized by Robert. Imagine that dentures are found but the body is not. Does this mean that something removed Robert's dentures?

This is another in the long list of cases where clothing is removed from someone who is missing. This is also a case where someone walked up in elevation when they were missing into heavier, deeper snow and more treacherous conditions. With the knowledge that Robert Winters hunted this exact area for twenty years, and with the knowledge that he was seventy-eight years old, it is very doubtful that he voluntarily climbed higher and into his demise, especially after telling his sons he would hunt at a lower elevation. SAR teams know that missing people rarely go higher in elevation when they are missing or when weather is turning sour.

An interesting question is, Whose tracks did the helicopter pilot spot at 7,100 feet just after Robert went missing? Surely, they were not his. He was too old and smart to go that high that quickly and risk death by exposure.

Chapter Summary

Missing People near Crater Lake by Age

Age/Missing Person	Date Missing•Location
8/Martin Ryan	05/03/60•Silver Falls State Park*
8/Derrick Engebretson	12/05/98•Rocky Point
8/Samuel Boehlke	10/04/06•Crater Lake Park
9/Nathan Madsen	10/22/89•Little Deschutes River*
10/Betty McCullough	06/21/41•Silver Falls State Park
14/Edward Nye	06/22/78•Prospect/Rogue River

19/Charles McCullar	10/14/76•Crater Lake Park*
21/Jason Franks	08/09/01•East of Chiloquin
29/Daniel Hilkey	01/22/85•Gold Hill
30/B. B. Bakowski	02/22/1911•Crater Lake Park
36/Robert Bobo	10/02/98•Union Creek
39/Wayne Powell	06/18/94•Dixonville
45/Corwin Osborn	06/17/01•Three Sisters Wilderness
48/Roy Stephens	11/16/05•Crescent
53/Celia Barnes	09/01/02•Gold Hill
78/Robert Winters	10/08/69•Sparks Lake*

*Denotes body was found.

Four boys have gone missing from the greater Crater Lake area in the last twenty-eight years. The facts behind their disappearances are troubling and do not duplicate themselves anywhere west of the Mississippi River. There is only one other national park that comes close to the amount of missing boys: Great Smoky Mountain National Park.

Missing males in the greater Crater Lake region outnumber females 14 to 2. As I stated earlier in this chapter, the two females who went missing could easily have been mistaken for men based on their physical appearance and clothing at the time they disappeared.

California

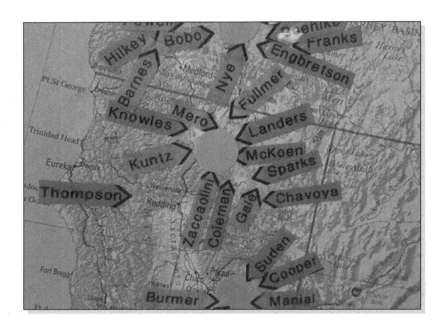

Introduction

It was easy to focus on northern California and Mount Shasta because the region is known for strange anomalies. Mount Shasta has a history of very strange events. The stories start with a strange craft circling the mountain to even stranger people living underneath a crater. It's an odd place but a beautiful location.

This chapter deals with people who have disappeared under extremely unusual circumstances where there is generally no evidence of where they are today. I start this chapter with a historical perspective of missing people in northern California.

Approximately seventy-five miles directly west of Mount Shasta is the coast of California and Del Norte County. Del Norte sits at the farthest northwest point of California, adjacent to Oregon. The area is lush with one-thousand-year-old redwood trees. It has many large rivers that bisect the county and is a haven for people who love fishing and the outdoors. The Smith River Recreation Area cuts through the county and is known throughout the western U.S. for its outstanding salmon and steelhead fishing. It is one of the last wild and scenic rivers in California.

In the late 1800s, the county was enjoying a boom of mining in the inland hills that stretched into southern Oregon. In 1896 the local newspaper, the *Crescent City News*, added a supplemental section called "The Hermit of the Siskiyous." This section dealt with many of the strange facts of the Siskiyou Mountain Range and featured some of the odd occurrences in this region. On page 78, L. W. Musick wrote about the disappearances of eighteen miners from different locations in an area near French Hill, a region just south of what is now known as the town of Gasquet. Gasquet sits directly on the Smith River approximately twenty miles east of the coast, near the Oregon border. It has a beautiful airport, a U.S. Forestry Office, and a small trailer park.

I have visited many of the older mines in this area (some can be found on old U.S. Geological Survey maps). The mines are isolated and difficult to locate, even with the help of historians. A Gasquet resident and organic farmer, Kirk Stewart, has taken me to a few of these mines. He confirms there is a certain aura at their locations that makes you feel "different." We didn't know which mines the people disappeared from, but the ones we found border areas where virtually nobody travels.

L.W. Musick wrote an article in the January 25, 1895 edition of the *Crescent City News*. It read: "It is said that of the eighteen disappearances around French Hill country, only one of the bodies has been found." All of the victims were miners living alone on isolated claims. There was never any indication that robbery was a motive.

We need to remember that in 1895 there wasn't the transportation system that we have today. Travel to many of these mines was a very cumbersome trek over rough and steep trails. It was a lonely existence, and it took extreme stamina to make the trip. It doesn't seem feasible that these people could simply disappear without locals, friends, or other miners knowing they were leaving. The stores and service businesses in the area were aware when people left to get supplies. The missing miners simply vanished and were never seen again. It would appear they were an easy target with little or no defense. What or who took the miners? Why were they taken? Where they were taken?

The idea that people started to disappear in the twentieth century in northern California and there is no history of these types of events occurring before then is completely not true. A little digging, thorough research, and tenacity has shown that this region of northern California has a history of people disappearing going back to the 1800s. These disappearances have many similarities to disappearances in the twentieth and twenty-first centuries, such as being alone in the woods, an easy target with few defenses, nobody nearby to render assistance, and no evidence of what happened to the victim. Don't think the odd incidents stop at the California border; they do not. There are incidents of people disappearing across the border into the southern Oregon Cascades.

The following stories reinforce the fact that people are continuing to disappear and law enforcement is doing little to understand why or how. I think a paradigm shift needs to occur in every missing person case that occurs in the wild.

Missing People in the Northern California–Mount Shasta Region by Date

Missing Person	Date Missing•Age•Sex
Billy Coleman	01/01/40•14•M
Greta Mary Gale	06/29/47•30M•F
**50 Year Gap	
Karen Mero	02/15/97•27•F
Hannah Zaccaglini	06/04/97•15•F
Carl Landers	05/25/99•69•M
Rosemary Kunst	08/18/00•70•F
Jerry McKoen	09/21/02•48•M
Angela Fullmer	12/05/02•34•F
Austin Sparks	01/04/04•15•M
David Knowles	08/17/06•43•M

Billy Coleman
Missing: 01/01/40, Viola, CA
Age at disappearance: 14

Mount Lassen is approximately seventy miles southeast of Mount Shasta. These mountains are the dominating peaks in the area. Lassen is a national park while Mount Shasta has a Wilderness Area designation.

The Colemans invited family and some of Billy's friends to their cabin at the foot of Mount Lassen for the New Year's Day weekend. The elevation of the cabin was near 4,500 feet, just above the snow line.

On New Year's Day at approximately 4:00 p.m., Billy was playing under a tree near the cabin. His mother checked on him and found that all was fine. Minutes after checking, she looked outside again and he was gone. She immediately started calling for him. Billy never answered and a search was started.

The first full day of searching produced an unusual find. Near a creek approximately 250 yards from the cabin, searchers found Billy's overalls, underwear, and other pieces of clothing. Billy's mother said he also had a large overcoat, a cap, and a shirt. The sheriff stated that they found tracks in the area of someone who appeared to have roamed aimlessly.

Searchers continued to look for Billy throughout January. There were up to five hundred people roaming the hillsides of Viola looking for the boy. Snow fell soon after Billy disappeared, and by the end of the search, over one foot of snow was on the ground near the Colemans' cabin.

Anyone unfamiliar with the hills below Lassen needs to understand that it is very cold in January. The idea that a young boy voluntarily stripped off clothes immediately after he left the safety of his cabin area is ludicrous. This is not a case of someone being hypothermic and stripping clothes, these were found the first day of the search. Five hundred searchers never found Billy; that's quite hard to believe. The local searchers were well fed, rested, and knew the country. Billy did not. According to news reports, searchers combed over twelve square miles, meaning they covered every foot of that region.

If you believe in coincidences, there are several in the disappearances of Billy Coleman and Austin Sparks. They were almost the same age when they disappeared. They were lost within twenty-five miles of each other and almost exactly thirty-six years apart. Both walked into the woods and were never seen again. Their parents couldn't explain the disappearance.

Greta Mary Gale
Missing: 06/29/47, 10:00 a.m., Lassen National Park
Age at disappearance: 30 months
John Tolan, a retired California congressman from Oakland, and his wife took their granddaughter, Greta Mary Gale, and her mother for a weekend trip to Lee's Vacation Camp in Lassen National Park in northern California. Mount Shasta is approximately seventy miles north of Mount Lassen, and Lassen was the location of the Tolans' summer home.

At 10:00 a.m. on Sunday, June 29, 1947, Greta was playing with other children in the camp. Sometime during the playtime Greta disappeared. Greta's mom was near the location where Greta disappeared. It was the feeling of people in the immediate area that there was a real possibility that the girl had been kidnapped.

Local law enforcement officials called the FBI and an agent responded. The state governor sent bloodhounds from Folsom State Prison in Sacramento to aid in the search for Greta.

Shortly after Greta disappeared, John Tolan suffered a heart attack and was rushed to a local hospital in grave condition.

Two days after Greta disappeared, searchers found the girl on the side of Mount Harkness. Greta was found on a thirty-five-degree slope approximately one mile from the family's cabin. An article printed on July 1, 1947, in the *Deseret News* had the following: "At Lee's Camp, experienced mountain men were amazed Greta could have climbed the sharp inclined slope and survived two nights in the sharp mountain air. Last night the thermometer dropped to 25 degrees." Greta was found wearing only panties. Her shirt, pants, and bib overalls were never found.

An article in the *San Jose News* the same day stated that local officials believed it was possible that the girl had been initially abducted and then released on the mountainside.

John Tolan died of his heart attack, but Greta was taken to the hospital and found to be in good condition despite the freezing temperatures on Mount Harkness. There were no follow-up articles indicating whether or not the FBI conducted an investigation.

Karen Elizabeth Knechtel Mero
Missing: 02/15/97, McCloud, CA
Age at disappearance: 27
5'8", 170 lb.

McCloud is a small community near the southern base of Mount Shasta. McCloud was once a logging community, but it is now a home for federal forestry workers. The area around McCloud is known for great trout fishing, beautiful hikes, and the Mount Shasta Wilderness just to the north. The 2000 census put the population of McCloud at just over 1,300 people. The town is geographically small, with no more than thirty roads in its main area.

Witnesses informed law enforcement that Karen Mero was last seen at the home of Ed and Deborah Henline on a street that borders Highway 89, the main highway going through the center of town. Karen lived at the house with her boyfriend, Ed Henline Jr. Karen was separated from her husband at the time and had disability payments as her sole source of income.

Karen wasn't reported missing until October 1997, eight months after she was last seen. It was believed that she had left on her own.

Four months after Karen disappeared, Hannah Zaccaglini also disappeared from McCloud. The day she disappeared, Hannah played guitar at a high school assembly. She was last seen at the apartment of her boyfriend. She left, walking to her residence adjacent to Highway 89, near the residence where Karen had previously lived. Hannah never arrived home and was never seen again.

She was a cheerleader and a promising model. Her parents and friends do not believe she would have left the area voluntarily.

Newspaper articles indicated that the Henlines were questioned by law enforcement about each girl's disappearance, and their residence was searched. There are several theories about the disappearance of each girl, but nobody believes they would have left the area voluntarily.

Hanna and Karen's cases are both active and open. No arrests have been made. The FBI has participated in this investigation.

Hannah Marie Zaccaglini
Missing: 06/04/97, McCloud, CA
Age at disappearance: 15
5' 5", 120 lb.
For narrative on this case, refer to the Karen Mero case above.

Case Summary

It's a guarantee that there are far more people missing in this region of California than what I have identified in this chapter—far more. Records were not maintained in the early 1900s like they are today, and even though an attempt was made to be as thorough as possible in my periodical search, I know I missed people. I continued to stumble upon missing person cases as I searched for other information on cases I was working. There are many others.

This section of California has a gorgeous coastal region, peaks up to 14,000', high desert, and lush tropical-type forests: it is very ecologically diverse. Some of the largest rivers in California traverse the region, including the Sacramento, Smith, Klamath, McCloud, and Pitt. This region also includes several of the biggest and most wild wilderness areas in the state, including the Shasta, Trinity, and Marble Mountain wilderness areas.

When people outside of California think of the state, they often envision Los Angeles, San Francisco, or San Diego; the image of thousands and thousands of square miles of open forests where no motor vehicles can travel is rarely broached. There are many areas of this great state where a human hasn't walked for decades, and maybe that's a good thing.

Carl Herbert Landers
Missing: 05/25/99, Mount Shasta, CA
Age at disappearance: 69
5' 9", 150 lb.

Carl Landers was born in Chicago and migrated to California. He met his wife, and they had two girls and a boy. The family lived in the upscale community of Orinda, just east of San Francisco, across the bay. Carl was an engineer by trade, but for ten years before his retirement he worked for Trane heating and air conditioning as a salesperson.

One of Carl's main hobbies for thirty years was running every morning. Carl's dream came true when he won a race lottery and was allowed to run the one hundredth anniversary of the Boston Marathon. Carl ran a highly respectable time of 5½ hours over the 26.2-mile course.

As Carl got older, he decided that he wanted to climb the highest peak in every county in California. Carl had hiked many of the peaks in the state and always had another on his agenda. In May of 1998, he headed for Mount Shasta. Carl did climb the mountain but didn't earn the summit. He slid down the mountain with his ice axe and vowed to return and conquer the beast.

In May of 1999, Carl was headed for Mount Shasta again. On this attempt he was going to be with two long-term friends, Milt Gaines and Barry Gillmore. Carl made the five-hour drive alone and met the other two men on his arrival.

At seventy years old, Barry Gillmore was the type of guy you'd go anywhere with. Barry graduated from the University of Oregon with a business degree and had no idea what he was going to do until a recruiter from the navy pitched being a pilot. From 1961 to 1966, Barry spent his military career flying aircraft for the navy off the carriers Midway, Hancock, and Enterprise. When Barry left the military, he joined American Airlines and flew for thirty-three years. He left flying the 767 for American.

Barry was a member of a local running club, and that is how he met Milt Gaines and Carl Landers. Carl heard that Milt and Barry were going to attempt a summit of Shasta and asked if he could join the group.

Barry stated that Carl wasn't an outstanding athlete, but he was a good runner. Barry said that he had gone scuba diving with Carl, and he wasn't the best swimmer; and he had gone skiing with him, but he wasn't the best skier; but he did enjoy the challenge of the sports.

Milt Gaines owned a wholesale warehouse and associated business in San Francisco. Milt had gone with Carl the first time he attempted a summit of Shasta. Milt had also been part of the running club for over twenty years and was in excellent shape.

The men stayed in a motel room in Mount Shasta City the night before they started their climb. They were well prepared: all had ice axes, crampons for their boots, and the proper attire for the climb. At 4:00 a.m. the men left the motel, and Barry drove them in his four-wheel drive to the trailhead at Bunny Flat for the Mount Shasta summit attempt.

This area is absolutely gorgeous. Hundreds of people attempt to summit Mount Shasta each year. There are sometimes dozens of climbers on the mountain simultaneously, and it can get hectic on the summit trail.

Milt and Barry explained that there were ten- to twelve-foot snow drifts at the start of the climb at Bunny Flat. The men decided to make the three- to four-mile hike up the mountain to a location where the Sierra Club had an old cabin called Horse Camp. The men stated that Carl was taking Diamox for adjustment to the altitude, and it may have had some adverse effect on his system. After a short time into the trip, Carl had to stop and go behind a tree or boulder because he had diarrhea. The men continued on and made it to a location called 50/50, approximately six hundred feet below Lake Helen, a major stop for most climbers. The lake is the spot most climbers spend the night before the last push for the summit.

The wind was blowing very hard in the early afternoon when the men decided to stop at 50/50. They dug their three-person tent deep into the snow and stayed there for the night. Milt and Barry remember Carl having to leave the tent for another bout of diarrhea, but other than that everything was fairly normal.

In the early morning hours, their tent was rattling badly as winds estimated at seventy miles per hour ripped around the mountain. The men saw people leaving Lake Helen and going back down the mountain. They stayed in their sleeping bags in the tent. The tent was positioned tight against the mountain between a few large boulders, and they were adequately protected. They waited a few more hours until the winds subsided and they saw climbers going back up the mountain.

As a group, Milt, Carl, and Barry, decided to hike the quarter mile to Lake Helen. In the back of their minds, they didn't think they would summit that day. But they thought they would go to the lake and see what might happen with the weather.

As Barry and Milt put the tent into their bags, they saw Carl standing and staring. He appeared to be getting cold. Milt told Carl to start walking for Lake Helen, and they would meet him there. The lake was just a short trip around the corner of the mountain and up a few hundred feet. Milt told Carl that he and Barry would finish packing and be on the trail quickly. Carl and Milt left the packed tent at 50/50, and inside of thirty minutes, they were heading for Lake Helen just a little behind Carl.

Approximately halfway between 50/50 and Lake Helen, Barry wasn't feeling well. He told Milt that he would head back to 50/50, grab the tent, and meet the men later at his car. Milt said that was fine.

Milt walked to Lake Helen and saw between twenty and twenty-four campsites. Milt asked a ranger supervising the area if another man had passed through and continued to climb. The ranger stated that only one man had gone up, and he had taken the "casual" route. Milt took off after the climber just in case it was Carl. He got within one hundred yards of the climber, but the guy was way too fast to catch and way too fast to be Carl. Milt turned back to Lake Helen.

Once Milt arrived at the lake, he again asked the ranger if anyone matching Carl's description had passed through. He said no. Milt then went back to 50/50, praying that Carl was sitting there waiting. He wasn't. Carl's and Milt's backpacks were still there, but Barry's was with him back at the car. There was another group now huddling at 50/50, and they had a cell phone. It was 5:00 p.m. Milt waited at 50/50 for another hour trying to decide what to do. Milt decided to take his pack back to Bunny Flats and leave Carl's at 50/50. Milt arrived at Bunny Flats at 7:00 or 8:00 p.m.

Once arriving at Bunny Flats, the men notified the Siskiyou County Sheriff's Office of Carl's disappearance. The search started the next morning.

The following morning the men went back to the trailhead and found U.S. Forest Service crews and the Siskiyou County sheriff on the scene. The first day the Shasta City schoolyard was the base for the search operations; after that the airport became the base. It was this morning that Barry called Bobbie Landers, Carl's wife, and notified her that Carl was missing. Bobbie stated, "I had a premonition something would happen." Later that afternoon another mutual friend of the men flew Bobbie and Milt's wife to Mount Shasta City to monitor the search efforts.

Milt reflected on his memory of that morning and adamantly states that there were no large crevasses in the area where Carl was hiking. There were a few large holes near some trees, but that was all. Milt stated that there really was no place for Carl to hide. He vanished.

Milt and Barry decided to hike back to Lake Helen and search the area. They got back to 50/50, and Carl's pack was still there. The ranger at Lake Helen again confirmed he had not seen anyone matching Carl's description.

As the search started to escalate, Griz Adams became the search coordinator assigned by the County. Griz was a veteran of hundreds of SARs and was the right person for the job. Griz ordered an Army National Guard helicopter pilot to take professional climbers to the summit, and then had them descend using separate routes to look for Carl. The climbers slowly descended and found no tracks, no helmet, no ice axe, and no evidence that Carl was ever on the mountain. There were twenty to twenty-four campsites at Lake Helen and fifty to one hundred people on the mountain, yet nobody had seen Carl.

The massive search on Mount Shasta didn't find one clue of Carl Landers' location.

There was one point after Carl vanished where Milt became so disturbed that he spoke with three psychics and asked for their assistance. One stated that Carl was in a body of water, and another stated that he was in a crevasse, and it would be many years before he was found.

When Milt was asked what he thought happened to Carl, he stated, "There's over a fifty percent chance that something very odd happened." He stated that Carl had a golden heart and would do anything for his friends. He further stated that everything on the mountain above Avalanche Gulch was covered with snow. Milt said that the color contrast would show anything that wasn't white but searchers saw nothing unusual.

Case Summary

I was very fortunate to have a long interview with Griz Adams, the SAR coordinator on Landers' search. Griz was then an SAR coordinator for the State of California, working out of Yreka, where we met. Griz stated that he had participated in over four hundred SARs in his career. He said it was remarkable that I was asking him about two specific SARs that he had been responsible for—Carl Landers and Rosemary Kunst (below)—and that they were the only two in his life where he never found one trace of the victims.

Griz stated that he had teams covering the forest area below the location that Carl disappeared, all working in a concise grid pattern. He obviously had the mountain above where Carl disappeared completely searched by professionals. This search lasted days, but nothing related to Carl was found by searchers. Griz reiterated what Milt had stated about the topography of the area Carl vanished: there was no place for him to disappear. It was generally felt that Carl must have disappeared somewhere between 50/50 and Lake Helen, but where? Griz stated that he prides himself in finding people who have disappeared, and he will stay at the scene until family members call off the search. It is their decision when to stop searching.

After cadaver-sniffing and human scent–sniffing canines found no scent to track in the entire area, hope started to quickly fade. Griz was also bothered by the fact that searchers weren't finding any of the equipment that Carl had been carrying. When people get distressed, they sometimes start shedding items they don't want to carry, but nothing of Carl's was ever found.

During the accumulation of information on Carl's disappearance, I heard the statement "It's like the mountain opened up and swallowed him" more than once. According to local legend, beings called Lemurians live underneath Mount Shasta. I heard from people close to this case that maybe the Lemurians got Carl. I was not sure if the people were joking or serious. I will always remember the statement made by Milt regarding what happened to Carl: "There's over a fifty percent chance that something very odd happened." That continues to ring in my head.

As you read through this book, you will notice that the disappearance of Carl Landers has many similarities with two cases of missing climbers in Colorado that also disappeared at high altitude.

Rosemary Theresa Kunst
Missing: 08/18/00, Spirit Lake, Marble Mountain Wilderness Area, CA
Age at disappearance: 70
5'3", 122 lb.

November 1, 1929, was a glorious day: Rosemary Theresa Kunst was born in San Francisco. The next sixty-nine years were very productive and successful. Rosemary married in 1950 to Charles "Bud" Kunst. They had six children and eleven grandchildren. The couple was active and enjoyed the outdoors. Rosemary was a licensed marriage and family counselor in their hometown of San Anselmo, California.

In 1998 the life of Rosemary and Bud got derailed. The couple was involved in a horrific traffic accident that took the life of Bud and nearly killed Rosemary. After months of recuperation and struggle, Rosemary came back and started to have the same energy level she did before the accident. Rosemary struggled with the loss of her husband and searched for a method to reach Bud's spirit. She decided to take a backpacking trip with the Earth Circle Organization in Yreka, California, operated by Karuk Chief and elder Charlie "Red Hawk" Thom.

Every year, the Earth Circle Organization went to the remote location of Spirit Lake in the Marble Mountain Wilderness Area just west of Mount Shasta, California. Red Hawk had built an altar at the lake, and every year he had a religious retreat that included a calling to the gods and a spirit dance. There were drums, singing, and dancing, all to bring the spirits awake and alive at the lake.

The lake sits at the base of a small bowl that would remind you of a mini volcano. There is only one way in and out. There is a side of the lake that drains into Wooley Creek. The area has an approximately seventy-degree fall, which is nearly impossible to climb. There are large trees in a portion of the bowl with significant ground coverage.

Rosemary read that there would be a group of approximately eleven people, including a cook, Red Hawk, and possibly his son. They would bring the food and tents into the area on horseback. It was a rigorous hike to the location, and it was remote. After reading about the trip and talking with organizers, Rosemary felt that this would be a good event for her. Rosemary was in excellent spirits as she headed off for the trip.

After being at the lake and establishing camp, Red Hawk had his ceremonial spirit dance and song after dinner on August 17, 2000. The entire group participated and attempted to call the spirits into the area and address their concerns.

On August 18 at 9:00 a.m., Red Hawk informed the group they were going to take a day hike to a nearby lake, and they would be back for dinner. Rosemary felt that she wanted to stay behind and enjoy the absolute beauty of Spirit Lake. The group left, and Rosemary asked Red Hawk's twelve-year-old son, Chalet, if he wanted to hike with her to the other side of the lake, a location that she hadn't explored. Chalet said he would stay behind with the camp cook. Rosemary asked for a small bag lunch to take with her, and the cook prepared it. Rosemary walked to the other side of the lake near the outflow to Wooley Creek.

At 5:00 p.m. the group with Red Hawk returned from their day hike and realized that Rosemary hadn't returned from her walk. A group was sent to get Rosemary, but after approximately one hour they returned and stated that they couldn't find her. It was at this point that a decision was made to contact the Siskiyou County Search and Rescue and declare an emergency. Within twenty-four hours there were nearly fifty searchers actively looking for Rosemary. Her family was notified and were en route from San Anselmo.

Through an archive search, I found out that the SAR commander on Rosemary's incident was Griz Adams. Griz stated that from the very beginning of this case he had a few very unnerving issues surrounding the disappearance. The first issue was that the south end of the lake, where Rosemary disappeared, did not have a path where a seventy-year-old woman could walk out of the lake basin. If she wanted to leave the lake, she would have had to walk by the cook and Chalet, which she never did. Another major issue was Rosemary's age. People confirmed that she was in excellent shape, but even a twenty-five-year-old in excellent shape isn't going to exit Spirit Lake through the south exit without ropes and climbing hardware.

Griz explained that the Marble Mountain Wilderness Area has split jurisdiction, and this disappearance was in Siskiyou County. He enlisted the assistance of several counties' SAR teams, a National Guard FLIR-equipped helicopter, a California Highway Patrol helicopter, canines equipped to track scent and find cadavers, ground searchers, and searchers on horseback.

As we talked about successes and failures on this search, it quickly became apparent that there were far more failures than successes. Griz explained that the canines could never pick up Rosemary's scent, which he thought was highly unusual since they knew exactly where she was headed and where she had walked. The cadaver canines never picked up any human scent. When asked about mountain lions and bears, Griz stated, "Mountain lions and bears are common in the Marbles, but attacks are almost unheard of." He further stated that if there had been a bear or mountain lion attack, there would be a defined location of the attack with blood and a scene defined by a fight for someone's life. Nothing like this was ever found.

They did find one tuft of hair under a bush approximately a half mile from the south end of Spirit Lake. The hair was never DNA tested, and to this day we don't know if this belonged to Rosemary.

This was the only possible evidence ever found. Her lunch and lunch bag were never found.

Griz confirmed that Rosemary's children were at the search headquarters, and they made the decision to terminate the effort after they had no other places to search.

Griz stated that there are two incidents in his thirty-five-plus-year career that will forever bother him: the disappearances of Rosemary Kunst and Carl Landers. He said that in both incidents canines never picked up a scent; not one piece of evidence was ever found; and they knew where the people disappeared but found nothing.

I had a very difficult time finding Karuk Chief Charlie Thom but eventually found where he lived and stopped by his house for a spur of the moment interview. Chief Thom was very polite but was initially a little apprehensive about discussing the incident. Once he understood that I already had considerable knowledge of the situation, he started to talk. He confirmed that they did conduct a spirit dance at his altar the night before Rosemary disappeared. He stated that he believes that Rosemary somehow got to a location called Devil's Back Canyon. He never completely explained why he thought she disappeared in that canyon, but he was fairly sure that is where she went. He had no idea why she would have left the safety at Spirit Lake.

Case Summary

The disappearance of Rosemary Kunst ranks near the top of my list for strange cases. Canines couldn't find a scent, and no evidence of her was ever found at the scene—no blood, no tracks, nothing. Since this area of California has a very long history of missing people, this case exemplifies the high strangeness of the region. The only photos we could find of Rosemary show her with very short hair, hair so short that from behind or at a distance she could be mistaken for a man. This may or may not have had any significance in her disappearance.

Any thoughts that Rosemary wanted to disappear or commit suicide were eliminated when Chalet confirmed that she had asked him to go with her to the south side of the lake.

Jerry Lee McKoen
Missing: 09/21/02, Medicine Lake Road, McCloud, CA
Age at disappearance: 48
6', 180 lb.

Jerry McKoen was a rancher and farmer in Merrill, Oregon, approximately two miles north of the California border. Jerry assisted in the family business and was an avid outdoorsman. He was single, lived at the family residence, and was a very caring son. Jerry was known throughout the area as an experienced hunter who truly went the extra distance to make it a sport. He didn't use a rifle; he used a bow and arrows. He would sit patiently and sometimes sneak up on his prey by being very stealthy and quiet, not letting his prey know that he was in the area.

On Saturday, September 21, 2002, at 5:30 a.m., Jerry left the family residence in a GMC pickup with a camper shell. He was carrying a Honda 185XL motorcycle in the bed of the truck that he would sometimes use to get into rough country.

Jerry's family didn't hear from him for four days, so they filed a missing person report on September 25. Neighboring farmers dropped their harvest work and immediately started to search for the forty-eight-year-old hunter. It was originally thought that Jerry might have gone to the Klamath Marsh or Christmas Valley to hunt, but both theories were incorrect.

A friend of Jerry's found his pickup and motorcycle approximately twenty miles east of Mount Shasta on Medicine Lake Road in an area known as Doorknob Snow Park. The friend also found Jerry's keys in a part of the truck where he normally hid them, indicating he had parked the truck there and gone hunting.

Seventy searchers were under the direction of the Siskiyou County Sheriff's Office, which headed the ground teams. There were as many as two teams of search dogs, four airplanes, and two helicopters, all searching the low and thick brush that covers the area. The area has small timber, but there is nothing that towers over the area. At the height of the search, over one hundred searchers were participating in an organized grid search of the area surrounding Jerry's pickup.

Several friends were interviewed near the time that Jerry went missing. Those questioned stated that Jerry was the consummate outdoorsman and could handle anything the woods could throw at him.

After several days of searching, the Siskiyou County SAR teams had nothing to show that Jerry was even in the area. Teams never found any of the equipment that he should have been carrying, and no arrows were found in the area. If someone became injured, they would slowly start shedding equipment. No equipment was found, and they did not find any animals he may have killed.

Case Summary

This is another of the many cases where an individual disappears alone in the woods. Even though Jerry was armed, he only had a bow and arrows. The stealthy nature of a bowhunter brings many questions about the possibilities of what occurred. Perhaps Jerry saw something that he shouldn't have and was killed, or maybe something snuck up on him when he wasn't expecting it.

The location where Jerry disappeared is still in the close shadows of Mount Shasta. It is a predominant presence in the area of a snowmobile park and is an area that is very, very desolate. The location of Jerry's disappearance is approximately twenty-five miles from McCloud. This spot offers some very mundane landscape compared to other missing people cases across North America. The hills are small; there are no huge peaks in the immediate area; and there aren't any large bodies of water nearby. Siskiyou County utilized helicopters in this search and hopefully utilized FLIR. This would be the ideal terrain for FLIR because it could easily penetrate small shrubs and identify a heat signature.

This case held my interest because of Jerry's outdoors experience, the fact that no equipment was found in the search, and the relatively tame topography where no evidence of the missing was ever found.

Angela Fullmer
Missing: 12/15/02, Lake Siskiyou, CA
Age at disappearance: 34
5'2", 120 lb.

On December 15, 2002, at 2:45 p.m., Angela Fullmer and her boyfriend drove to an area west of Mount Shasta near the West Fork of the Sacramento River, just west of Lake Siskiyou. The lake has a gorgeous setting at the base of the city and the mountain. According to published reports, the couple had supposedly been drinking the entire day. At some point during the festivities, possibly near 6:45 p.m., the couple got into a dispute. Angela walked away from the truck and into the woods toward South Fork Road, located near an old logging road in the Twin Pines area. She was never seen again.

Angela's boyfriend reported her missing to the Siskiyou County Sheriff's Office. There was an extensive search, but only tracks in the snow were found.

At the time of Angela's disappearance, she was the mother of five children and was unemployed. The Siskiyou County Sheriff's Office has never named a suspect in Angela's disappearance, but they do believe she was probably killed in the forest.

Austin Sparks
Missing: 01/4/04, Montgomery
Creek, CA
Age at disappearance: 15
5', 115 lb.

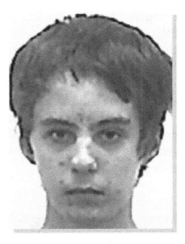

Austin was home sick from school with his dad on January 4, 2004. He awoke at 7:00 a.m. and walked to the Acorn Café, which is located on Highway 299 in Montgomery Creek, California. The town sits to the northeast of Shasta Lake and close to the Pit River, which flows into the eastern side of the reservoir. The area just to the west of the town is extremely remote and rugged.

Austin walked in the snow from his residence to the café and entered it twice. People at the café saw Austin—the last confirmed sighting of the boy.

Austin was reported missing by his father and a search of the area quickly ensued. He was wearing a special type of shoe that had a very unique and identifiable sole. The county sheriff tracked Austin's shoe prints for over two miles in a westerly direction through snow that was sometimes over a foot deep. Deputies eventually made their way to the banks of the Pit River where the tracks were lost.

Deputies who tracked Austin to the banks of the river specifically stated that the area is extremely remote and very rugged. It was virtually inaccessible to their personnel, and they couldn't understand how Austin had made it that far. Deputies performed a thorough search of the river, and they believe that Austin may have drowned. Austin's dad said the boy had never been to that location before, and he wouldn't have entered the water in the middle of winter, at least voluntarily. The dad believes that Austin somehow became disoriented, got lost, and died in the elements, even though his body was never found.

Case Summary

This is another case in which law enforcement cannot understand how a victim got to the location where they believe he disappeared. If experienced law enforcement personnel can barely get into the dense wilderness near the Pit River, it's difficult to understand how a small and frail fifteen-year-old boy could get there, especially since he'd never been there before. The better question is, Why would Austin ever make this journey? There is nothing out there except twenty miles of wilderness consisting of rivers and extremely steep and rugged mountains.

All of the publicly available facts are presented here; however, it's hard to imagine there isn't much more information that law enforcement and the family don't know about what really happened to Austin. The location is inhospitable even in the warm summer months, and the freezing conditions of winter make this area absolutely remote and dangerous. I don't believe there is any chance that Austin voluntarily entered the freezing Pitt River.

David Clarke Knowles
Missing: 08/17/06, Sims Flat Campground, Castella, CA
Age at disappearance: 43
5'7", 175 lb.

David Knowles was last seen at the Sims Flat Campground just east of Highway 5, approximately thirty-five miles south of Mount Shasta. The area to the east of the Sims Flat Campground is very desolate, with essentially no development for twenty miles, just open forests. David left his campsite to use the bathroom two hundred feet away and never returned. The area where he was staying is adjacent to the upper Sacramento River and is a well-maintained and highly used camping area.

David had intended to meet two friends at the campsite and fish the Sacramento River with them. David arrived first, set up his camp, and appeared to be set for a few days of camping. David was an experienced camper and quite comfortable in the woods.

David's friends arrived late and noticed that David wasn't at the site. All of his property and his vehicle were there. The friends contacted law enforcement and David's fiancé, Heidi Lindholm, who lived in Orland, California.

Heidi works for the Glenn County Welfare Department. She was very cooperative during my interview and was appreciative that someone was talking about David's disappearance. She told me that David had a good job as a truck driver and that nobody has heard from him since he disappeared. David's mom and dad put the down payment on the house where David and Heidi lived in Orland. Heidi told me that she didn't believe that David had had a life insurance policy. Heidi said what happened to David is a huge mystery.

Northern California and the Sierra Nevada

The region covered in this section includes the Sierras north of Lake Tahoe to just south of Mount Lassen.

Missing Person	Date Missing
Teddy Thompson	01/29/38•4•M
Dickie Tum Suden	11/01/45•3•M
Dana Cooper	08/04/71•13•M
Jo Anne Burmer	02/25/73•38•F
Debra Manial	12/12/82•29•F
Gary Lee Chavoya	07/30/83•10•M
Todd Lucchesi	05/31/99•28•M

Teddy Thompson
Missing: 01/29/38, p.m., ten miles north of Covelo, CA
Age at disappearance: 4
Note: This incident occurred in the coastal foothills but is included in this section because it fits the profile of missing people in northern California.

Charles Thompson was employed by the U.S. Forest Service in northern California. He and his wife lived a very rural lifestyle at their home adjacent to the Eel River near Ham's Crossing. This is a very wild region that is now predominantly known for great salmon and steelhead fishing and for marijuana cultivation. In 1938 there wasn't much of anything happening in this region.

On January 29, 1938, four-year-old Teddy Thompson had lunch and went outside to play with two friends. A short time after lunch, his mother had to reprimand and spank the boy for wandering from the yard. After the spanking, all of the children stayed quite close to the Thompsons' house.

As dinnertime approached, Mrs. Thompson went outside to tell Teddy it was time to eat, but none of the kids knew where he had gone. Mr. and Mrs. Thompson scoured the area and then placed a call to the sheriff and other USFS employees for assistance. The initial response came from fellow USFS employees, who searched through the night.

Just after Teddy disappeared, a major storm hit northern California, dumping several inches of snow on the coastal hills and greatly inhibiting search efforts. Searchers did find what they believe were Teddy's barefoot tracks on a nearby trail, but the boy never responded to their calls. Bloodhounds and search dogs were brought into the area to assist with the SAR, but they never found the boy.

The search for Teddy lasted weeks at a formal level and additional weeks informally. The local sheriff understood that the USFS employees knew the mountains where Teddy disappeared, and the idea that the boy couldn't be found bothered the sheriff greatly.

On February 1, 1938, the *Oakland Tribune* ran a story and statement from Sheriff E. L. Williams: "I am not satisfied with the theory that the boy merely wandered away from home, or that he was the victim of a wild animal." The sheriff further stated that he didn't believe the boy could survive in the mountains more than three days wearing just overalls and a sweater. The sheriff had a strong feeling that foul play was involved.

On March 28, 1938, Arthur Carpenter was riding his horse two miles from where Teddy was last seen. Arthur's dog alerted him to something under a thick Manzanita bush. He dismounted his horse and walked to see what the dog had found. Arthur located the body of Teddy Thompson. A March 29 article in the *Oakland Tribune* had the following: "Constable Charles Lovell said he was convinced the child had frozen to death the first night he was away from home. Both legs had been eaten off by animals and the body was horribly mutilated, he said, but he discounted the theory that Teddy had been carried off by a mountain lion."

Case Summary

The area where Teddy disappeared is very remote and rugged. Sheriff Williams felt that Teddy would never have voluntarily walked into the mountains dressed as he was; thus, he felt there was foul play involved. The location that Teddy disappeared was so remote that the thought of foul play seems a little spooky. Sheriff Williams was aware that Teddy had been spanked for wandering from his yard just prior to his disappearance. My mind questions why Teddy walked away a second time knowing that he would probably be punished again, or was there some other element to this disappearance that we don't understand?

How did the constable know that Teddy had died the first night? This is ridiculous. He wasn't a coroner. Articles stated the body was well preserved; thus, you could probably determine what had been chewing on the boy. No article I found ever addressed this. Articles did state that the body was found within twenty feet of where searchers had been. It also seems odd that Teddy would crawl under a thick and prickly Manzanita bush.

Dickie Tum Suden
Missing: 11/01/45, Goodyears Bar, CA
Age at disappearance: 3

Joseph Tum Suden was the wealthy son of a San Francisco entrepreneur. Joseph was married to Sally Tum Suden, and they had one son, Dickie Tum Suden. The family lived a majority of the year in San Francisco, but during most of the summer months, they stayed in Goodyears Bar in the northern Sierra foothills of California.

Joseph's father owned the Brush Creek Gold Mine just outside of Goodyears Bar. Joseph was the assistant superintendent of the mining facility. The Sudens were known as socialites in San Francisco, and the community knew they were quite wealthy.

On November 1, 1945, Sally was at their residence in Goodyears Bar with Dickie. Dickie was playing outside the house with his pet sheepdog, Heide. During the short amount of time Sally allowed Dickie to play outside, he and Heide disappeared. Sally ran up the trail and called for the dog and her son, but no answer came back. She ran back to the house and flagged down the first car that came by. In it was Dr. Guy Cahoon, a professor of education at Ohio State University who was vacationing in the California Sierras. Dr. Cahoon walked up the trail alone and eventually found Heide. He brought the dog back, but he could not find Dickie.

Soon after the young boy went missing, Sierra County Sheriff W. Dewey Johnson arrived and a formal search was initiated. Late in that first day of the search, evidence was located. A *Milwaukee Sentinel* article from November 3, 1945, reported the following: "One of Dickie's gloves was found late in the day on a high crag. Searchers doubted the lad could have climbed onto the rock without some assistance." They actually found one of Dickie's red and blue gloves, which he was wearing when he disappeared.

The second day of searching brought hundreds to the scene, including many of the top field scouts and trackers in the western United States. Among them was John Black, an expert tracker who owned two Russian shepherd dogs. John had participated in other missing person cases and had always found the missing. He announced that the dogs had "shown no interest in the only clues found so far." According to the November 5, 1945, issue of the *San Jose News*, John stated that the dogs were "taken to a spot a quarter mile from the home of Dickie's socially prominent parents, Mr. and Mrs. Tum Suden, where a mitten was found and to a more remote point where small footprints were discovered, but failed to pick up a trail."

As the days went on, soldiers from Camp Beale tried unsuccessfully to find Dickie. They searched the river, grounds, crags, and mountains, but found nothing. Small footprints were found in the mud quite a distance from the residence, but the dogs were not interested in tracking that scent.

A second set of dogs were brought to the scene and again taken to the same locations where evidence had been found. Al Tousseau and Bill Thompson were the owners. On November 5, 1945, the *News and Courier* ran a statement from the dog handlers: "The dogs appeared unable to pick up a scent." It should be noted that these two dogs were claimed to have found over one hundred missing people.

The first night after Dickie disappeared, there was a rainstorm. Also, there were several rains and snow flurries during the first seven days of the search, all slowing the results and hampering the efforts.

In the middle of the first week of search efforts, FBI agents arrived at the search headquarters and appeared to monitor the activity. Joseph Suden asked if the FBI would join the search, but they declined. The press was interested to know why the FBI was at the search headquarters if they were declining to participate. A November 6, 1945, article in the *News and Courier* included this statement about the FBI: "The agents have declined to give their names or even admit they are interested in the case."

On November 7, the formal search for Dickie came to an end. Over 250 soldiers, seventy-five volunteers, trackers, forest rangers, and sheriff deputies had searched for the young boy. The only evidence they ever found was one mitten and small footprints in the mud.

After the formal search was completed, there were additional searches but no results. The Sudens moved back to the San Francisco Bay Area. There were a few harassing calls and claims about Dickie, but there was no solid evidence about where the boy may be or what might have happened.

In a very unusual twist of events, the FBI announced on November 15, 1945, that one of their best kidnapping experts was going to formally undertake the Suden case. Assistant FBI Director E. J. Connelly left his post on the East Coast and took up residence in San Francisco. He claimed that his job was to investigate the Suden case and the case of a girl who went missing on her way home from school in San Jose (there was no link between the two cases). The November 15 article that announced Connelly's arrival was printed in the *Telegraph Herald* and also stated that under federal statute the FBI may enter a case after the person has been missing seven days if there is evidence of kidnapping.

The Sudens had been claiming that they felt Dickie was kidnapped since a very early point in his disappearance. There was significant evidence in the mind of the Sudens to show that Dickie didn't leave the yard voluntarily.

Case Summary

There is much to support the contention that Dickie Suden was forcibly taken from his yard. The river near the residence was searched thoroughly by soldiers and volunteers. The searchers didn't find the body, and the body never surfaced. I don't believe that Dickie went into the river. It was too cold of a day, and evidence does not point that direction.

The first day of the search, the sheriff found one of Dickie's mittens high up on a rocky crag at least a quarter mile from the residence. The boy's dog was found a short distance from the residence in the opposite direction of the river. There are two aspects of finding the glove that should have raised the concern of the searchers. First, the mitten was found high above the trail in an area where

Dickie could not have gone by himself. Children normally do not start to climb when they are lost: they usually go downhill, not uphill. If the sheriff stated that he didn't think Dickie could have gotten to that location without assistance, I believe him. If you start to track specific elements in each of the disappearances in the western United States, you start to understand that evidence (tracks, clothing, etc) are sometimes found in locations that completely baffle searchers.

One major aspect of many disappearances in this book is bad weather. Rain and snow hit the Goodyears Bar area soon after Dickie disappeared. Many, many instances of missing people have rain or snow hit the area where they went missing very soon after they are reported.

Another unusual element common to many of the searches in this book is that tracking dogs cannot find the scent of the lost individual, or they refuse to track. Tracking dogs love to search for people; they live for this adventure. If you have ever seen a dog on a track, you know they are excited. They view it as fun. The dogs in many of the searches outlined in this book are uninterested and want no involvement, as is the case with Dickie Suden's search.

There was never a validated ransom demand in Dickie's case, and the FBI never arrested a suspect. To the best of my knowledge, Dickie Suden's body was never found and this should still be an open case.

I never found Dickie Suden's name on any missing child database anywhere in the United States.

Dana Cooper
Missing: 08/04/71, Camp Arcade, Soda Springs, CA
Age at disappearance: 13

Camp Arcade is a school for mentally challenged children. The summer retreat is located six miles south of Soda Springs, California, in an area with dozens of small lakes and many square miles of granite-faced cliffs and exposed rock.

Dana Cooper, a thirteen-year-old boy with red hair, was on an "ecology hunt" sponsored by the camp when he apparently wandered off. The group was walking down a dusty dirt road near the camp at the time of the disappearance. Dana's parents described the boy as having the mental capacity of a five-year-old, and he did not have the ability to speak.

The Placer County Sheriff's Department was the lead law enforcement agency heading the search for Dana. The agency brought in helicopters, equestrians, hikers, bloodhounds, and scores of volunteers to search the region around the camp. For four days searchers found nothing to indicate where Dana may have been.

Late on the fourth day of searching, volunteers heard a "sound" in an area near the base of Devil's Peak adjacent to Long Lake. Numerous newspaper articles claim people did hear a sound, but there was no description of what was heard. It was too late on Saturday to search the area, so searchers waited until Sunday morning.

Searchers moved into a very rugged area approximately 1½ miles from the location Dana was last seen. The searchers were moving down a dry creek bed when they heard something in nearby bushes. An August 9, 1971, article in the *Daily Review* stated: "Dana was found in head high brush sitting in the shelter of three fallen trees that had formed a sanctuary." Dana was described as "tired," and he had lost his shoes and socks. Dana had been missing almost exactly five days in very rugged country at an elevation of 6,800 feet. How fortunate and convenient for Dana to find the shelter where he was resting.

Dana was transported to a regional hospital for an examination by Dr. Charles Kellermyer. The same article quoted earlier stated, "Kellermyer said that Dana apparently stayed in the same place the entire time he was lost because his feet were not scarred and he had no sunburn. He seemed frightened more than anything else." The doctor diagnosed Dana with mild pneumonia, dehydration, and exposure, and he was kept at the hospital for observation.

The doctor couldn't have known if Dana had stayed at the one location the entire time. He may have been carried to that location, at which time his shoes and socks were taken to ensure he wouldn't wander off.

Case Summary

Many newspaper articles state that the area where Dana was found had been thoroughly searched in the days prior to his discovery. Dana's shoes and socks were never found. Where were they? If Dana's feet were not scratched or scarred, and his shoes and socks couldn't be found, how did he get to the location of his discovery?

Searchers and volunteers reported hearing "sounds" in the area where Dana was found, and it was those sounds that led searchers back into that area on Sunday. What were the sounds that people heard? If Dana can't talk, well, Dana couldn't have made the sounds.

Many articles describe the location where Dana was found as a location where three trees had fallen and formed a "sanctuary." Was it pure luck that Dana found this sanctuary, which subsequently protected him from the weather elements?

Dana was found near the base of Devil's Peak. I'd like to know how and why the peak got that name.

Jo Anne Burmer
Missing: 02/25/73, Nevada City, CA
Age at disappearance: 38
5' 3", 135 lb.

Jo Anne was a mother who lived just off Highway 80 in the Sierra foothills of Colfax, California. She had friends throughout the region and enjoyed socializing. Her parents lived in Reno, approximately eighty miles east.

On February 25, 1973, Jo Anne left her child with good friends in Colfax. She stated that she was going to visit friends who were staying at a cabin in Nevada City. Jo Anne's car was later found on the roadway near the cabin, as were tracks in the snow leading toward the cabin. She never arrived at the cabin and has never been seen again.

On June 13, 1973, Nevada County Sheriff Wayne Brown utilized fifty inmates from the California Youth Authority and searched the area where Jo Anne disappeared. Searchers found one comb on the ground, but that was all that was discovered. Sheriff Brown stated that he waited until June to conduct the search so snow on the ground could melt and they could potentially find evidence.

A June 13 article in the *Nevada State Journal* reported the following statement from Sheriff Brown: "It's pretty rugged country." Brown was referring to the type of terrain. The area had many huge trees and some ground cover typical for the Sierras. Brown confirmed that no trace of Jo Anne has ever been found, and he did not know if or when he would reinitiate a search.

I know that many people will quickly discount the importance of this story but understand, a life has been taken. How does someone vanish on a short walk to a cabin? These types of stories defy common logic and need a closer look.

Debra Kay Manial
Missing: 12/12/82, Dobbins, CA
Age at disappearance: 29
5'4", 112 lb.

The holidays are usually fun and exciting times for everyone. When you live in a mountainous area of California, you can obtain a permit from the USFS to cut your own tree. It appears that is what Debra Manial and her friends were doing on December 12, 1982.

Debra and friends were in an area called Dobbins, approximately thirty-five miles east of Marysville. The group had gone out in the morning and split up to look for a tree. In the early afternoon, the group couldn't find Debra and a search was initiated. Soon after it was confirmed that Debra could not be found, the Yuba County Sheriff was called.

During the week of search efforts, two helicopters, ground teams, and canines covered the hills where Debra was last seen. They found no evidence of Debra ever being in the area. Immediately after Debra disappeared, the *Los Angeles Times* published an article about the incident, stating: "During the time the woman has been missing, the area has been blasted by rainstorms, snowstorms, and freezing temperatures." This is another of the long line of cases where bad weather hits an area immediately after someone is reported missing.

The weeklong search for Debra was unsuccessful. The area where she disappeared is heavily wooded, with large and small trees and heavy ground cover.

Like others, Debra had a very short haircut when she disappeared. Looking at Debra from a distance, it could be possible that she was mistaken for a male and attacked. Her body has never been found.

Note: Debra is one of two people who have disappeared while looking for Christmas trees in the forest. Derrick Engbretson went missing in southern Oregon while looking for a Christmas tree with his father and grandfather. He was never found. The Engbretson case is documented in the Crater Lake section (Oregon).

Gary Lee Chavoya
Missing: 07/10/83, noon, southeast of Quincy, CA
Age at disappearance: 10

Gary went on a fishing trip with his stepfather, Steve Avery. They had traveled to a very rural area of the Plumas National Forest, southeast of Quincy, California. At approximately noon, Steve and Gary became separated and Gary disappeared. Steve looked for the boy throughout the area and, when Gary could not be located, he notified authorities.

Plumas County officials and USFS personnel searched the Sierras for six days but still could not locate the boy. During the SAR, one team of professionals thought they heard the sounds of a small child calling for help, but they couldn't locate the exact position of the call. Another search team found what was believed to be Gary's socks.

On the sixth day of the SAR, Steve Avery was with a team at an elevation of six thousand feet. They called out the boy's name and he answered. They walked a short distance and found Gary. What is remarkable about this is that Gary went missing at an elevation of four thousand feet. He was found three miles from where he vanished and two thousand feet higher in elevation.

Gary had scratches on his legs and was slightly dehydrated. The boy told searchers that he had made a cave from leaves to sleep in. He also told searchers that he had not "eaten any berries." The mystery is why the boy had specifically stated that he had not eaten any berries, and why he had chosen to climb two thousand feet upward in elevation.

Todd Edward Lucchesi
Missing: 05/31/99, Sierra City, CA
Age at disappearance: 28
5'5", 135 lb.

The Luchessi family owned a summer home near the banks of the North Fork of the Yuba River in Sierra County. Their son, Todd, loved the outdoors and enjoyed the serenity of the cabin and the river.

On May 29, 1999, Todd went to his family's summer home to take a short vacation. When he still hadn't returned after Memorial Day, his family called the Sierra County Sheriff.

During the weeklong search, Sheriff Lee Adams separately utilized four tracking dogs. Each dog tracked Todd from the steps of his cabin to within five feet of the Yuba River, where they all stopped. Todd Luchessi's body never surfaced, and there has been no activity on his bank accounts. The sheriff stated that he believes he has done all he can and does not have any additional information or new areas to search.

The Luchessi case has some similarity to the Austin Sparks case in Mount Shasta. Both individuals were tracked to a river where the trail inexplicably stops.

Yosemite National Park

Yosemite National Park sits approximately one hundred air miles southeast of Sacramento, California, in the heart of the Sierra Nevada.

Yosemite is the third oldest national park in the U.S. and consists of 1,189 square miles, or 760,917 acres. Yosemite Falls is one of the top five highest waterfalls in the world at 1,430 feet.

Yosemite was first occupied over eight thousands years ago by Miwok Native American Indians. The Miwok held the Yosemite Valley in high regard and felt it was sacred. It is believed that the first white man stepped foot into Yosemite Valley sometime after

1850. On October 1, 1890, Congress passed legislation establishing Yosemite National Park. Since Yosemite was formally made a national park, visitor numbers to this gorgeous granite spot have slowly increased. In 2000, 3.4 million people visited Yosemite.

Yosemite is known as a spot where there are a great number of black bears. People visiting Yosemite are continually warned about the population of bears and how the bears will visit campsites at night and steal food. The bears have become so innovative that they often climb onto the hood of a vehicle that harbors food, use their claws to pull down the metal frame of the window, and break the window to gain entry. These bear break-ins have been known to cause car owners hundreds of dollars in repairs and hours of humiliation. In 2009 there were 529 "incidents" involving bears at the park, and twenty-nine accidents where a bear was hit by a vehicle.

Yosemite is known as the world's foremost spot for rock climbing. Half Dome has a sheer face of granite that challenges the top climbers in the world. On any summer day, you can see climbers on the face of Half Dome creeping up the granite. Bring your binoculars because the climbers look like tiny specks on the huge granite walls.

Yosemite Village is the city located in the valley inside the park. The city has a beautiful first class hotel called The Ahwahnee. Reservations for the hotel are required months, and sometimes years, in advance. It is open year-round. There are tents that are permanently stabled in the park that visitors can rent and utilize as their home base when in the valley. There is a large store with fishing supplies and maps, and there are even instructors who will teach you how to climb at the Yosemite Mountaineering School.

There are thousands of miles of hiking trails in Yosemite Park. Bring your hiking shoes, camera, personal locator transponder and a friend—and be ready to be active.

Alphabetical Listing of Missing People in the Yosemite Region

Missing Person	Date Missing•Age•Sex
Andrews, Christopher	10/03/08•42•M
Arras, Stacey Anne	07/17/81•14•F

Barnes, Timothy	07/05/88•24•M
Bartholomew, Elizabeth	01/08/91•80•F
Bier, Theresa	06/01/87•16•F
Burke, Kieran	04/05/00•45•M
Claasen, Fred	08/01/03•46•M
Estes, Jeff	05/24/76•25•M
Ficery, Michael	06/15/05•51•M
Good, Leah	04/30/73•49•F
Gordon, Walter A.	07/20/54•26•M
Green Jr., Anthony	11/06/09•31•M
Griffen, Donald R.	08/22/63•4•M
Gunn, John	07/28/67•19•M
Holt, Emerson	07/18/43•55•M
Hesselschwerdt, Jeanne	07/09/95•37•F
Huckins, David	02/04/86•21•M
Jacobus, Ruth	06/07/89•76•F
Klein, Kenneth	07/28/67•23•M
Laughlin, Carol	09/09/79•19•F
Madden, Michael	08/10/96•20•M
Mayo, Nita	08/08/05•64•F
McPherson, Richard	05/26/38•10•M
Miller, Kenny	06/24/92•12•M
Opperman, Tom	08/08/67•21•M
Pearce, Doug	04/21/05•86•M
Price, Bernice*	03/22/23•Unknown•F
Reinhard, Walter	09/20/02•66•M
Scott, David Allen	07/13/57•2•M
Von Laass, Orvar	10/09/54•30•M
Walsh, Michael	03/01/01•56•M
Wondrosek, Godfrey	04/26/33•26•M

*Details on the disappearance of Bernice Price can be found in the chapter on farmers in the second book of this series, *Missing 411: Eastern United States*.

Totals
33 Cases Cited
24 Males
9 Females

Females
Oldest case: 1923- Bernice Price
2 cases occurred in June
2 cases occurred in July
Youngest: Stacy Arras, 14
Oldest: Elizabeth Bartholomew, 80

Missing by Month

January	1 Female
February	1 Male
March	1 Male, 1 Female
April	1 Female, 3 Males
May	2 Males
June	2 Females, 2 Males
July	2 Females, 7 Males
August	1 Female, 4 Males
September	1 Female, 1 Male
October	2 Males
November	1 Male
December	N/A

Several items on this map need to be addressed. It is obvious that if there are more people vacationing in a national park, more people will disappear; however, more people also means more assistance, more witnesses, and better facilities. Trails would be easily identified; help and transportation would be close. I don't necessarily believe that just because there are thousands of people visiting Yosemite every year, that this would mean an immediate upsurge of missing people.

I have been very concerned about the attitude that the NPS expresses about missing people. There is no national database in the NPS system identifying missing people. There is no local database for each park identifying missing people. There is no list in each park identifying the people, the circumstances, locations, dates that they disappeared. This is very disturbing. How would a large park or a regional district ever know if there was a serial killer utilizing the park as a location to abduct victims? Answer: they wouldn't. It's hard to imagine that a giant government law enforcement agency such as the National Park Service doesn't monitor and track these basic statistics. This is beyond inept; it borders on complete stupidity, unless this is a calculated maneuver.

I requested a list (not the case files) of all missing people inside Yosemite National Park from the western regional information director, Charis Wilson. After thirty-five days elapsed, I had to send another e-mail. I again asked for the list and how much the park service would charge me for this information. Ms. Wilson responded that it would take 750 man-hours to accumulate a list of all missing people inside the park. Yes, it's an unbelievable estimate for information that should be at the fingertips of an administrator in any park at any time. I literally almost fell over when I read her estimate.

The primary law enforcement in every national park is the law enforcement body of the NPS. They have agents which are equal to a city detective. Imagine a series of disappearances that occur at three different national parks over a thirty-year period. They are all boys, ages eight to fifteen, all missing for a substantial period of time, some found, some never found. Imagine that these boys were being escorted by the same man with disappearances occurring at intervals of six to eight years. The way the NPS agents transfer—rangers move park to park—the acquisition of case information would only be occurring if the law enforcement officials stayed in a specific area their entire careers. According to Ms. Wilson, there is no database that detectives can refer to and track missing people, witnesses, and specific data that could show trends. Imagine that this exact scenario could be playing itself out in any of the large national parks.

What if the NPS understood that the number of missing people inside their parks represents a staggering figure, a number that would concern the public and have a direct effect on visitations? What if they knew they were not successful in finding vast numbers of missing people, and they were worried this information would be publicized? The inability to find large numbers of missing people would reflect poorly on the NPS, so perhaps for this reason they choose not to keep those statistics. What if they developed a system of merely declaring the person "probably deceased" after a period of time, a method of internally justifying the lack of tracking missing people and keeping an ongoing list? These are not *what ifs*. This is a reality, and they are doing this today.

In my thirty-plus years of investigating a variety of criminal and civil issues, I have never seen a governmental agency approach such a serious issue with such a laissez-faire attitude. There is a reason the NPS is not releasing statistics on missing people inside their system. I know they have the data; they don't want you to know the numbers!

I've heard the statement that they cannot afford a computer system to track the number of missing people, and the parks don't have the infrastructure to maintain the lists. How stupid do they think we are? Any modern-day laptop computer would suffice for tracking missing people across the entire park system. I could devise a clipboard with a legend at each park that would maintain a list of missing people, where they went missing, time, date, location last seen, etc. Each major national park has a special agent assigned that works like a detective. These agents have been trained at the National Law Enforcement Training Center, so they understand the need to track trends. I can't imagine any major county or city in the United States that doesn't maintain a database or list of all missing people in their organization. It just doesn't happen (except inside the nation's national parks).

The United States has a mandatory reporting law regarding the tracking of the disappearance of any juvenile. Once the law was enacted, all jurisdictions were forced to comply. During my investigation of missing people in national parks, I accidentally came across the case of Stacy Arras, who was fourteen years old at the time she disappeared (07/17/81). Stacy was not listed in the National Center for Missing and Exploited Children. I asked the NPS why Stacy wasn't listed in the national database. The formal answer was that Stacy disappeared prior to the 1984 requirement. Everyone needs to understand that most jurisdictions list children as missing regardless of how long ago they disappeared. When I asked the director of a state criminal investigative agency about the NPS's response regarding Stacy, he was shocked and dismayed. He literally couldn't believe what I was telling him.

Stacy Arras not being listed in the National Center for Missing and Exploited Children and the NPS's response to my inquiry don't make sense. Dennis Martin was seven years old when he disappeared June 14, 1964, from the Great Smoky Mountains National Park, and he is listed in the national database. The more I looked into the Stacy Arras case, the more questions arose and the more concerned I became. You will read more about her case later in this chapter.

The people below all went missing in or near Yosemite National Park. Some of the disappearances occurred on the periphery of the park but are consistent with other cases in this chapter.

Christopher Andrews
Missing: 10/03/08, Iceland Lake, Tuolumne County, Emigrant Wilderness, CA
Age at disappearance: 42

Amy and Christopher Andrews were married and lived in the wealthy community of Hillsborough, California. Christopher was employed by the Oracle Corporation, and he had actually left school one semester early to take the job.

In October 2008 Christopher took a five-day break from work and headed to the Emigrant Wilderness Area, a region on the northern perimeter of Yosemite National Park. He was an experienced and avid hiker. He was safety-conscious to the point of carrying a personal safety transponder. Christopher was in the wilderness when the transponder was activated on Friday, October 3. The transponder sent the signal to emergency services via satellite. Emergency services contacted the Tuolumne County Sheriff's Office and notified them of the location of the signal—Iceland Lake. The signal was received late Friday and rescuers were not able to get started until Saturday morning because of high winds and a storm that hit the area.

The location where Christopher activated his distress signal has large areas of exposed granite. The transponder signal was coming from an area between Relief Lake (at 7,200 feet elevation) and Iceland Lake (at 9,200 feet elevation). There is a very open and easy hike between the two locations, and there would be no need to climb to the top of a large granite spire. Christopher would have known bad weather was moving into the area; it would have been obvious. The last place you want to be in bad weather is on a peak as this exposes you to the elements of weather, lightning, wind, rain, etc.. There were very good areas near Relief Lake to protect himself from the elements, and there was no need to take to a peak. There are three separate and obvious valleys that lead into Relief Lake from Iceland Lake. A few are very protected and are areas where you could sit out a storm.

On October 5, a helicopter went into the area. At the same time, the personal beacon shut down. They were unable to locate Christopher at that time.

Rescuers initially had difficulty locating Christopher. It wasn't until the weather cleared and a helicopter flew into the area that they were able to find him wedged in the bottom of a crevasse near the bottom of a granite spire. He was dead. Officials believe that Christopher had climbed to the top of the spire, slipped on a wet surface and fell to his death in the crevasse.

I have personally read hundreds of SAR reports outlining almost identical circumstances. The hiker is always alone and falls to his death in an area he should not have been in. Christopher was a very smart hiker. What would cause him to climb to the top of a granite spire in bad weather?

Stacey Anne Arras
Missing: 07/17/81, three miles
southeast of Tenaya Lake, Yosemite National Park, CA
Age at disappearance: 14

If there is one story in this
section that caused me to stop
and take notice of the dangers in
Yosemite, it is the disappearance
of Stacey Anne Arras.

Stacey was fourteen years
old when she and her dad joined
a group of ten people and their
guide for a trip through High
Sierra Camps on horseback.
The group had stayed together,

stopped for lunch at Upper Cathedral Lake, and then headed for
their first night stop at Sunrise High Sierra Camp, approximately
three miles southeast of Tenaya Lake and 1½ miles from Sunrise
Lakes. The trip parallels Highway 120, approximately one mile
southeast.

Stacey had some aches and pains from riding all day and quickly
went to the old cabin she shared with her dad, showered, and then
wanted to take a short hike to stretch her legs. She started to leave
her cabin in sandals when her dad stated that she had to put on hiking boots if she was going to walk on a trail. She did. At an elevation
of 9,200 feet, it would be a slow hike with a vast amount of exposed
granite. The lack of trees makes this a spectacular arena for sightseeing. Gerald Stuart, seventy years old, was also on the ride and
volunteered to join Stacey on her hike.

Stacey and Gerald started the short 1.5-mile hike to Sunrise
Lakes. The hike is across giant slabs of granite with small clusters
of large trees that surround many of the hundreds of small lakes in
the area. After only a few minutes, Gerald got tired and explained to
Stacey that he was going to sit and rest. It was at this time that the
trail guide for Gerald and Stacey's trip, Chris Grimes, happened to
look fifty yards up the hill from his position in the corral and caught

the last glimpse anyone on Earth would ever see of Stacey Arras. Stacey stood on a large boulder and stared into the distance and walked into the sunset.

On page 467 of Butch Farabee's book, *Off the Wall*, he states that the nine-day search for Stacey included 8,004 man-hours, fifty-seven hours of helicopter time, four separate agencies, and not one clue about what happened to Stacey. The search cost the NPS $99,845 in 1981.

The potential value of the NPS tracking missing people cases may become more evident with the disappearance of Stacey. Maybe the NPS does not want this publicized, or maybe they don't realize the following relationships exist between Stacey's disappearance and the disappearances of others in the same area.

I requested the NPS case file on the Stacy Arras disappearance. This request was identical to many others I have made to the NPS system for people who have disappeared and never were found. One of the many cases I requested and received was the disappearance and subsequent investigation of a missing employee/ranger. Up until the point I requested Stacy's case file, I had never been denied my request on a missing person case.

Prior to the formal denial by NPS in supplying me with the Arras case file, special agent Yu for the park service from Yosemite called and asked me a series of questions. He wanted to know why I was requesting the case. This is a violation of the Freedom of Information Act. Any citizen can ask for any federal file and the government cannot ask why you are seeking it, this cannot be grounds for refusing to comply. The agent stated that I was not going to get the case file, ever. I advised him that I had several case files on missing people in the NPS, and they were all still active and open. He stated that he didn't believe me (a rather rude comment). I advised him to call the local FOIA administrator in Denver, Charis Wilson, and confirm what I was stating.

The agent did clearly state that there were no suspects in the Arras disappearance; the case is still classified as a missing person; there are no leads; and there is no apparent sign that the classification will change in the near future. So, I confirmed that this is just a missing person case. When I told him she wasn't listed in the

National Center for Missing and Exploited Children, he stated that he didn't believe me.

I have never had such a negative conversation with anyone in the NPS. He denied access to the case file. His arguments why I could not have the file included that there was a possibility that the case may develop a criminal lead. Excuse me, the case was thirty years old. By his own admission they had no leads. The closest person to Stacy (Gerald Stuart) at the time she disappeared would be over one hundred years old today. Why would he make such a statement when I had already received many cases from the NPS that were open and active?

Fact: Stacy Arras was not listed in any database as a missing person. Fact: The NPS had denied me all access to the case file. I'm not a great believer in conspiracy theories, but why has this case been withheld from the public? What is in Stacy's case file that the NPS does not want released to the public? It would appear that the NPS has kept Stacy's case out of public view for thirty years. Why?

In the fall of 2011 I appealed the Stacy Arras decision by Special Agent Yu to another branch of the NPS, I was again denied access.

Missing People in the Area Stacy Arras Disappeared and Timeline:
09/08/68, Tenaya Peak
Two off-duty San Jose police officers found a man's body in a crevasse. The body was never identified. Tenaya Peak is approximately one mile directly north of Sunrise Lakes, where Stacey disappeared. See narrative in this chapter for additional details.

05/25/76, Snow Creek Trail
En route to May Lake, Jeff Estes disappears. On a map you could draw a straight line through Sunrise Lake, Tenaya Lake, and May Lake, each almost equal distance apart (approximately 1½ miles). See narrative later in this chapter for additional details.

07/17/81, three miles southeast of Tenaya Lake
Stacey Anne Arras disappears.

07/15/88, Murphy Creek Trail
The Murphy Creek Trail starts at Tenaya Lake and goes northeast a half mile to Polly Dome Lake. Timothy Barnes disappears. See narrative later in this chapter for additional details.

Each of the four above incidents occurred in proximity to each other. Each incident has its own bizarre and unexplainable story. How can a body be found in the middle of a national park and never be identified? How did the man get there, and where did he come from? Where is the camping equipment, backpack, and supplies that Jeff Estes and Timothy Barnes were carrying? How can a search party encompassing eight thousand hours of work not find a trace of a fourteen-year-old girl missing in an area largely of exposed granite with limited tree coverage?

The incidents listed above had five to eight years between each occurrence. Three of the four incidents involved white male adults. Two of the incidents happened in mid-July, almost to the date.

Again, the NPS wanted to charge me over $30,000 for a list of missing people inside Yosemite National Park. The idea that these are the only missing people in this area would not be accurate. It was an extensive periodical search that produced these results, and there are others. Stacey Arras, Timothy Barnes, and Jeff Estes did not disappear. Human beings cannot disappear. They are probably somewhere inside that park. Why are we giving up the search when we know exactly where they disappered??

I believe the paradigm of searching for missing people needs to drastically change. Why should we ever give up searching for people when we know exactly where they were located fifteen minutes prior to their disappearance? How far can a fourteen-year-old girl travel on her own? I can guarantee that the loss of Stacey Arras was the worst life-changing event in her father's life. I have no idea how a parent would cope with the loss of a child; it would be horrific. I also don't understand how the NPS can stop searching for a girl after just nine days. They know this child is still in the park. Why aren't they continuing to search? Do they know something that allows them to reconcile this decision in their minds? In a remote set of circumstances, some adults may walk into the wild with the intent of disappearing, but not a fourteen-year-old girl. When children are abducted off a city street, detectives understand that they can be transported hundreds of miles in just a day; a search in a national park is much different, much more confined. The NPS knows the environment. They know the geography. And they know exactly the parameters of how far a girl can travel in one day. Why are these searches terminated so quickly? Why aren't visitors informed of the dangers associated with some regions of the park?

James Arthur
Missing: 07/28/08, Beasore Road, Iron Lakes Reservoir, Madera, CA
Age at disappearance: 67
6', 189 lb.

James Arthur was a retired lieutenant colonel in the California Air National Guard. He was a lifetime military man with excellent survival skills. On Monday morning, July 28, 2008, he told his family that he was going to drive to the area of Star Lake to take photos. He told the family that he would be back before it was dark. He never returned. The family called the Madera County Sheriff.

During the height of the search, over one hundred SAR team searchers participated in covering the hills and valleys of the area. The teams centered on three separate regions: Iron Lake Trailhead, Grizzly Lake, Junction Lake and Bear Island Lake. This area of the Sierra National Forest has many small lakes that are very picturesque. This region was logged fifty years ago but has since grown over. It is very dense and rugged, with many large rock outcroppings.

On Tuesday at 12:30 p.m., searchers found James's Dodge Ram pickup parked at the entrance to Iron Lakes Reservoir on Beasore Road. The sheriff stated that there was no evidence of foul play at the truck. James's truck was found at an elevation of seven thousand feet.

Searchers were told that James was wearing an orange shirt and carrying a walking stick. Madera County Sheriff John Anderson stated that he had known James for over twenty years: "If he was up and around and walking, we would have run into him."

This case presents some elements that are very confusing. How could a man that has military and survival skills simply disappear on a beautiful summer day? There was a notation in the search record that canines were utilized in the search. Obviously, they were not successful. It is very doubtful that James ventured off any of the main trials. He was carrying a camera with the intent of taking photographs. Did James attempt to photograph something that he wasn't suppose to see? Could he possibly have been abducted? This is doubtful as he was a big man.

The statement of the sheriff regarding the fact that there was no evidence of foul play "at the truck" concerns me. Did the sheriff use his language skills carefully by stating there was nothing found "at the truck" but things were found elsewhere? There was a notation that searchers were able to interview two different parties that saw James on the trail. What did they say? The area east of where James disappeared is very wild, very open, and extends for over thirty miles without any large roadways or cities. The fact that James was wearing a bright orange hunting vest would indicate that he should be easier to spot, yet James has not been found.

Timothy John Barnes
Missing: 07/05/88, Murphy Creek Trail, Yosemite National Park, CA
Age at disappearance: 24
6'4", 180 lb.

Timothy Barnes loved the outdoors. His six-foot-four frame gave him an excellent stature to view the beauty of Yosemite, where he was hiking on July 5, 1988. Timothy started his hike from an area near Highway 120 east of Tioga Road at approximately 9:00 a.m. He had told friends that he would hike up to Polly Dome Lakes via the Murphy Creek Trail. He left the area near the highway and was never seen again. Friends called law enforcement the next morning, but a massive search by several SAR crews found no evidence of Timothy Barnes.

The area where Timothy started his hike is at an elevation of 8,200 feet, and Polly Dome Lakes is at 8,775 feet. It is only one air mile from the highway to the lakes where Timothy was heading. The area has massive open granite with sparse coverage of large trees. The Murphy Creek Trail runs through a small valley, which contains the creek and is bordered on two sides by huge, exposed granite walls.

Elizabeth Barbara Bartholomew
Missing: 01/08/91, Midpines, CA
Age at disappearance: 80
5', 140 lb.

Elizabeth Bartholomew and her husband lived on the outskirts of Midpines, California, near the intersection of Carstens and Plumbar Creek roads. There is a small valley near the intersection with an elevation of 2,800 feet. The valley has a small lake surrounded by heavy timber and vegetation in the Sierra National Forest. The Bartholomew's lived on their daughter's 230-acre ranch and worked regularly on the maintenance of the property.

On January 8, 1991, Elizabeth was riding the family tractor with her husband as they graded a winding dirt road on the ranch. Elizabeth stated she wanted to get off and head back to their residence. Bill, her husband, complied. He let her off the tractor and kept her in sight for a few minutes. He then looked back to where she should have been and she was gone.

The Mariposa County Sheriff's Office immediately responded and started an area search for Elizabeth. They said the vegetation around the ranch was so thick that they didn't believe that she could have penetrated it. At times there were 150 searchers trampling over twenty-five square miles in search of Elizabeth. A total of nine thousand search hours were contributed in the effort.

Law enforcement officials believe that Elizabeth became disoriented, lost, and walked away. Law enforcement conducted an extensive search and found no evidence of her.

This is the type of case that I have a very hard time understanding. The victim was eighty years old. How far could she go? It's hard to imagine how law enforcement truly could not find any evidence of Elizabeth in the area where she vanished. If the county sheriff truly believes she just wandered away, she should have been located by canines, heat-seeking helicopters, etc. Elizabeth should have been found.

Theresa Bier
Missing: 06/01/87, Shuteye Peak,
Sierra National Forest, CA
Age at disappearance: 16
5'5", 110 lb.

If there is only one case in this book that strikes the reader as odd, this is it.

Theresa Bier was Russell Welch's neighbor. Welch gained permission to take sixteen-year-old Theresa on a camping trip to the area of Shuteye Peak at an elevation of 8,200 feet in the Sierra National Forest. There is a road that goes to the summit, and the area immediately around the summit has large areas of exposed granite.

Russell claimed to be an expert on the topic of bigfoot, and the two were supposedly looking for the biped. Sometime during the trip, Russell claims that Theresa was abducted "by a tribe of bigfoot." Yes, that was the wording he used in 1987. Russell came back to his Fresno home and then reported Bier missing to law enforcement.

He took officials to the area where he claimed Theresa was abducted, but no evidence of any kind was ever found. Russell was charged with the abduction of Theresa Bier, but the charges were later dropped. Follow-up searches of the area around Shuteye Peak did not produce any evidence of the girl.

The Theresa Bier case inspired me to conduct additional research on the Shuteye Peak area. It is interesting that Theresa disappeared in an area that topographically matches many associated with missing people in the greater Yosemite area: rocky, large granite outcroppings, etc.

The case of Theresa Bier got major press in the Fresno, California, area at the time it occurred.

Kieran Burke
Missing: 04/05/00, Yosemite National Park, CA
Age at disappearance: 45
6', 180 lb.

Kieran Burke was a resident of Rothfamham in Dublin, Ireland. His family stated that Kieran was a very adventurous and interested traveler who enjoyed the experiences associated with foreign travel.

On April 5, 2000, Kieran reserved a hotel room just outside of Yosemite National Park. He went into the park and proceeded into the heart of the main village, Curry. He took his camera and went on a day hike never to be seen again. Witnesses state that he had a camera but few other supplies. The search for Kieran was delayed six days because nobody realized he was missing until family members got involved. A massive search of the park failed to find Kieran or his camera.

Fred Claasen
Missing: 08/01/03, Whorl Mountain, Yosemite National Park, CA
Age at disappearance: 46
5'10", 150 lb.

Martha and Fred Claasen loved the outdoors and spent time in remote areas to experience isolation. In late July 2003, the pair had just returned from a backpacking trip in the Ansel Adams Wilderness Area. Fred had two additional days of vacation and asked Martha if it was OK for him to go back into Yosemite for two more days of recording audio and video of thunderstorms. Martha told him to enjoy himself and she headed home.

Fred headed to the northeastern section of Yosemite, specifically the Sawtooth Range in the Hoover Wilderness. The hike plan called for Fred to hike through Mule and Burro Pass to Crown Lake and then to Twin Lakes via Matterhorn Pass and the Horse Creek drainage. The last confirmed sighting of Fred was August 1 at Crown Lake. Searchers found his car where he had parked it near the trailhead.

Fred was an expert with audio and video equipment. When he disappeared he had microphones and video equipment with the intent of filming a thunderstorm that he had predicted to hit the area.

The Mono County Sheriff's Office and Yosemite officials conducted an extensive search but were unable to locate any evidence of Fred Claasen.

After Fred's disappearance, Martha moved to Lee Vining to be closer to the search location and to monitor activity in the area. During a camping trip, an off-duty ranger remembered seeing what she thought was a backpack in the backcountry. She reported it to park officials, and SAR was organized. The backpack and Fred's body were found at the base of Whorl Mountain.

Whorl Mountain has an elevation of 11,500 feet with a razor-thin summit. There is a thousand-foot cliff running the east side of the mountain, and it appears that is where they found Fred. He was last seen at Crown Lake, approximately two air miles from where his fall would have occurred. Fred would have had to cross two large valleys or walk a treacherous two-mile ridgeline to get to the point he is believed to have fallen. Again, it makes no sense.

Fred was a carrying a heavy pack. He would have known the risks of carrying heavy equipment at a ridgeline on a summit. The width of the ridge in the area, coupled with the winds at that height, would have made the trip very dangerous. Fred was on the trip to capture video and audio of thunderstorms, and he would have known the extreme danger of being on a summit during a storm. He would never have positioned himself at the top of Whorl Mountain if a thunderstorm were in the area. I'm sadly pleased that Martha has resolution to Fred's death, but the circumstances surrounding his death still disturb me.

Jeff Estes
Missing: 05/24/76, Snow Creek Trail, Yosemite National Park, CA
Age at disappearance: 25

I found this listing in a book called *Vanishing* by Ray Jones (page 62). There is nothing available on any local, state, or national database regarding Jeff Estes.

The entry in *Vanishing* states that Jeff was a bus dispatcher in Yosemite but took the day to drive to Tioga Pass on Highway 120 and take the Snow Creek Trail to May Lake. He had intended to spend the night and return the following morning. He never returned. A massive search did not locate Mr. Estes.

In a peculiar and odd coincidence, Snow Creek runs one valley east of the trail that Timothy Barnes disappeared on July 5, 1988. These two locations are less than a half mile from each other and only one valley apart. Both are located on Tioga Pass Road at an elevation of near 8,500 feet.

Michael Ficery
Missing: 06/15/05, Hetch Hetchy Reservoir, Yosemite National Park, CA
Age at disappearance: 51
5'10", 165 lb.

Michael Ficery, a resident of Santa Barbara, obtained a wilderness permit for the backside of Hetch Hetchy Reservoir on June 15, 2005, the date he was last seen. Michael had initially taken the north end trail but changed his path and decided to take the Pacific Crest Trail. The wilderness permit expired June 19, and Michael did not return. On June 21, the Ficery family contacted the National Park Service and an SAR was initiated.

Searchers found Michael's backpack off the trail near Tiltill Mountain, not in a location which he had planned to be. Searchers described this area as "extremely rugged and hazardous" and could not find evidence of Michael. Missing from the backpack was his camera, water bottle, and topo map. Michael disappeared in proximity to Walter Reinhard on September 20, 2002, near White Wolf.

Karen Caldwell was the Yosemite press information officer at the time of Michael's disappearance. She stated that Michael was very physically fit, and the searchers had a good opportunity to find him. Karen stated that four helicopters, search dogs, and ground searchers were utilized on the SAR for Michael. He was never found.

Leah Oliver Good
Missing: 04/30/73, Yosemite Village, CA
Age at disappearance: 49

Leah was the wife of John Good, the assistant superintendent of Yosemite National Park. The family lived on the park's premises and knew the area very well. Leah enjoyed the park atmosphere and regularly took hikes in the area.

On Monday, April 30, 1973, Leah decided to take a hike on Mist Trail leading to Vernal Falls. It was the start of spring in the park. According to an article in the *Merced Sun Star* on May 2, 1973, Leah had left a note for her husband stating that she was going to pick wildflowers. Leah didn't return and John reported her missing.

The park initiated a massive search with sixty men and a navy helicopter combing the area for Leah Good. The search party did not find Leah, but a visitor found her in a pool of water below Vernal Falls. In *Off the Wall* (41, 499), Farabee reports that Leah had terminal cancer. The coroner's report indicated "possible suicide by jumping."

As someone who has investigated dozens of suicide cases and read as many books on the topic, this story doesn't make sense. Why would Leah leave a note at her residence indicating that she was going to pick wildflowers and then jump to her death? Most people leave a note to their loved ones cleansing their souls of guilt and explaining their actions and apologizing. Leah apparently did not do this. Leah disappeared in an area where nine other people have disappeared, and three bodies have been recovered under questionable circumstances.

On November 8, 1976, John Good left Yosemite and became park superintendent of Everglades National Park.

Walter A. Gordon
Missing: 07/20/54, Camp Curry, CA
Age at disappearance: 26

Walter Gordon was a summer employee of the Camp Curry Company and held a job as a desk clerk. During the school year, Walter was a student at the University of California at Berkeley. (In a remarkable twist of fate, Orvar Von Laass, another UC Berkeley graduate student, went missing in Yosemite on October 9, 1954. See Von Laass section for more details.)

Walter had left Curry Camp in the morning hours of July 20 for a hike to the 7,200 feet elevation of Glacier Point. Walter was never seen again. An organized search covered the area where others believed he had hiked.

On October 27, 1954, the relatives of Walter and Orvar Von Laass wrote to then President Eisenhower asking for additional resources for a search for both men. The families cited the use of bloodhounds, climbers, helicopters, and organized search teams, but nothing was found of either man. The father of Von Laass stated, "The situation in which there has been no indication of what happened to either man is unsavory." Both families stated that the evidence points to a mysterious disappearance and gives rise to many unanswered questions. Mr. Von Laass stated what I have been saying numerous times throughout this entire book, something unusual is occurring.

Anthony Green Jr.
Missing: 11/06/09, Happy Isles, CA
Age at disappearance: 31
5'7", 200 lb.

Anthony Green called relatives from a pay phone in Happy Isles on the perimeter of Yosemite National Park and explained where he was going. Relatives didn't hear from Anthony for several days after his initial call and phoned authorities. A search found Anthony's car at the trailhead to the park in Happy Isles.

Green was found approximately five miles south of the location of the disappearances of Timothy Barnes and Jeff Estes.

Circumstances of Anthony's body being found are difficult to understand. We do know that his driver's license was found at the top of Nevada Falls inside the park. The following day searchers found additional bones along with Anthony's wallet. Park officials told the mother they were 99 percent sure that they had found Anthony. Blood samples and DNA testing were taken from his mother with results to follow in the coming weeks.

I could never find absolute confirmation that Anthony was found.

Donald Roger Griffen
Missing: 08/22/63, 8:30 a.m., Huntington Lake, CA
Age at disappearance: 4

On August 22, 1963, Don Griffen (35) and his wife, Gladys (30), were camping in their trailer with their two children, Susan (5) and

Donald (4). They had picked a location in the Deer Creek Public Campground adjacent to Huntington Lake at an elevation of approximately seven thousand feet. On this morning everyone was up and moving, and Gladys was preparing at approximately 8:30 a.m. The aroma of freshly made eggs and bacon were in the air when they noticed Donald was missing. Don and Gladys started to search the area around their campsite and then slowly started to look in a more far-reaching area. Very quickly it was becoming apparent that their yells and screams for Donald were not going to get any response, and they called the forest service and the sheriff.

Inside of twenty-four hours, there were over two hundred searchers combing the High Sierras for Donald Griffen. There were sheriffs on horseback and SAR personnel on foot. Quadrants were being thoroughly covered and searched.

SAR leaders were frustrated because they hadn't found footprints or other evidence of where Donald may have gone. Canines were brought into the area but couldn't pick up the boy's scent. For four days there was no progress in the effort to find Donald.

Early in the morning of the fourth search day, a team was again covering the Potter Pass Trail, a trail they had searched several times before. They were higher in elevation than they thought necessary, but still in an area that they had been in the past. The team was in an area they felt they should search. They actually felt they'd never find Donald six miles from his campsite and three thousand feet higher in elevation. The team was near timberline when they came across a freshly fallen pine tree. Lying face up across one of the larger branches was Donald Griffen. The boy had apparently walked through some extraordinary, rugged wilderness to get to the point where he was found. SAR teams told news sources that they had been on this same trail "scores of times" and never saw what they found at 4:20 p.m. on August 26. An August 27 article in the *Los Angeles Times* expressed the feelings of searchers: "'It's a complete mystery why he went up,' said Robert Stiver, member of the Altadena Mountain Rescue Squad." Searchers were clear that they did not feel that Donald took any trails to get to where he was found. They felt he took a rugged and steep boulder-strewn route to get to that location, an amazing feat for a hungry four-year-old!

Kevin Klein
Missing: 7/28/67, Camp 4, Yosemite, CA
Age at disappearance: 23

John Gunn and Kevin Klein were work associates at the Yosemite National Park and Curry Company gas station in Yosemite Village. They started at 11:30 a.m. and were going to hike from Camp 4 to Upper Yosemite Falls and Eagle Peak. The pair did not return from the trip and an extensive search ensued. According to an article in the *Modesto Bee*, searchers found Kevin's car at Camp 4 and his motorcycle at an old entry point of a stagecoach road. The rangers theorized that the pair were going to ride the motorcycle back to the valley via another route.

SAR teams questioned backcountry packers and searched by air and horseback, but found nothing of the pair.

Five weeks after they disappeared, hikers found the submerged body of John Gunn in a deep pool in Yosemite Creek, upstream from Lower Yosemite Falls. According to what Butch Farabee documented in on page 384 of his book, "*Death in YosemiteOff the Wall*, "He had drowned and he somehow had sustained a broken neck." Kevin was never found; no death certificate was ever issued; and he is still presumed to be a missing person.

Here is another case where two employees inside Yosemite go missing. One is found dead under highly suspicious circumstances. When a coroner's report indicates the cause of death is drowning, it means that the person was alive when they entered the water and inhaled water into their lungs. It would appear from Farabee's statement that he found it slightly unusual that John had a broken neck.

Jeanne Hesselschwerdt
Missing: 07/09/95, Glacier Point, Yosemite National Park, CA
Age at disappearance: 37
5'2", 120 lb.,

Much of the information in the Jeanne Hesselschwerdt disappearance was gleaned from the reports obtained from the NPS through an FOIA request. The park service did not furnish all of the forms I requested, and they did not state why those forms were withheld. The NPS did not have a legal reason to withhold reports, as this case has been closed with the finding of the victim's body.

In June of 1995, Mike Monahan and Jeanne Hesselschwerdt were living together in Arlington, Massachusetts. The couple had been dating for over ten years and had recently gotten engaged. Relatives stated that it was a perfect, loving relationship. In June the couple left their home for a planned trip to the Sierra Nevada to go backpacking and sightseeing in the mountains.

Jeanne and Mike made a stop near Lake Tahoe, where they joined a Sierra Club–sponsored backpacking excursion into a wilderness area. The weeklong trip went well, and they decided to head for Yosemite to see its beauty firsthand.

The couple took Tioga Pass Road up into the mountains on Highway 41 and entered Yosemite National Park at 10:12 a.m. They turned east on Glacier Point Road and continued until they reached a paved turnout near Summit Meadow. The road that the couple was driving is very desolate and is only open during the summer months. There is absolutely no traffic on this road for a majority of the year. There were patches of snow in this specific area at the time of the couple's visit.

Jeanne and Mike exited their car and decided to take separate short hikes, agreeing to meet up in fifteen minutes at a designated location. Both took off in different direction. Mike reached the location where they had agreed to meet and waited a little longer than fifteen minutes. Jeanne never arrived and he started to panic. He immediately started to search the area but found no trace of Jeanne. After fifteen minutes he made his way to where he saw a park service employee emptying a garbage can and asked for his assistance. It was now 12:30 p.m. Within forty-five minutes there were park rangers in the area looking for Jeanne. At 2:15 p.m., the rangers asked for additional assistance.

The search quickly escalated and expanded to forty square miles, utilizing over one hundred searchers and eight different dog teams. The public at this time started to be concerned about bear and mountain lion attacks. The concern was addressed by Yosemite spokesperson Kris Fister in a July 18, 1995, article in the *San Francisco Chronicle*: "Our bears don't maul people. We haven't had a negative encounter here between a mountain lion and a park visitor. It's not impossible, but I'd say the likelihood is pretty slim."

After two weeks the National Park Service stated that they were giving up the search for Jeanne. Searchers had found two clear boot impressions that had belonged to Jeanne: one near the spot where she disappeared and another crossing one of the largest trails in Yosemite (which made no sense). Why would a lost person cross a trail when everyone knows that a trail will eventually lead to other people and safety? Searchers didn't believe that she would purposely not take a trail, so the impression was discounted. Rangers who were initially on the scene asked Mike what he thought Jeanne did when they separated. He thought she may have gone to some boulders and lain on them to get sun. They then asked him how long they were separated before he realized something was wrong. Mike said no more than ten minutes.

Several search dogs were placed in the area where Mike stated that he had last seen Jeanne. None of the dogs were able to pick up her scent. The dogs either refused to track or didn't smell anything. One handler told authorities that he didn't believe Jeanne was ever in the area and thought Mike was hiding something.

Federal law enforcement officials asked Mike if he'd take a polygraph examination so that he could be cleared from any suspicion. He agreed. Detectives working the case stated that Mike passed the polygraph without any question. He was completely vindicated of any involvement.

On June 24, 1995, the family of Jeanne formally asked the FBI to become involved in her disappearance. After a slight delay, they agreed. Their investigation was going to include involvement in both the Boston area and Yosemite. The FBI interviewed family members, Mike, and friends. Then they searched for witnesses that were in the Glacier Point area when Jeanne disappeared. The mere fact that the family was asking for the FBI to become involved clearly states that this wasn't a normal missing person case in the eyes of the family. For the FBI to agree to enter the case indicates that there must have been some great concern on the part of the park service and the FBI that something criminal in nature may have occurred.

At the culmination of the formal search for Jeanne, the NPS had expended sixty-six hours of helicopter time, countless ground searches, bloodhounds, vehicle searches, and interviews of possible witnesses.

On September 3, 1995, Yosemite Valley resident Mike Ulawski and a friend were fishing three-quarters of a mile above Bridal Veil Falls, which is approximately three miles from where Jeanne disappeared. As they were fishing and walking the river, they came across a human body in a small pool. They notified the park service. A helicopter had to wait until the following day to exhume the body because of high winds. It was obvious to rescuers that the body had been in the river for several weeks and visual identification would be impossible. Mike was interviewed by reporters and asked to describe the area where they had found the body. "The area is really inaccessible to anyone other than rock and mountain climbers. It's very rugged," he said.

Through a dental comparison, the body was positively identified as Jeanne Hesselschwerdt. The body was found completely nude except socks and one boot. Rescuers and the park service were becoming increasingly puzzled by how Jeanne's body ended up where it did. A park spokesperson stated that the body could not have gotten to that location by water transport because there were too many large blockages. The park confirmed that Jeanne disappeared at an elevation of seven thousand feet and was found at 5,300 feet, a huge drop in less than three miles.

Case Summary

This is one of the cases from Yosemite that is quite unsettling. You have conflicting facts that don't make sense. First, several teams of search dogs either refused to search or failed to find any scent of Jeanne in the area she disappeared. Searchers found two boot prints in an area that would have corresponded with her direction of travel. Her boyfriend lays out facts that are supported through a federal polygraph examination (strong evidence he told the truth). The most significant and disturbing detail is that park officials and the witnesses who found the body stated that only rock and mountain climbers can get in and out of the area where Jeanne's body was found. How did Jeanne get there?

It's obvious from the FBI's involvement that there must have been some suspicion, however remote, that Jeanne had been the victim of a crime (probably an abduction). I think we all would agree that a rock climber can't abduct a human and forcibly carry her up granite cliffs. Again, thinking through this rationally, if Jeanne couldn't have gotten to that location under her own power and skill level, and the creek didn't wash her downstream, then what carried Jeanne to that spot?

I did file an FOIA with FBI to obtain their reports on this incident, I was denied. The explanation for the denial was privacy concerns for the victim. I asked for an explanation, I was denied.

Emerson Holt
Missing: 07/18/43, Merced Lake, Yosemite National Park, CA
Age at disappearance: 55

A group of close friends decided to hike from the floor of Yosemite Valley in an easterly direction to fish Merced Lake. The group of fishermen were within sight of the lake when one of the party, Emerson Holt, stated he was sweaty and a little tired and wanted to rest. The remainder of the group stated that they were going to hike on and they would meet at the lake. Emerson was never seen again.

The area where the hikers left Emerson was near the banks of the Merced River. The river in this area moves very slow, does not have any deep pools, and offered no threat of swift water or drowning. The meadow did have a grove of very large trees. The area where he disappeared is a small bowl surrounded by huge granite walls. The only trees are in the valleys and crooks of the granite.

There was a July 22, 1943, article in the *San Mateo Times* in which Park Superintendent Frank Kittredge considered the disappearance to be "almost supernatural." A July 24 article in the *Los Angeles Times* quoted park rangers describing the disappearance as "mystifying." Park officials stated that the river in the area of the disappearance did not pose a significant danger, and there were no cliffs near the location where Emerson could have fallen.

He had complained of being tired and had pains in his legs when he sat to take a rest. The man wasn't going to walk anywhere other than to the lake because his legs hurt too much. The group was on a trail, and there were no cars for five miles. The disappearance of Emerson Holt is a true mystery.

David Huckins
Missing: 02/04/86, Camp Curry, CA
Age at disappearance: 21

David Huckins was an employee at the Ahwahnee Hotel in Yosemite in February of 1986. He was last seen near his residence in Camp Curry. His dad stated that he last saw David wearing a jogging outfit and was told that he was going to go jogging in a westerly direction. David was reported missing and a subsequent search failed to find him.

According to articles printed in the *Fresno Bee* and the *Modesto Bee* and Farabee's *Off the Wall* (475), on July 6 a human arm was found near Lower River Campground, though two reports indicate it was Lower Pines Campground. One day later and two miles away, David's torso and other pieces of him were found in the Merced River near Happy Isles. On October 11, David's scapula and distal humerus were found one mile above the Happy Isles footbridge.

I scoured every news service for additional articles about David Huckins' disappearance and could find nothing. This is a very disturbing case from many angles. David disappeared in February according to the *Modesto Bee*. February in Yosemite can be very cold, and bears are in hibernation. What would have chewed David into pieces? Could normal decomposition have accounted for David being found in pieces? It seems very odd that a piece of David is found on land and other pieces are found in the river. It's amazing that there were not additional news stories about this disappearance. It almost appears that the story was not talked about because of the potential for bad press.

Ruth Alice Jacobus
Missing: 06/07/89, noon, Amador County, CA
Age at disappearance: 76
5', 115 lb.

Facts surrounding the disappearance of Ruth Jacobus are few. Investigators believe that Ruth wandered away from her remote home and got lost in the wilderness. The area around the home has steep and rugged mountains that make hiking the area treacherous. She was last seen by her husband near noon. A search by the sheriff could not find Ruth.

Carol Laughlin
Missing: 09/09/79, Camp Curry, Yosemite, CA
Age at disappearance: 19

This is a case that the National Park Service does not want the public to know about. I filed two separate FOIA requests for all information related to the Carol Laughlin case and was repeatedly denied. The NPS would not even send me the press releases they made regarding Carol's disappearance. I did find one article in the *Merced Sun* dated May 2, 1980, titled, "Body of Park Employee is Discovered." The article stated that the body of Carol Laughlin was discovered by two men descending Castaneda Wall near Big Oak Flat Road. The article stated that the NPS was conducting an investigation, and they added that Carol was an employee at the Curry Village Gift Shop.

Without the special access that Butch Farabee had to Yosemite records, we would not know the following details, which he included on page 528 of *Off the Wall*:

Carol lived in tent #51 in Curry Camp #6. Friends of Carol stated that she was very responsible and would not have left without proper notifications.

The chief law enforcement officer at Yosemite at the time was Lee Shackleton. Lee was completely stumped as to what happened to Carol and eventually turned to San Francisco Bay Area psychic Kathleen Rhea for some direction. Kathleen stated that Carol was located beneath a large steel grate of some type. Since there were very few of these types of structures inside the park, this made the job to find the location very difficult. Lee did order every park crew to investigate every grate in an effort to find Carol, but she wasn't found.

On April 28, 1980, two climbers took a paper bag to the Yosemite visitor's center and placed a human skull on the counter. The climbers stated that they had found the skull above Cookie Cliff and the rest of the remains and clothes still lay on the granite in that area. Rangers Norm Hinson and Dick Martin were taken to the site by the climbers. The location is a quarter mile above the cliff, five hundred yards up Old Coulterville Road from where it intersects Highway 140. The exact spot is four hundred feet below the longest tunnel on Big Oak Flat Road. Carol's remains were directly under the air vent of the longest tunnel in the area. Rangers found scattered bones, beer cans, and other trash in the area. Every bone that was found was inside a fifteen-feet radius.

This tunnel and associated side shaft are seventy-five feet long and tall enough to ride a bicycle through. The side shaft is perpendicular to the roadway. In 1980 the grate to the tunnel was open; it is now closed and locked. The tunnel did have a great view of the Merced River below.

Lee Shackleton determined that Carol Laughlin was a homicide victim. There was never a suspect arrested in this case, though many witnesses were interviewed.

This case is nearly thirty years old and still has not been solved. It is extremely doubtful that any investigator has even looked at the case in years. Knowing how far forensics has come in thirty years, one immediate question comes to mind: Did investigators collect the beer cans in the area? If the cans were collected, there is a chance that DNA could be collected and matched against known and even unknown suspects within the California prison system. Unfortunately, we will never know more specifics of this case because the NPS will not release *any* documents.

This area is in a rugged valley with an elevation of approximately five thousand feet. Just to the northwest is a location known as "The Devil's Dance Floor," which describes the location very well.

There are many questions that arise from this case. How would anyone find the location of this extensive tunnel system? It was implied by Shackleton that this was a location where people went to drink. This means the cans found may not specifically belong to the killer(s). This area is very desolate and the surrounding area is quite remote. It would have been quite possible and probable that bears and other animals spent their winters inside these tunnels before they were barred. It is troubling when agencies refuse to release *any* information on a thirty-year-old case. It's hard to understand why the NPS can't allow press releases, photos of the victim, etc., to be released since this was already done once. It's almost as though the park service does not want any information about this case placed in front of the public.

Michael Larry Madden
Missing: 08/10/96, Sand Bar Flat, Sonora, CA
Age at disappearance: 20
6'1", 195 lb.

Michael Madden was home on summer break from California State University at Humboldt. He took his dog, Mathilda, in his Chevrolet Cavalier and drove to the Sand Bar Flat Campground by the Middle Fork of the Stanislaus River, east of Sonora. He was going there to meet a group of friends. Michael had been to this area several times with his father and felt very comfortable camping in the area. Michael arrived before his friends. He set up camp and fished the area alone.

His friends arrived a day later and found Michael's car and some equipment, but he and his dog were gone. Friends of Michael notified authorities of their disappearance. An extensive search was performed without finding any evidence. Four days after Michael disappeared, Mathilda wandered into the campsite, dehydrated and tired. Searchers tried to get the dog to lead them to Michael, but that was unsuccessful.

Michael's mother died in 2004, and his father passed away in 2008.

Michael Larry Madden has never been found.

Nita Mary Mayo
Missing: 08/08/05, Donnell's Vista Lookout, Sonora, CA
Age at disappearance: 64
5', 140 lb.

Nita Mayo was a resident of Hawthorne, Nevada, and a licensed practical nurse at Mount Grant General Hospital. She decided to take a day trip to Sonora, approximately 2½ hours from her home. She drove westbound on Highway 108 in her silver 1997 Mercury Sable station wagon. At 2:00 p.m. Nita stopped at the Strawberry store and purchased postcards, a sasquatch refrigerator magnet, and possibly gas. Nita drove to the Donnell's Vista lookout on Highway 108. This gorgeous spot has a commanding view looking north to the Sierras. Something happened at the lookout and Nita disappeared. Nita's family and fellow employees at the clinic in Nevada reported her missing.

A Caltrans (California Department of Transportation) worker found Nita's car at the lookout the same day she disappeared, but he didn't know at the time she was missing. On August 10, he heard of Nita's disappearance and called the sheriff's office. They processed the vehicle. Inside the car they found Nita's purse, car keys, and cell phone. Her car was locked but had a keypad for entry. After a conversation with her family, the only items confirmed missing were her camera and her prescription sunglasses.

Deputy Ed Warnock from the Tuolumne County Sheriff's Office helped manage a massive search for Nita. Motorcycles, jeeps, dog teams, SAR ground searchers and volunteers combed the area of her disappearance without finding Nita.

Nita's car door was locked and her keys were inside, but she could open the door with her keypad. It would appear that she was standing outside her car taking photos of the landscape when something happened. The vista point is in a very large, open area. It was the middle of a clear and gorgeous day. An abduction by vehicle could possibly have occurred, but there were huge risks. If the abduction wasn't extremely quick, the possibility of being seen by other motorists was likely. Even if the abduction was fast, other motorists would have seen a vehicle near Nita's—evidence that no serial abductor wants. An abduction in broad daylight at a major vista point along a primary highway seems almost unbelievable. However, Nita didn't fall over the edge, didn't walk away, and didn't voluntarily disappear. Something very unusual and very dark happened to this nice woman.

Richard Mcpherson
Missing: 05/26/38, Rock Creek, four miles south of Shuteye Peak, Madera County, CA
Age at disappearance: 10
A *Nevada Star* newspaper article from May 27, 1934, stated that USFS Ranger Chester McPherson was assigned to the Shuteye Peak Lookout Station. On May 26, 1934, his sons, Richard and Robert, and their cousin, Howard Ibbotson, went fishing at the headwaters of Rock Creek. A storm moved into the area and dropped snow as the boys were fishing. The boys camped at the site all night and then Robert decided to leave to get assistance. Howard later stated that Richard had disappeared from the campsite, unknown exactly when. The boys were eventually able to contact authorities and a search ensued. The Civilian Conservation Corps was organized and, in conjunction with forty USFS rangers, searched the area.

The headwaters of Rock Creek is approximately four miles south of Shuteye Peak. The elevation of the creek in the gully starts at 5,400 feet and quickly declines. The creek starts in an area adjacent to Whisky Ridge in the Sierra National Forest.

On May 28, an article appeared in the *Fresno Bee* explaining that search crews had found the body of Richard McPherson two days and three nights after he became separated from the other two boys. The article stated that the "body was only lightly covered against the rain, sleet and snow which alternately has swept the Shuteye Peak region during the time he was missing. His overalls had been removed, presumably because they had become wet in the stream Friday night." Wait a minute. His overalls had been removed? That makes no sense. Rock Creek is a creek, not a river. And where they were, it's a small creek. I have spoken to many survival experts about the "overall" statement, and it doesn't make sense to anyone. It was raining and snowing in the days just prior to Richard being found. I don't think a ten-year-old would be stripping his clothes off; he'd be looking for more clothes.

The issue of the overalls being off the body obviously struck the writer of the article as being so odd that he included it in his summary and even attempted to logically explain it away. I don't think it can be.

Two extremely odd and unrelated disappearances have occurred in the Shuteye Peak area in the last forty nine years—almost forty nine years years to the day (a very, very odd coincidence). The disappearance of Theresa Bier and the body found of Richard McPherson. If you have time at this point go to a computer and Google "Shuteye Peak, CA," look at the vastness of the Sierra Nevada and imagine the odds that Theresa and Richard both disappeared in nearly the exact same spot.

Kenny Miller
Missing: 06/24/92, Meiss Meadows, CA
Age at disappearance: 12
Meiss Meadows is fifty miles north of Yosemite in the High Sierra area. It is located just north of Highway 88 and just west of the intersection of Highway 88 and Highway 89.

Kenny Miller was developmentally disabled. He was twelve years old but had the emotional age, according to newspaper articles, of a four-year-old. Bob and Sharon Miller had taken Kenny and their ten-year-old daughter, Cindy, on a short vacation in the mountains. The family had driven from their home in Oakhurst, California, to enjoy the summer weather near Carson Pass.

The Millers took a hike from their vehicle up a small hill into Meiss Meadows. This is a very tranquil spot with mostly exposed granite and very little foliage. There is a small creek and an old cabin in the area. Kenny found entertainment by throwing small pebbles into the creek, which was flowing from the snow at upper elevations. Bob and Sharon took Cindy a short distance away to look at the old wood cabin. The family was cut off from Kenny by tall grass, and after a few minutes, they went back to his location and found he was gone. The family spread out and screamed his name, but they did not receive a response. The group soon contacted forestry officials and a search was started.

Kenny was lost at an elevation of 8,400 feet. There are few places to hide in this area because it's above timberline. This area looks very similar to areas around Yosemite because of the exposed granite. Searchers combed the entire area for several days. They were hampered by heavy wind, rain, lightning, and at times snow. Searchers found tracks zigzagging from the area of the creek where Kenny was last seen, but the tracks then disappeared.

After nine days of freezing, wet weather and not finding one clue in the disappearance of Kenny, the search was terminated. Three counties had participated in the search efforts and everyone was very depressed.

On July 4, more than ten days after Kenny disappeared, a group of hikers saw a small body lying on a ridgeline at 9,800 feet, 2½ miles and 1,400 feet higher in elevation than where Kenny was last observed. It was on Stevens Peak ridge that hikers found the body of Kenny Miller. The boy was in the fetal position and clad only in a T-shirt and cotton shorts. An autopsy of the body indicated that Kenny died of exposure.

I found eleven pages of articles on the Kenny Miller disappearance, and not one inquired why the boy would be over 1,400 feet higher in elevation than where he went missing. Not one made a mention of the lack of shoes, socks, etc., found on the boy. Not one article mentioned that the boy's body was at one of the highest points in this area of the Sierras—a very, very high ridge far from the comfort of his parents. In an odd twist of fate, Bob Miller is a school teacher at the Yosemite school.

Tom Opperman
Missing: 08/08/67, Tuolumne Meadows, Yosemite, CA
Age at disappearance: 21

Tom Opperman was a porter at Curry Company in Yosemite Village. Tom was originally from Fresno and was a California State University cross country and wrestling champion. He had left his residence in Yosemite to climb Mount Clark (11,522 feet) via Tuolumne Meadows. He planned to go through the eastern ridge via Merced Lake. Tom was going to do this route during his two days off. He was traveling alone.

Tom was due back on August 11 but did not return. His parents were staying in the valley and reported him missing. A search included marines from the special warfare center, park rangers, and many others. Two weeks after starting the search, having not found any clues of Tom's whereabouts, the park service gave up.

Tom was the son of Joseph Opperman, a reverend from Fresno, California. His family was staying in the park during his trip and knew that he was well prepared for his two-day trek. He was never seen again.

Doug Pearce
Missing: 04/21/05, Chowchilla
Mountain Road, Summit Camp,
Mariposa, CA
Age at disappearance: 86
5'10", 160 lb.

Doug Pearce was a retired nuclear and chemical engineer. At 86, he was in very good health and spent a portion of his time volunteering at the Woodland Elementary School and Mariposa Middle School in Mariposa. Doug was very active in the community and was a very mentally sharp person. The last confirmed sighting of Doug was on April 21 in Modesto.

Doug's 1990 Ford Ranger pickup was found on Chowchilla Mountain Road near Summit Campground. The vehicle was found stuck in the mud and had suffered severe fire damage. A subsequent law enforcement investigation revealed that the truck was not intentionally burned.

Law enforcement officials theorized that when Doug's truck caught fire, he attempted to walk out of the area, got lost, and died in the wild. They admit that they have no evidence to support this theory and that no possibilities are being ruled out.

Doug disappeared approximately four miles southeast of Devil's Peak and four miles from Star Lakes, the area where James Arthur disappeared. The area of Doug's disappearance is on the southwest perimeter of Yosemite. The elevation where Doug's truck was found is 5,500 feet. Shuteye Peak and the area where Theresa Bier and Richard McPherson disappeared are less than five miles from where Doug vanished.

Walter Reinhard
Missing: 09/20/02, White Wolf Area, Yosemite National Park, CA
Age at disappearance: 66

Walter is not listed as missing on any county, state, or national database, and there are no articles indicating he has ever been found.

On October 2, 2002, the National Park Service issued a one-paragraph statement indicating that Walter was from Oro, Arizona, and was on a day hike in the White Wolf Area of Yosemite. Walter's family reported him missing on September 19. The park service was able to confirm that Walter used his credit card to check into a hotel near the park on September 19, and that was the last time he was seen.

White Wolf is on Highway 120 adjacent to Hetch Hetchy Reservoir, the main water source for the City and County of San Francisco. The elevation in this area is approximately 8000'eight thousand feet.

This is in very close proximity to the location of Michael Ficery's disappearance.

The lack of information available regarding Walter's disappearance is disturbing. The NPS is under no legal obligation to publicize this disappearance or include his name on any national database. This needs to change.

Unusual Deaths in Yosemite

Evelyn Consuela Rosemann
Discovered: 10/19/68, Base of Nevada Falls, Yosemite National Park, CA

Investigators determined that Evelyn Consuela Rosemann was employed in San Francisco as a masseuse. Evelyn had prior employment in the city at a strip club. She decided to take a trip to Yosemite, apparently alone, and was out hiking when something terrible happened.

On October 19, 1968, a group of three hikers found Evelyn's body badly battered east of the base of Nevada Fall, near the Merced River. She had a pair of badly torn, tan corduroy pants that were pulled down near her ankles; her sweater had been pulled up over her head. Another of Evelyn's sweaters was lying on a rock near her feet.

Investigators determined that Evelyn had either fallen or been thrown off the top of Nevada Falls, a height of 594 feet. Law enforcement officials also believe her body had been assaulted after the fall (more on this later).

Investigators combed the scene for additional evidence to explain how Evelyn became located so far from the base of the waterfall. Fifty feet from the body, probably the point of impact or close to it, in the middle of the stream at the base of the falls, they found a portion of Evelyn's brain. Halfway to the base of the falls, they found traces of corduroy from her pants.

Evelyn's body was sent to the coroner's office for an autopsy. It was found that she had massive internal and brain trauma, probably caused by the fall. A more unusual and highly strange comment in the report indicated that Evelyn had bloodless lacerations in her vagina, which indicates sexual assault either just before or even after her death. Investigators believed that it was possible that Evelyn was the victim of a sexual assault after she went over the falls. The coroner stated that Evelyn had been dead approximately twenty-four hours when hikers found her.

Readers must remember that this happened in mid-October, a time of the year when rivers and creeks run low, and the flow is at its most minimal point. The idea that Evelyn fell into the creek and went over the falls isn't viable for a multitude of reasons, least of which is the water flow. As Butch Farabee stated in his book, "She had somehow launched off the top of it," meaning she had somehow been thrown a distance off the cliff that wouldn't indicate a fall. The initial reports of this incident by law enforcement indicated that Evelyn had been "thrown" off the top of the falls. Who has the strength to throw a grown woman? What type of person would then go to the base of the falls and rape the corpse, and risk being seen? It's obvious from the reports that the body was moved after the original fall. Evelyn was dead, and whoever threw Evelyn probably moved her.

I extensively searched the archives on this incident. I never found one report or advisory from the NPS to visitors regarding the need to be cautious about a possible stalker or murderer in this area.

One interesting coincidence involving several of the missing people is that several were photographers, and several were residents of Yosemite Valley. I'm not sure what to think of the unusual aspect of several of the people being respected photographers, but the idea that many of the missing were residents of Yosemite is troubling. The residents should be inherently knowledgeable of the dangers associated with Yosemite and take precautions. The strange death of an assistant superintendent's wife (Leah Good) exemplifies the point that it doesn't matter what your economic profile is in the park, everyone is vulnerable.

David Allen Scott
Missing: 07/13/57, Mono Village, Bridgeport, CA
Age at disappearance: 2

It was mid-July when Robert Scott left his job as a plastering contractor in San Diego County and decided to take his trailer and his family on vacation to Mono Village in the eastern Sierras for a wilderness excursion. Mr. and Mrs. Scott placed Tony (4), Cindy (6), and David (2) in their car and motored to an area fourteen miles east of Bridgeport, California. This area of the Sierra Nevada does not get the amount of tourists that the western Sierras get. From major population points in Los Angeles and San Diego counties, it can take several more hours to reach points on the east side of the Sierras than the west side.

The area where the Scotts were traveling (Mono Village) was on the eastern fringe of the Hoover Wilderness Area, a very wild and rugged area of the Sierras that has peaks nearing twelve thousand feet. There are many mountains with gorgeous exposed granite peaks and very rugged trails and summits. The Hoover Wilderness borders the eastern edge of Yosemite National Park and the Mono Village camping area and is just three miles from Yosemite's border.

The Scotts arrived at Mono Village and set their trailer at the far western end of Twin Lakes. The small village has a small store and improved areas for camping. The entrance to the campsite coming from the east is on a road from Bridgeport. The road terminates at the village, and this is where the wilderness begins. The elevation of the village is 7,100 feet, and the mountains immediately to the north shoot vertically and abruptly to over ten thousand feet. There are several large groves of big trees around the village, but the trees stop just outside the perimeter of the lake and the village. Most mountains in the area have no ground cover and consist of exposed dirt, boulders, and granite.

The Scotts arrived on a Friday afternoon and were having a great time enjoying the gorgeous setting of Mono Village. It was mid-afternoon on Saturday when the family saw David approximately one hundred yards from their trailer. They weren't too concerned because he wasn't moving very fast. It was going to be David's birthday on Monday, and they were starting to think about how to celebrate. David was near a large group of trees in an area with significant ground cover. David's folks entered the trailer momentarily. When they came outside, they didn't see the boy. They quickly went to the area where they last saw him and couldn't locate him. There were no other people camping in the immediate area. After an hour of searching, the Scotts contacted authorities.

Mono Village is in Mono County, California. The county is 3,044 square miles and has a population of just over twelve thousand. The county is not wealthy. In 1957 the Mono County sheriff was Cecil Thorington, and he was on the scene soon after the Scotts declared David was missing. The sheriff's office quickly called for assistance from the USFS and other nearby agencies. The first place that was searched was the general camping area and meadow on the valley floor. Daylight doesn't last long in the Mono Village Valley because of the huge mountains that surround it. Night came quickly and David Scott had not been found.

The next morning the Scotts told the press that they felt David may have been kidnapped. They knew that the only reasonable places that David could be had already been searched, and ponds and the lake were about to be dragged for a body. On July 15, Sheriff Thorington ordered an all-points bulletin asking all law enforcement agencies to check cars leaving the Bridgeport area for the possibility that David Scott may be inside.

There were 250 searchers on the scene at this time, with the added assistance of the U.S. Marines from nearby Pickerel Meadows Cold Weather Training Facility. An article in the *Youngstown Vindicator* on July 15 stated, "Mild weather has aided and diminished fears the boy may have suffered from exposure."

Late on July 15, Bloodhounds arrived from a facility in Los Gatos, California. The dogs sent to Mono County had an exceptional record of finding lost people. Once the dogs arrived, they were given pieces of David's clothing and immediately set off following what appeared to be David's scent trail. The owner of the dogs stated that he was sure that his dogs were following David's trail, which led them to a very steep mountain slope behind Mono Village. The dogs and searchers stayed with the hunt until late that night when the dogs appeared to lose the trail.

Canines and marines started the search for David Scott early in the morning of July 16. A marine found one of David's canvas shoes at an elevation of ten thousand feet. This encouraged searchers but they were also confused because they were hiking almost straight up a very steep hillside on the outskirts of the village. This is so steep that someone hiking the hillside can turn around and see the campsite below. The search continued up the hillside until it peaked at just over ten thousand feet. Searchers then went down the back side of the mountain that now put Mono Village out of sight. The back side of the mountain went down to 9,500 feet. Here is the base of 11,821-feet Eagle Peak. U.S. Marine Staff Sergeant Robert O'Brien was trying to imagine where an extension of the scent trail may lead. He played a hunch and started to search the base of Eagle Peak. On a hillside ridden with huge boulders, Sgt. O'Brien found the body of David Scott. The body only had a T-shirt and a red-white-and-blue sock on one foot. There were no pants, no shoes, or coat. Sgt. O'Brien fired one round from his weapon indicating to searchers that he had found the body. Fellow marines carried David Scott back to his parents.

A July 16, 1957, article in the *San Mateo Times* stated, "The boulder-studded mountain was so steep the searchers said it was hard to believe that the child was able to make his way up the peak." On July 17, an article in the *Dispatch* quoted searchers as saying, "Scott was found among boulders on the steep slope. He had climbed an incredible 3,000' higher than his camp." A July 17 article in the *Schenectady Gazette* stated, "Asked if there was any signs of violence [on David's body], O'Brien stated, 'I don't know, that is out of my line.'"

Case Summary

I started a review of this case by looking at a Google map of the region and switched to the Terrain perspective. It's not surprising that searchers were shocked that a two-year-old child was found three thousand feet above his camp by supposedly hiking a huge mountain. There are few things in life that I describe as impossible, but this is an impossible scenario. David did not have shoes or water. He had absolutely no motive to climb that huge mountain. Reality check: this boy was two years old—climbing this mountain would have been impossible. The book *Lost Persons Behavior* by Robert Koester has graphs for SAR commanders about the likelihood of finding people based on age. A child one to three years old will be found 99 percent of the time climbing upward less than 2,300 feet. You need to understand that this may mean a gradual path leading slowly upward in elevation, not a steep mountain going vertically—that's even more unbelievable.

There is only one reason that Robert Scott got his son's body back: the Bloodhounds. There is no way that a search party would ever have searched the base of Eagle Peak for a two-year-old child. The idea that the child would have ended up at that location would have been deemed impossible, unless kidnapped. Even a two-year-old knows the difference between up and down, and David would have known by looking down the hill that warmth and safety at his mom and dad's trailer just below him. He could have seen it.

I would be very interested in the condition of David's feet when he was found. Were the socks tattered and worn? Were the soles of David's feet scratched, worn, and injured? They must have been if he had hiked that distance without shoes. Where were David's pants? From the vast amounts of archived articles I have read about this incident, David's pants were never found. How could this happen?

Children at two years old are known to take the path of least resistance. In this case, that would have been the valley floor. Most two-year-olds are afraid of heights and would never climb a huge mountain. The idea that law enforcement didn't understand that this case needed much more investigation is absurd. One of the articles I read stated that the cause of David's death appeared to be dehydration, exposure, and exhaustion. The sheriff stated early in this search that the weather was very mild—not hot and not cold. The general belief was that David would have done fine in the temperature range that existed during this time period. Dehydration is an interesting angle. Remember, David supposedly hiked a three-thousand-foot mountain with two huge lakes in the valley below (yes, lakes with lots of water). I have read cases from the early 1900s in which coroners made claims that people had died of exhaustion, but you don't hear that today. I'm not sure if anyone can die of mere exhaustion.

Early in this SAR operation, Mr. and Mrs. Scott told the press that they felt David had been kidnapped. Understanding that there wasn't substantial ground cover in the area of their camp, and there were very large trees, the idea that David walked away and wasn't immediately found was a major red flag. Parents have a keen sense when something is wrong—probably a sixth sense that people just haven't fully developed.

The last key element of this case was the observations made by Sgt. O'Brien when he found David's body. A member of the press asked if there were signs of violence on the body. O'Brien didn't answer the question. The marines carried the boy's body off the mountain. The soldier would've been able to see odd marks on the child. If O'Brien *hadn't* seen something strange, I think he would have stated that. It must have been a shocking sight to see a nude boy's body in a boulder-strewn field on the side of a mountain.

This case most closely resembles the disappearance of Garrett Bardsley from Utah and David Griffen from Huntington Lake. Garrett disappeared while fishing at a high altitude lake with his dad. He got wet, left to go back to the camp, and was never seen again. Searchers found one of Garrett's socks high above the lake among boulders, but Garrett was never found. David Griffen disappeared from Huntington Lake camping with his family and was found deceased three thousand feet up in elevation and six miles from camp. The distance from Huntington Lake to the spot where David Scott was found is approximately seven miles.

Orvar Von Laass
Missing: 10/9/54, Sugar Pine Bridge, Ahwahnee Hotel, Yosemite Valley, Yosemite National Park, CA
Age at disappearance: 30

Orvar Von Laass, his wife, Marilyn, and her parents were staying at the beautiful Ahwahnee Hotel in the middle of Yosemite National Park. This is the centerpiece of the park. It is an older hotel and grand in style. It is made of natural wood and huge granite boulders, and it has the luster of the early 1900s. Orvar was a graduate student in the economics department at the University of California–Berkeley. Friends and family have described Orvar as a genius. The family had stated that Orvar was an experienced hiker and was comfortable in the outdoors.

On Saturday, October 19, 1954, at approximately 2:00 p.m., Orvar asked to borrow his wife's binoculars and stated that he was going on a short hike. He told his wife that he'd be back at 4:00 p.m.

A search was immediately started Saturday night when Orvar's wife reported that he hadn't returned. The number of searchers participating continued to escalate for almost ten days. At one point canines joined the search. On two separate occasions, the dogs tracked the scent to the base of Royal Arch Cliff behind the hotel. Rangers Henneberger and Morehead climbed the lower half of the arch in an attempt to search for Orvar, but nothing was found. Marilyn had advised searchers that Orvar was only wearing a light shirt and trousers, not climbing gear.

Eight days into the search, a group of helicopters from Stockton hovered over Yosemite Valley for several hours searching for any sign of Orvar.

On October 11, 1954, Yosemite Chief Ranger Oscar Sedergren made the following statement regarding Orvar Laass: "It is difficult to understand how a man could get lost in the area where Laass disappeared because there are many trails and roads through it and park visitors frequent it constantly."

Only three months earlier, another UC Berkeley graduate student, Walter A. Gordon, disappeared inside Yosemite. Walter was on summer break from school and was employed in Camp Curry, a short distance from the Ahwahnee Hotel. Gordon, 26, went hiking and never returned. Refer to the section in this chapter on Walter Gordon for more information on his incident

On October 27, 1954, the parents of both men wrote letters to then President Eisenhower. The letter stated that there are no indications that Orvar or Walter disappeared voluntarily. They asked that the government assign special warfare troops that work in the mountains so they may assist in the search for the men. One portion of the letter stated, "Nothing points to voluntary disappearance in either case. There are various aspects of these disappearances which bear investigation." The families stated, "The men's fates may exist in remote corners of the national preserve." There was no explanation for this statement..

Walter and Orvar were never found. The searches were finally terminated in late November. The family never felt there was an adequate explanation about what happened to the two men.

Michael James Walsh
Missing: 03/01/01, Alpine County, CA
Age at disappearance: 56
6', 140 lb.

There are very few details about the Walsh case other than he disappeared March 1, 2001, from rural Alpine County.

Godfrey Wondrosek
Missing: 04/26/33, between Camp 7 and Half Dome, Yosemite National Park, CA
Age at disappearance: 26

Godfrey Wondrosek and his sister Josephine made a trip to Yosemite from Chicago. On April 26 Godfrey told his sister he was going to hike toward Half Dome. That was the last time Josephine saw her brother. She reported him missing that night and a search immediately started.

For people who have never hiked to the top of Half Dome, it is treacherous. There is a rope and cable that climbers use to make it to the summit. During the off-season, the rope and cable are taken down to ensure people don't try to climb. It is essentially a very, very steep hike up a slippery granite wall. You don't need to be an experienced climber to hike Half Dome, but you do need the right shoes and be in reasonably good shape.

The cables and ropes to the top of Half Dome were not available on April 26, as there was still snow near the summit. Rangers still made the climb to the summit under the belief that Godfrey may have made the attempt. At the summit they stated they found footprints. They also stated that they found some footprints on the trail at the bottom and others near the summit, though some looked old. They said there was no way Godfrey could have made the summit before dark as this would have made his trip down extremely treacherous. Rangers also noted that other tracks were found in the area of the summit, but they didn't guess how old those were. Rangers inside the park stated that making it to the summit of Half Dome without cables was possible for an experienced climber, but it was very treacherous. There are no indications in anything I read that Godfrey was an experienced mountain climber or had climbing tools or equipment.

The park service enlisted the aid of employees and American Indian trackers in an effort to find Godfrey. According to reports, the searchers dealt with continuous rain and snow during their search. They found nothing.

Park officials theorized that Godfrey made the summit attempt and fell. If Godfrey fell, where is his body? All indications from family and friends show that Godfrey was quite intelligent. Why would any intelligent person attempt a near-suicidal attempt to climb Half Dome without ropes and cables? How could Godfrey even know the correct route to the summit without the cables? Who made the footprints and tracks?

My statement to the National Park Service: People Do Not Disappear. Where is Godfrey's body?

Bodies and Bones Found

I have always stated that it is important to understand how people succumbed to the elements to assist in public education and avoid as many disastrous results as possible. I include here a small list of bones and bodies that have not been identified because I want all readers to understand how dangerous this region can be.

These people had to have gotten to Yosemite in some manner. If these victims drove a vehicle to a location near where they disappeared, the NPS would have the auto information and, hopefully, could connect the dots. If these people were with others, their friends reported them missing. Again, one hopes the NPS could connect the dots.

The victims on this list appear to have been on a cliff, climbed up a cliff, or even down a cliff, because their bones were found in close proximity to a cliff. I've always stated that I believe people are more careful traveling alone than traveling in pairs. If these people were traveling alone, how in the heck did they get in the strange places where their bones were located? Could these people have disappeared in a completely different location in the Sierras and somehow ended up in Yosemite? I would concede that a very small amount of people are murdered by a serial killer in Yosemite, driven to the park, and their body dumped (Farabee discusses this in his book). This would not explain bodies that had fallen off cliffs or were stuffed in crevasses, nor would it explain other odd contortions and strange injuries. I submit to you that if these incidents were occurring in any major city in the U.S., a regional task force would be developed to understand exactly what and how it was occurring. It's difficult to understand why the NPS is not tracking this information. It's bizarre.

Butch Farabee is a retired U.S.N.P. Ranger and a long-term employee at Yosemite. He had access to information that the public will never get. Because of this he was able to write an outstanding book about life and death in Yosemite: *Off the Wall: Death in Yosemite.* Included in the book is a section about bodies and bones that were found in the park and were never identified. It would seem that in the twenty-first century and with the advancements of DNA identification, all bones and bodies would be able to be identified and a name placed with the corpse. Unfortunately, this isn't always the case.

Butch lists eleven different instances where bones were found and the name of the deceased could not be confirmed. Please think about this carefully: eleven cases exist in which the park service could not identify the name of the deceased. Why? Could the reason be that they are not tracking the locations and names of the people who have disappeared inside their parks and thus cannot connect the dots? Could it be possible that these people disappeared in other regions of the Sierras, in California or maybe even Nevada, and somehow got to Yosemite? These are all perplexing questions that need to be addressed.

Here I include a few of the instances in a section titled, "Found but Neither Identified Nor Known to Be Lost," from *Off the Wall.*

Washington Column, 06/01/38

A member of the Sierra Club found portions of a human skeleton at the base of Washington Column. Forensics showed the bones had been there six to seven years; race, sex, and age of the victim could not be identified.

Tenaya Peak, North Face, 09/08/68

Two off-duty San Jose police officers and a friend found the nude body of an eighteen- to twenty-five-year-old bearded WMA who had been deceased two to four weeks. The body was wedged into a large, diagonal crack four hundred feet below the summit. The victim had a broken ankle and crushed chest. The FBI got involved in this case and was requested to assist in identifying the body. They were unable to identify the victim.

Midway between Half Dome and Mirror Lake, 06/07/75

One thousand vertical feet above the floor of Yosemite Valley, climbers discovered human bones in a small creek. No identification was ever made of these remains.

North Dome Gully, 11/25/77

A climber came across a human skull hundreds of feet above the valley floor near the North Dome Gully. Rangers found additional bones, but identification of the victim was never accomplished.

Half Dome, below northwest face, 07/26/87

A climber was looking for water and found a human skull, mandible, and Maxilla. The bones were determined to belong to a male, eighteen to twenty-five years old. The bones had been in that location for two to fifteen years. The front of the skull was fractured, suggesting a possible fall.

100 feet east of Lower Yosemite Falls, base of Sunnyside Bench, 09/14/90

A human jawbone was found set atop a rock next to a trail. The mandible was collected, but the identity of the victim was unable to be made.

Old Tioga Road, Yosemite Creek Campground, 07/13/05

A human skullcap was found on Old Tioga Road east of the campground and west of Tioga Road. The victim was a forty-five- to fifty-year-old female who could not be identified.

Chapter Summary

The seven cases listed above make up a short list of the people and bones that have *not* been identified inside Yosemite National Park. Don't be misled: the NPS does not want the public to know this information. They have made it essentially impossible for even a published author to receive information through a Freedom of Information Act request. They refuse to furnish it without paying tens of thousands of dollars in research fees. Readers, this is very, very basic law enforcement data that every legitimate law enforcement agency in North America maintains. Where people disappeared, how they disappeared, and when they disappeared are all essential elements if you are to track missing people trends and possible crimes.

The NPS told me they do not maintain any logs, lists, or databases of any missing people. Yes, you read this correctly: no lists, no logs, and no databases of anyone missing in any of their parks, monuments, or properties. When I inquired about how this information is tracked, they said through the memories of longtime employees. Huh? This is not just completely incomprehensible to any law enforcement detective, it's completely inappropriate and reckless to manage any investigative information in this manner. The victims' families should be outraged and demand a congressional investigation. When I asked for a list of all missing people inside of Yosemite National Park (and I asked them to include the location where the victim went missing), I was advised it would take 750 hours of research time by NPS employees and I'd have to pay that research fee.

Once you understand the NPS claim that they don't keep logs of missing people, you start to understand their complete inability to identify bones and skeletons of people found in the wild, they don't have the ability to connect the dots. The NPS' inability to connect those dots is a complete infrastructure failure to every victim and their family who has disappeared in a national park.

Why would an author/researcher have to pay for a list of missing people when it's a basic investigative need and practice that the NPS should be following? Maybe the answer to this complex equation is that the NPS does not want the public to know how dangerous it is trekking alone in the backcountry of our national parks. The cases I am citing in this book are only a fraction of the total number of missing people in the woods, and it's still a staggering number.

Southern California

There are two distinct small clusters described in this chapter: One group consists of the missing children in the Newhall area, and the other in the Big Bear Lake area. Joey Barkley, Cecilia Mitchell, and Jill Hatch all disappeared in a relatively small area of north Los Angeles and south Ventura counties. David Gonzales, Wayne Bowers, and David Baumgarten disappeared from Big Bear Lake. Gonzales and Bowers each disappeared in July. It's interesting to note that all of the individuals missing from the vicinity of Big Bear Lake are males less than ten years old.

Missing People in Southern California by Date

Missing Person	Date Missing•Age•Sex
Cecilia Mitchell	05/02/32•3•F
David Baumgarten	05/11/38•2•M
Wayne Bowers	07/05/47•3•M

Joey Barkley	03/11/53•2•M
Thomas Bowman	03/23/57•8•M
Jill Hatch	11/02/57•7•F
Bruce Kremen	07/13/60•8•M
Travis Zweig	03/10/93•2•M
Jonathan Aujay	06/11/98•38•M
David Gonzales	07/31/04•9•M

Cecilia Mitchell
Missing: 05/02/32, 12:30 p.m., mountains near Newhall, CA
Age at disappearance: 3
Blonde hair

Geneva Mitchell was a housekeeper at the Hovden Ranch, located approximately fifteen miles north of Newhall in the Tehachapi Mountains in northern Los Angeles County. On May 2, 1932, Geneva's youngest child, Cecilia, went into the back area of the ranch to pick wildflowers with two older children—her sister Mary (6) and a ranch friend, Ronald Offendahl (8). The kids picked flowers for a short while, and then Ronald and Mary returned without Cecilia. At 12:30 p.m. Geneva asked the kids where Cecilia was, but they did not know. Geneva went into the back area calling Cecilia's name. There was no answer. Geneva called the Los Angeles County Sheriff's Department for assistance.

The sheriff, area ranchers, farmers, and other volunteers searched for Cecilia for almost a week before they found their first clue. Searchers located a toy sled that Cecilia had been pulling a half mile from the ranch residence. The sled was found twelve feet off the valley floor on a rock ledge, an unusual location to find a child's toy. The searchers concentrated on the area around the sled for another week but still could not locate the girl.

The area of the search is a desert-type environment with wild hogs, rattlesnakes, and some deer. Airplanes flew over the area constantly, but they still could not find the girl. Searchers continued to look for Cecilia for six weeks, but they never found her.

Fourteen months after Cecilia first disappeared, two boys were hiking near the pump house at Quail Lake, approximately two miles from the location Cecilia was last seen. The hikers found the bones of what appeared to be a small child. The Los Angeles County Sheriff's Department was called, and they determined that it was the skeleton of Cecilia Mitchell. The coroner later stated that Cecilia must have died from exposure and starvation.

Law enforcement officials believed that Cecilia must have taken the ridge route from her ranch to the location she was found. This would have meant that the girl climbed in elevation off the valley floor to eventually get to the area near Quail Lake.

It is approximately fifty air miles from the location where Cecilia was found to the spot where Jill Hatch was located (in the mountains near Camp Scheideck). Considering how remote and isolated both communities are, and considering that both victims were young girls, it seems like an odd coincidence, especially considering this area was lightly populated in the early 1900's and these are the only two cases I could find in the historical archives of both areas.

David Baumgarten
Missing: 05/11/38, noon, Pine Knot, Big Bear Lake, CA
Age at disappearance: 2

Leon Baumgarten was a food company representative. He took his wife and son, David, with him on a sales trip to Big Bear Lake. At noon on May 11, 1938, Leon stopped at a country store on the north side of the lake to visit the owner. Sometime during the visit to the store, David disappeared. The Baumgartens did not wait long before calling the sheriff and asking for search assistance.

San Bernardino County Sheriff Emmett L. Shay responded with several deputies and canines to look for the boy. The search continued nonstop through the night and went into the snow-covered hills east of the store.

Thirty hours after David disappeared, Leon was searching an area east of the store on an old wagon road when he thought he saw faint prints in the snow from the prior night. Leon stated that when he saw the prints, he kneeled in the snow and prayed that he'd find his son. He continued up the hill and found his son lying facedown and unconscious in the snow and mud four miles from where he had disappeared. David Baumgarten was alive.

David had three deep scratches on his face but was otherwise in very good condition. The boy survived. Why David was walking uphill into heavier snowfall and colder temperatures is something we will never know.

Wayne Bowers
Missing: 07/05/47, Big Bear Lake, CA
Age at disappearance: 3
Blonde hair

Master Sergeant Claude Bower was stationed at the U.S. Marine facility in Barstow, California, when he took his family for a weekend retreat at Big Bear Lake. The family stayed in a cabin on the southeast side of the lake.

Sometime during the day on July 5, 1947, three-year-old Wayne Bowers disappeared from the family cabin. Locals assisted the family in searching for the small boy until they realized they needed additional assistance.

Sheriff James Stocker of the San Bernardino Sheriff's Department joined the hunt and assigned search areas to a contingent of deputies, volunteers, and local residents. The sheriff stated that two groups of canines followed the boy's scent four miles from the cabin to an area near the state highway. Stocker stated that there was the possibility that the boy was abducted.

Fifty-six hours after the blonde-haired boy disappeared, searchers found tracks up on Moon Ridge Road near Sand Canyon, four miles from the cabin. The sheriff threw all available resources into the area. Two hours later an SAR member was re-searching an area that had been searched the day before. The searcher found Wayne Bowers asleep at 4:35 p.m. lying against a log. The boy had scratches on his body but was in reasonably good condition. Wayne was taken to a local hospital, where he was given fluids and declared to be in good condition.

Joey Barkley
Missing: 03/11/53, 1:00 p.m., Placerita Canyon, Newhall, CA
Age at disappearance: 2
Blonde hair

Joey Barkley was playing on a knoll at his new prefabricated home in Placerita Canyon on the outskirts of Newhall, California. At approximately 1:00 p.m., Joey's mom went to look for the boy and discovered that he and his dog were gone. A search was started for the boy, but he could not be found. The Los Angeles County Sheriff's Department was called for assistance.

A two-day search for the boy included all of the sheriff's resources, including air teams, horsemen, ground troops, and canines. The sheriff eventually obtained three hundred searchers to assist in finding the boy. The searchers covered ten square miles in their efforts.

Throughout their search, SAR members found many broken twigs, which confused them. At 8:50 a.m. on March 11, searchers were in a draw off Orosino Canyon, and they spotted Joey's Doberman. The searchers looked further and found Joey huddled under a mesquite bush.

Joey stated that he had been sleeping under a ledge during daylight hours. This confused his parents. He claimed that he had seen rabbits, which excited the boy.

Joey disappeared approximately fifteen miles south of Cecilia Mitchell, who had disappeared twenty-one years earlier and was found deceased.

Thomas Eldon Bowman
Missing: 03/23/57, 7:00 p.m., Altadena, Arroyo Seco Canyon, Angeles National Forest, Los Angeles County, CA
Age at disappearance: 8
4', 47 lb.
Blonde hair

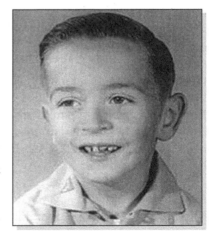

On March 23, 1957, after the family ate dinner, eight-year-old Tommy Bowman and his father, Eldon, took a hike above Altadena in the Arroyo Seco Canyon near Devil's Gate Dam. Tommy and Eldon had hiked out on the trail and were walking back to the parking lot when Tommy said he was going to run ahead to the car. Eldon reached the parking lot a few minutes after Tommy ran ahead, but the boy was not there.

The Los Angeles County Sheriff's Department responded to the call for assistance by the Bowmans. The area of the search was small and well defined. There was not a huge distance between the trail, where Tommy started to run, and the parking lot. After several weeks of formal and informal searches, the SAR teams had little to show for their work. Searchers did find one maroon sock in a bush off the trail near where Tommy disappeared. It was never confirmed if the sock did belong to Tommy.

The Bowmans went through hell with the disappearance of their son. Law enforcement said it was possible that Tommy had been abducted. The sheriff investigated field calls from people claiming they had the boy or knew where he was located, but all of the calls appeared to be hoaxes. Tommy Bowman was never found.

This disappearance occurred on the southwest side of the Angeles National Forest on the side of the Los Angeles Basin.

Jill Hatch
Missing: 11/02/57, 11:00 am, Camp Scheideck, CA
Age at disappearance: 7

Mr. and Mrs. William Hatch left their home in Santa Barbara for a two-hour ride inland into the Los Padres National Forest for a weekend of fishing and camping.

Camp Scheideck is a very small town in the middle of nowhere. There is one bar/restaurant in the town and a small, beautiful creek that starts in the mountains behind the town and runs down through the main street. The road dead-ends at a campground that surrounds Reyes Creek. The creek in this area is stocked annually with trout and offers an oasis in the middle of the desert.

Camp Scheideck is near the base of 7,510-foot Reyes Peak. The eastern side of the peak is covered with huge, beautiful trees and a lush ground cover. This is the only mountain within thirty miles that has a lush green environment and large trees; everything else resembles a desert.

The Hatch family arrived Friday at 4:30 p.m. and set up their camp near the creek. They brought their cocker spaniel, Chips. The family walked around the area, ate dinner, and went to sleep early.

On Saturday morning the family had breakfast and fished the area inside the camp. At approximately 11:00 a.m., Mr. Hatch told the family that he was going upstream to fish a remote area away from other campers. Jill Hatch said she would go with her dad and take Chips. Mr. Hatch walked up the valley with Jill. She sat on a rock with Chips, and her dad walked another hundred yards upstream. After several minutes of fishing, Mr. Hatch came back downstream and found that Chips and Jill were not on the rock. He walked downstream to the campsite and looked around for his daughter, but she was not there. The family searched the area for the girl until 4:00 p.m., at which time Chips arrived back in camp without Jill. It was at this point the family notified the forest service.

Just as the Ventura County Sheriff's Office and U.S. Forest Service teams arrived, snow started to fall near the camp and up in the mountains. Within twelve hours of the girl disappearing, there were five airplanes in the air, forest rangers, pack horses, Bloodhounds, and a helicopter from Hamilton Air Force Base, all searching for Jill. In total there were three hundred people looking for the missing seven-year-old.

Twenty-eight hours after Jill Hatch went missing, searchers were near the summit of Reyes Peak in very rugged country. When they were descending, they saw Jill Hatch on the side of the hill. Jill was nearly 7,500 feet up the mountain lying in fresh snow. She had her heavy coat tied around her waist. She was in a crawling position.

Jill was found five miles from her camp and an incredible 3,500 feet up in elevation from where she disappeared. I personally went to visit Camp Scheideck. The camp sits two small hills away from Reyes Peak, and it would appear that Jill had to cross those to reach the side of the peak where she died. Remember, this is the only large mountain in the entire area that has large trees and a lush environment. It would seem nearly impossible for Jill to think she was heading in the correct direction because the environment where she was found is completely different than the chaparral ground cover where she had been camping. She must have known she was too high.

The coroner said it appeared that Jill died of exposure, but there were no definitive statements.

Bruce Kremen
Missing: 07/13/60, Buckhorn Flats, Angeles National Forest, CA
Age at disappearance: 7
4'5", 65 lb.

In the summer of 1960, Bruce Kremen attended a YMCA camp in the Angeles National Forest with eighty other children. Bruce was with two other boys on a trail a half mile from camp when he was momentarily left alone and disappeared.

Search parties scoured the Buckhorn Flats area and interviewed many of the children at the camp. No leads were developed. The formal search lasted eleven days, but it went on informally for weeks.

An *APO* article dated July 14, 1961, stated the following: "'We have sent crews back many times,' Fontaine said, 'but it's like the other unsolved cases in the forest.' The reference was to Brenda Howell and Donnie Baker, youngsters who rode their bicycles into the forest in August and never returned, and to Tommy Bowman, who disappeared while hiking with his father a year later. The forest, a mountainous and heavily wooded area, covers 691,052 acres."

The case involving Baker and Howell was resolved through the arrest of a suspect in their murder. Bruce Kremen's and Tommy Bowman's cases were never resolved. The location of Bruce's disappearance is approximately fifty miles south of where Cecilia Mitchell disappeared.

Travis Zweig
Missing: 03/10/93, 10:30 a.m., Pinyon Pines, CA
Age at disappearance: 2

Sixty-five miles south of Big Bear Lake is Pinyon Pines, California. It is a rural area with cabins on the border of a desert and a forest of big, lush trees. Many people from the Los Angeles Basin have summer homes in the area. The area sits between Palm Springs and Oceanside at the coast and has an elevation of approximately four thousand feet.

Kevin and Travis Zweig made the trip to a friend's cabin where he was a caretaker. The area was inside of the small community of Pinyon Pines, an area the boys had visited in the past. The Zweigs had also taken their golden retriever, Baby, with them.

On March 10, 1993, at approximately 10:30 a.m., Travis was playing fetch with Baby while Kevin cut firewood and fixed a chain saw. Travis was out of Kevin's view for just a short time, but when Kevin returned to the side yard, Travis was missing. Friends searched for the boy for several hours and then called the Riverside County Sheriff's Department.

Searchers scoured the area of the cabin but only found a few small prints in the chaparral that surrounds the cabin. The night that Travis disappeared, snow and rain hit the region and greatly hampered search efforts.

Despite several weeks of searching and continued efforts by neighbors and friends, Travis was never found and is still listed as a missing person.

Jonathan Aujay
Missing: 06/11/98, Devil's Punchbowl, Angeles National Forest, CA
Age at disappearance: 38
6', 165 lb.

Jonathan Aujay was a fifteen-year veteran of the Los Angeles County Sheriff's Department when he disappeared. He was working in a unit that handled critical situations in the field, but he was off duty when he vanished.

The Aujays were residents of Palmdale and lived with their ten-year-old daughter. The morning of June 11, 1998, Jonathan drove to a parking area adjacent to Devil's Punchbowl to go hiking. The deputy never returned from his hike, so his family called the sheriff.

Jonathan's car was found in the parking lot of the hiking area, and subsequent searches found tracks near the ridges of Mount Baden Powell at 7,500 feet. Formal and informal searches lasted months but never found the deputy.

The sheriff's department felt it was possible that the deputy had stumbled onto a drug lab or transaction while hiking. The department started an undercover operation in Antelope Valley called "Operation Silent Thunder." The object of the operation was to thwart continued drug use and sales but also to develop intelligence on Jonathan's disappearance. Nothing was found.

It's strange that two people missing in the vast Angeles National Forest have disappeared in areas with "devil" in their names: Deputy Jonathan Aujay went missing in Devil's Punchbowl, and Tommy Bowman at Devil's Gate Dam. How did these areas get their names?

David Gonzales
Missing: 07/31/04, 8:00 a.m., Hanna Flat Campground, Big Bear Lake, CA
Age at disappearance: 9
3'10", 52 lb.

Jose and Resenda Gonzales left their home in Lake Elsinore, California, on a late Friday afternoon. The family made the trip to the Hanna Flat Campground on the north side of Big Bear Lake in the San Bernardino Mountains. The campground was near

Fawnskin. The family spent the night at their camp and awoke early Saturday morning.

At 8:00 a.m. on Saturday, their son, David, woke and asked his mom if he could walk the fifty yards to their van and get cookies as a snack. She said yes. David took the keys and was quickly out of sight. After five minutes the family went to look for him, but he couldn't be located. At 9 a.m. the family called the sheriff's department.

The sheriff utilized every conceivable resource to find David Gonzales. Seven days after he disappeared, searchers found shoe prints similar to David's 1½ miles from the camp. This gave them hope. The searchers scoured the area for another three days and then terminated all efforts. They never found the boy.

On May 29, 2005, hikers walking near the Hanna Flat Campground found the bones of David Gonzales. He was found very near the area where he disappeared. David's family had made statements that they felt their boy was abducted by a predator and then dumped back at the camp. They continued to make those statements after the boy was found.

After the initial SAR was terminated, the San Bernardino County sheriff gave the case to the homicide department, where it stayed until David's bones were discovered. This may be some evidence that the sheriff may not have believed that David simply walked away and got lost.

Fifty-seven years to the month after Wayne Bowers disappeared from Big Bear, David Gonzales disappeared and was found deceased, could there possibly be a connection?

Chapter Summary

There are many more children missing from the Southern California region, but I needed to reduce the size of this book (it was getting huge). To all of the parents of children not included in this chapter, I am truly sorry.

If you look at the ages of the children missing in this section, it is mostly children under ten—an unusual age cluster. The only adult missing from this region (and fitting the criteria) is also unusual because he was a deputy sheriff.

SOUTHWEST UNITED STATES

Arizona

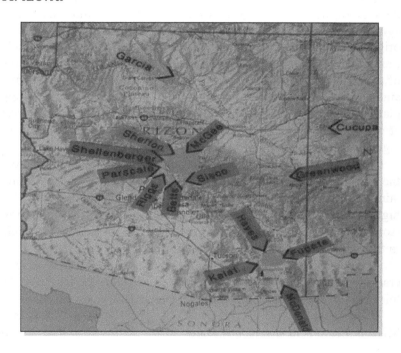

All of the Arizona cases are within two hundred and fifty miles of each other. They are located in a very small and confined area of the south central and southeast corner of the state. When you view a map of Arizona and the vast open areas that exist, it's remarkable that these clusters of missing people are in such a small area. There are no other pairs or clusters of missing in rural Arizona that even come close to the numbers that exist in these two location. The cases of Betts, Parscale, Riggs, Shelton, Shelenberger, and Sisco are extremely unique, as they all disappeared in the same mountain range. Also, only one woman is missing in this group: Joan Shelton.

Saguaro National Park and the Catalina Mountains are one solid piece of continuous mountain stretching south to north across the eastern border of Tucson, Arizona. This range is no more than thirty miles and is the second cluster in Arizona and harbors some extremely dark secrets.

The city of Tucson includes 195 square miles and sits just to the west of the mountains. It was settled over twelve thousand years ago. Tucson is one of the oldest cities in the United States. It was originally an American Indian village called Stook-Zone, which translates to "water at the foot of the black mountain." The elevation of the city is 2,400 feet. Tucson is the county seat for Pima County and sits 118 miles south of Phoenix. The 2009 census puts the population of the city near 550,000, with the entire metropolitan area at over one million. The average annual temperature in Tucson is eighty-two degrees.

Tucson has four main mountain ranges that sit on its perimeter; the Santa Catalina Mountains to the northeast, the Tucson Mountains to the west; and the Santa Rita Mountains to the south. The highest points being Mount Wrightson, in the Santa Rita Mountains (south) with an elevation of 9,453 feet, and Mount Lemmon, which in the Santa Catalina range sits at 9,157 feet.

American Indian culture proliferates throughout Arizona with several reservations and housing areas. It is claimed that the first to settle this region were the Paleo-Indians over twelve thousand years ago.

Missing Persons in Arizona by Date

Missing Person	Date Missing•Age•Sex
Jerry Hays	11/10/38•5•M
Ronald McGee	02/07/42•2•M
Mike McDonald	10/30/45•2•M
Jerry Garcia*	08/12/56•NA•M
Danny Greenwood	06/08/67•5•M
Randy Parscale	01/13/69•10•M
Paul Fugate	01/03/80•41•M

William Sisco	06/12/94•32•M
Donald Shelenberger	07/03/94•35•M
Abraham Kalaf	07/24/96•79•M
Joan Shelton	02/07/04•79•F
Jonathan Betts	10/20/06•32•M
Dwight Riggs	01/21/09•61•M

*Details on the disappearance of Jerry Garcia can be found in the "Sheepherder" chapter of *Missing 411: Eastern U.S.*

Jerry Hays
Missing: 11/10/38, Rucker Canyon, Chiricahua Mountains, Douglas, AZ
Age at disappearance: 5

Fifty miles north of Douglas, Arizona, and forty miles west of the New Mexico border is Rucker Canyon, a rugged region in the Chiricahua Mountains. The area is not what most people visualize when they think of Arizona. This region has an elevation of 6,000–7,400 feet and is lush with heavy timber.

In November 1938 the Hays family was camping in the canyon on an annual hunting trip. They set up a hunting camp in a valley with a dry wash basin running at its lowest point. The camp was at an elevation of approximately 6,200 feet. At some point on November 10, 1938, the camp lost track of little Jerry Hays. They searched the area extensively but could not find the boy. The family called the local sheriff, and he responded with a posse of men. Within days, over one thousand people were working specified quadrants in the effort to find Jerry. It was a mystery to the sheriff what might have happened to the boy because the family was camped in a canyon surrounded by high mountains, and there weren't a lot of places a lost little boy would normally go. It was also a major mystery because Mrs. Lauren Hays had told law enforcement that Jerry was a frail boy who had a severe case of rheumatism. He wasn't a rugged child that was known to wander far.

After a week of searching the Chiricahua Mountains, search leaders became more and more concerned about the welfare of Jerry. One of the searchers gave an interview to the *Prescott Evening*

Courier on November 17. It read: "He speculated on the theory a hunter had shot him accidentally and hidden the body, or that the child had been spirited away out of the hills in some unexplained manner." The statement by the searcher explains how confused they were in not finding the boy. Also, in that same article, it stated that soldiers who were assisting in the search "found barefoot tracks about a mile above tracks reported two miles from the camp." These tracks were outside the bounds of the original search perimeter and confused searchers.

A November 18 article in the *Prescott Courier* had the following: "A few indistinct footprints were the only trace of the missing child found by searchers, CCC enrollees, sheriff deputies and citizens in their search over an area of more than 150,000 acres. Sheriff I. V. Pruitt said he had 'no idea what could have happened to the child.'"

On November 19 a group of searchers had wandered off on their own into an isolated and remote area following subtle clues associated with missing Jerry. The searchers thought they found tracks going uphill and started to follow them. The searchers knew this made no sense because small frail children don't usually climb mountains when they are lost, yet that was exactly where these tracks led. The searchers followed the indicators up a steep boulder- and brush-covered slope on the side of a mountain, climbing one thousand feet in elevation. The searchers were 4½ miles from the Hays' hunting camp when they came across the body of Jerry Hays. USFS employees Ben Wheeler and Jimmie Coryell fired their pistols three times indicating they had found the boy.

The searchers were shocked to find the boy did not have his shoes or socks. His coat was also missing. This was another aspect of the search that was puzzling because temperatures in these mountains during the search had been in the low thirties. Jerry Hays' body was found to have many scratches. The coroner reported that Jerry Hays died of exposure.

Case Summary

Jerry Hays disappeared in the same mountain range approximately fifteen miles south of where Paul Fugate vanished forty-two years later (The Fugate Story is located later in this chapter). As

I have stated many times, you learn much more by studying the circumstances of a missing person who has been recovered than by studying a case where the person was never found. The case of Jerry Hays defies every logical explanation as to where he was found and the circumstances of his discovery.

His parents described Jerry as a "frail" child who wasn't rugged and wouldn't go far. This kid not only went far (4½ miles), he climbed up a steep mountainside for over one thousand feet, challenging conventional SAR criteria that children, when lost, do not usually climb uphill. In another mysterious twist to this story, all of Jerry Hays' footwear and coat had disappeared and were never found. Remember, the child was outside in thirty-degree weather climbing up a hillside of rocks and brush, a location where you'd need footwear. I would like to have understood the condition of his feet as this would indicate if he was carried or he made the trip on his own.

Do I believe a frail boy would voluntarily walk out of a camp, walk 4½ miles, shed his only protection from weather elements, and then climb one thousand feet into colder weather and a harsher climate? No. What really happened to Jerry Hays in 1938 we will never know.

Ronald McGee
Missing: 02/07/42, a.m. hours, a half mile northwest of Congress, AZ
Age at disappearance: 2
Blonde hair

Congress, Arizona, is a small and isolated community approximately sixty miles northwest of Phoenix. Congress sits close to two small mountain ranges. The elevation of Congress is three thousand feet, and the highest peaks in the area get to 5,500 feet. There is a small body of water, the Billingsley Reservoir, which sits six miles north of Congress and supplies the city's water.

On a cold February morning in 1942, two-year-old Ronald McGee and his four-year-old brother, Elwood, were playing in a small wash approximately a half mile north of town. Late in the morning, Elwood returned home to see his mother but Ronald did not. The family immediately started a search, but the boy wasn't found. The family called the sheriff in Prescott and a posse was formed to conduct a search.

The sheriff orchestrated a comprehensive search for four days. It included airplanes, bloodhounds, and over two hundred volunteers and professionals, but the boy could not be found. Nearly everyone in the small mining community contributed in some way to the search for Ronald. The Army Air Corps sent planes and the local prison contributed men to search.

Searchers were running out of locations to look for the boy, but they continued to move north toward rugged mountains and across a major roadway. A February 10 article in the *Deseret News* stated, "'It's just like the earth opened up and swallowed him,' asserted the sheriff, who leans more and more to the theory that foul play may have been involved. 'We haven't even been able to find a footprint.'"

At 10:30 a.m. on the fourth day of the search, two expert trackers, Jack Crist and John Bond, thought they found faint tracks in a very isolated area far north of Congress. Highway Patrolman James Cramer and Sheriff Homer Keeton joined the trackers after they inexplicably saw tracks going up the side of Tenderfoot Peak, an unbelievable twelve miles north of Congress. Four hundred and twenty-eight feet up from the desert floor in an area strewn with large boulders and small bushes, searchers found the body of Ronald McGee. A February 11, 1942, article in the *Brownsville Herald* had the following article about finding the boy: "The body of two-year-old Ronald McGee, lost since Saturday, was found 'horribly scratched and torn' Wednesday on the side of Tenderfoot Peak." A February 12, 1942, article in the *Albuquerque Journal* had the following: "Fear was written on the child's tear-stained face. The sight of the body, which they said was 'horribly scratched,' shocked hard-boiled sheriff's deputies."

Case Summary

The coroner listed the cause of death as exposure.

What happened to Ronald McGee is a modern-day mystery. No, I don't think anyone believes that a two-year-old boy could walk across twelve miles of desert and climb a four-hundred-foot peak, especially when the coroner reported that he felt the boy died the first day he was missing. I did not find one article that reported a theory on how Ronald arrived at the location where his body was found or how his body was torn—yes, torn—and horribly scratched.

Mike McDonald
Missing: 10/30/45, a.m., Sulphur Springs Valley, AZ
Age at disappearance: 2

Sulphur Springs Valley is in southern Arizona, west of the Chiricahua Mountains between Bisbee and Douglas. The valley is home to the Whitewater Draw Wildlife Area and has a huge lake and swampy area. This is the only location in the southern region of Arizona that has a water source in the middle of an otherwise dry valley. The valley is relatively flat, with mesquite brush and few large trees. The valley sits between the Chiricahua Mountains to the east and another smaller range that includes Mount Ballard to the west.

On October 30, 1945, Mike McDonald was playing in his yard with his mixed-breed dog. Sometime in the morning hours, Mike disappeared. The family immediately started to search for the boy but could not locate him. Local law enforcement, ranchers, farmers, and other community volunteers all looked for Mike.

The morning after Mike disappeared, Joe Mauzy, a Bisbee businessman, and Mike's father, Ed McDonald, were riding their horses looking for the boy and were slowly working their way away from the McDonald home. The cowboys were a remarkable fifteen miles from the McDonald home when Joe saw a dog sitting on a dirt mound. Joe directed the men to the mound and Ed confirmed it was his dog. The men dismounted their horses and walked toward the dog. They found a small cave dug into the dirt. Through the two-foot-wide opening, they found Mike McDonald sleeping inside. The boy had a small cut on one foot but no other injuries.

Case Summary

According to SAR books, children one to three years old will be found less than 5.6 miles from the point they were last seen 95 percent of the time. Mike had traveled nearly three times this distance. He was found in a small cave in the middle of the valley floor. What would the statistical chances be that Mike happened to stumble upon a cave in the vast Sulphur Springs Valley, especially since none of the fifteen cowboys who participated in the search had ever known it existed?

Danny Greenwood
Missing: 06/08/67, 1:00 p.m., Reservation Lake, Mount Baldy, AZ
Age at disappearance: 5
Blonde hair

The Greenwood case is included in this chapter because the facts supporting the disappearance match others found in this book yet it is not a part of either cluster in Arizona.

The Greenwood family lived in Socorro, New Mexico, approximately 140 miles east of Reservation Lake in eastern Arizona. Raymond Greenwood had decided to take Danny (5) and Martin (12) to Reservation Lake for a long weekend of fishing.

Raymond, Danny, and Martin slept in their camp Wednesday night and then got an early start on fishing Thursday morning. Just after lunch, Danny told his dad that he was going to walk back to their campsite. Raymond said that was fine. The Greenwoods' camp was fifty yards down a small and defined trail, and Danny walked directly to the camp. After a short time without seeing the boy again, Raymond walked back to their campsite and couldn't find Danny. He summoned authorities. Within four hours the Apache County Sheriff's Office and Arizona State Police had arrived at the area where Danny had gone missing. The Apache County Sheriff's office and Fort Apache Indian Reservation rangers headed the search for little Danny.

Searchers found small prints believed to be the boy's moving away from the family's campsite and up into a boulder-filled area toward the summit of Mount Baldy. Mount Baldy looms large over Reservation Lake to the west and is on the Fort Apache Indian Reservation. The entire Mount Baldy area is a designated wilderness area. A wilderness area designation means that nothing with a tire can go into the area. Only people on foot or horseback are allowed in a wilderness area.

Searchers scanned the lake and shoreline, and eventually had to believe the boy had walked almost directly uphill toward the summit. This path taken by Danny made no sense to searchers. Regardless, the search teams broke into quadrants and continued to make their way toward the top of Mount Baldy. On Sunday morning, searchers found Danny Greenwood.

A June 12, 1967, article in the *Yuma Daily Sun* had the following: "The three-day search for the five-year-old Socorro, New Mexico, boy ended Sunday when posse members found his body twenty feet from the summit of 11,600-foot Mount Baldy, the highest peak in eastern Arizona." The article later states that the boy was found fifteen miles from his family's campsite. "James Sparks, manager of White Mountain Recreation Enterprise, said, 'No one could imagine a boy that age climbing that mountain alone.'" A helicopter airlifted Danny's body off the peak, and a physician later stated that Danny had died of exposure, probably on Friday night.

In his book, *Lost Person Behavior*, Robert Koester states that a child four to six years old—if climbing upward in elevation—will be found 95 percent of the time after climbing 1,303 feet or less. Danny left Reservation Lake at 9,000 feet and made it up to 11,580 feet, a vertical climb of 2,580 feet. Koester also states that the child will be found in under 3.7 miles if walking uphill. Danny had walked fifteen miles uphill (into freezing temperatures and thin air).

Case Summary

There is nothing in the disappearance of Danny Greenwood that makes sense. He walked fifty yards back to his campsite, his father saw him walking that direction. The weather dropped below thirty degrees at night at this elevation, yet Danny walked uphill, where it got colder. He would have been able to turn and see Reservation Lake behind him, and he knew his father and brother were there.

This case has hauntingly similar facts to the disappearances of Garrett Bardsley and Raymond Ewer from Utah. Both of these males disappeared while walking back to their campsites after fishing with family. Neither was ever found. I doubt that Danny would have been found if searchers had not found the tracks leading uphill.

Very few searchers would have climbed to the top of Mount Baldy searching for Danny, as most SAR manuals state that the odds of finding a child at the summit are almost zero.

It's very difficult for me to believe a five-year-old boy could or would climb up an eleven-thousand-foot mountain where air is very thin and temperatures very cold. He walked through a boulder field to get to this location. Garrett Bardsley's sock was found in a boulder field in Utah. Even though Garrett was never found, this may have indicated the path he took. Boulder fields seem to be a common location where missing people are recovered.

There is a long ridgeline that emanates near Reservation Lake. It goes in a northerly direction toward the summit of Mount Baldy, but the last four hundred feet of the mountain is an almost sheer cliff coming from the southern end. The only easy route to the summit (or to get within twenty feet of the summit) is from the north—the opposite direction Danny would have had to come from. I do not see it humanly possible that a five-year-old boy could make the journey from the lake to within twenty feet of the summit of Mount Baldy. I would encourage all readers to go to Google Maps, search for Mount Baldy, Arizona, and examine at the terrain.

Randy Parscale
Missing: 01/13/69, Peppersauce
Canyon, AZ
Age at disappearance: 10
4'6", 70 lb.

Randy Parscale was a third grader at Roberts Elementary School in Tucson. On the weekend of January 13, 1969, he took a hike into Peppersauce Canyon near Oracle, Arizona. Randy was with his father and two brothers as they made their way through the rugged region on the edge of Tucson. Peppersauce Canyon has its share of kids who run the trails (there is a Salvation Army camp that hosts kids of all ages for weekend trips).

Randy ran ahead of his family and momentarily went out of sight. When the family reached the end of the trail, they could not find the boy. A report was immediately filed with law enforcement and a massive search was conducted. Hundreds of searchers scoured the mountain—on horseback, by air, and in abandoned mines. In a horrible twist to this case, a searcher died of a heart attack while conducting the search.

The current theories about what happened to Randy include: he may have fallen into an old mine shaft, or he might have been abducted and taken from the scene. Peggy Foley, Randy's mom, is one of the surviving members of his family that continues to campaign for a follow-up on his whereabouts. Since Randy has disappeared, both of his grandfathers and his father have died.

This case has many similarities with the disappearance of Thomas Bowman from Los Angeles County. Thomas ran ahead of his father while they were on a hiking trail and his dad never saw him again (refer to the section on Southern California for details on the Thomas Bowman case).

Paul Braxton Fugate
Missing: 01/13/80, Chiricahua
National Monument, AZ
Age at disappearance: 41

Paul Fugate was a twenty-year National Park Service ranger, though he was not a traditional ranger in the sense of his appearance or his history with the NPS. He wore long hair in a ponytail and had a large moustache. His career ended in 1971, when the park service terminated him for failing to trim his hair and moustache. Paul was a fighter: he went to the American Civil Liberties Union and filed an unlawful termination suit. After half a decade of legal proceedings, Paul was awarded his job back (1976), along with back pay and other benefits.

On January 13, 1980, he was at work wearing his traditional NPS attire. Paul was the supervising ranger in the park that day because the superintendent was away on a hunting trip. At 2:00 p.m. he told a co-worker he was going to take a hike. He put on an orange-lined U.S. Park Service coat, left his radio in the charger, and walked toward the park entrance and a house that was being donated to the park. Paul was never seen again. This is the lone case in the history of the NPS that a ranger disappeared and was never found.

Paul was forty-one years old when he disappeared. After a lengthy investigation, the superintendent and other park officials claimed they had no real clue regarding his disappearance. On February 23, 1982, the NPS sent his wife, Dody, a letter claiming that Paul had abandoned his job with the NPS and then terminated him from their employment. They then filed paperwork against Dody to retrieve $6,000 that had been paid to her—half of Paul's salary, a benefit to all widows. This hostile action against the wife of a missing ranger caught many in the community by surprise. Many writers penned stories asking how the park service could do this to a woman who was obviously in stress and missing her husband.

Dody Fugate had friends at the Antioch School of Law in Washington, D.C. With their assistance she filed a $250,000 lawsuit against the park service. The case loitered in the courts for months, but Dody eventually prevailed and won all back pay and benefits deserving of a widow.

The NPS organized one of the largest searches in their history. It included U.S. Customs, Border Patrol, Southern Arizona Search and Rescue, and Cochise County Sheriff Search and Rescue. Airplane, helicopter, and four-wheel drive searches were all completed. A total of eighteen square miles were extensively searched without finding any evidence of Paul. The combined reward for information leading to Paul had reached $25,000.

Paul left behind a 1955 Chevrolet that he was restoring, $300 in cash, traveler's checks, and his personal vehicle. He was also midway through completing several projects for the park that were important to him. Paul lived in an apartment at the monument and would travel home to Tucson to stay with Dody on weekends.

On January 15, the Cochise County Sheriff's Office entered the search for Paul. This started the massive investigation that lasted until January 27. The investigation into Paul's disappearance turned up one tantalizing clue. Richard Horton stated he saw Paul riding in the front seat of a pickup truck between two men on January 13, 1980. The interesting clue to this is that Paul was not wearing his glasses. Paul was nearly blind without the glasses. The witness described Paul as appearing "dejected." Lt. Craig Emmanuel from the sheriff's office was the lead investigator in the case and claims that the description of Paul in the pickup is the only clue they have about his disappearance. A total of twenty-eight psychics assisted on the case—some even mentioned a pickup and two men way before the witness account was released.

Dody believes that her husband left the park office and headed to the Faraday Ranch, an area that had suffered vandalism in the past and was going to be donated to the park. Once at the spot, she thinks Paul interrupted some type of crime that was in progress. Paul did not have his radio and was alone. Dody believes he was kidnapped and taken from the scene.

During the course of researching this story and others, I filed an FOIA request to the NPS for all files related to the Paul Fugate case. Months after the filing, I received a large box of materials in the mail. One of the more interesting and informative documents that I received was a letter written by Charles E. Scott, a private investigator from Mesa, Arizona. The letter, dated October 29, 1985, was addressed to Dave Lennox of the Western Region National Park Service in San Francisco. It appears the NPS retained the investigator to provide independent investigative services into the disappearance of Paul. One portion of the report dealt with information law enforcement received from another investigator, Michael Erickson of Racine, Wisconsin. Michael had received information from a city resident that a person claimed he killed a cop in Arizona and then buried his body in the desert. A suspect was identified and named. This information was given to Lt. Emmanuel at the sheriff's office, and he subsequently called the suspect on November 18, 1982. (I personally don't know of any detective in any homicide case that would call a suspect by phone and question him about his involvement.) Emmanuel received a defensive answer, and the suspect immediately retained an attorney. The suspect took two polygraphs—one inconclusive and one that could not be completed. Charles's report states: "(The suspects name removed) maintains his boasting of killing a cop was the result of being intoxicated and to impress people. If this was the case, it could be easily explained and suspicion removed."

Charles went on to interview Bill Bangs, a polygraph examiner for the Arizona Department of Public Safety. Bill stated that he conducted the polygraph with the suspect and that the suspect had "registered deception in all questions which pertained to the missing police officer [Paul Fugate]." The results of the polygraph left Bill with the opinion that Paul Fugate was dead.

At the time of publication, Paul is still considered missing by law enforcement, even though Dody had him legally declared dead by a judge. Every file I read that was forwarded by the park service indicates that Paul would not voluntarily leave his position or vacate his employment. He loved his job. The best guess by law enforcement appears to be that Paul was abducted by someone somewhere and is probably deceased.

I think it's an interesting policy by the NPS to release a file on one of their own rangers that was never found and is still considered an open case yet they won't release the Stacy Arras case from Yosemite.

William Marshall Sisco Jr.
Missing: 06/12/94, Happy Valley, AZ
Age at disappearance: 32
6'1", 165 lb.

William Sisco and his prospecting friends were in a remote area near Happy Valley and adjacent to the Saguaro National Park. On the evening of June 12, 1994, William said he wanted to leave. His friends said they did not. William decided to leave the prospecting site alone and was never seen again.

Law enforcement investigators believe that William met with foul play or died of exposure in the desert. His body has never been found.

Donald Kenneth Shelenberger
Missing: 07/03/94, Mount Lemmon, Tucson, AZ
Age at disappearance: 35
5'11", 160 lb.

Donald Shelenberger was making arrangements to meet a friend on Mount Lemmon in the northeast section of Tucson, Arizona. They were going to meet and hike the mountain. Donald was never seen again and details about this case are few.

Abraham Kalaf
Missing: 07/24/96, Gleeson, AZ
Age at disappearance: 79
5'8", 185 lb.

Abraham Kalaf was the supervisor of a drilling team working in an isolated region between Tombstone and Gleeson, Arizona. On July 24, 1996, he left Tucson and headed for the site. He never made it to the site and was reported missing.

In October, his 1989 Dodge Ram pickup was located stuck in rugged mountains seventeen miles from the drill site. All of Abraham's personal items, checks, and work items were in the vehicle. Authorities responding to the scene found tape in the area that appeared to be placed by Abraham as an indication of what direction he walked. Law enforcement followed the path, which led toward the Dragoon Mountains. At one point the path changed direction and headed toward civilization. As the trail started to evaporate, law enforcement brought in significant resources but were unable to find Abraham.

Joan Phyllis Shelton
Missing: 02/07/04, Catalina Foothills, Northeast Tucson, AZ
Age at disappearance: 65
5'3", 103 lb.

In 2004, Joan Shelton was staying at an assisted living facility on East Sunrise Drive in Tucson, Arizona. The facility is very close to a mountainous area between the Santa Catalina Mountains and Saguaro National Park. It is located just under Mount Lemmon.

Joan checked out of the facility at 2:10 p.m., and people were unsure exactly where she was going. She was an avid hiker, and it's possible she went into the mountains. A large search of the area failed to find Joan Shelton. Joan's body has never been found.

Jonathan Betts
Missing: 10/20/06, Saguaro National Park, AZ
Age at disappearance: 32
5'10", 190 lb.

It appears Jonathan Betts drove his Mazda Protégé to Saguaro National Park. According to the receipt found in his vehicle, Jonathan paid upon entering; the stamp shows he arrived at 4:00 p.m. After a three-day search of the park, searchers eventually found his vehicle. The car was parked at the Loma Verde Loop Trail, slightly off the main roads.

Jonathan was an avid hiker. His parents are from the East Coast, and he was a student at Pima Community College. Law enforcement states that there were no indications of foul play. An extensive search of the park and his residence failed to uncover any evidence of his location. Jonathan's body has never been found.

Dwight Alan Riggs
Missing: 01/21/09, Rural Pima County, AZ
Age at disappearance: 61
5'11", 175 lb.

Dwight Riggs lived in a rural area on the outskirts of Tucson, Arizona. His residence abutted an area between the Santa Catalina Mountains and Saguaro National Park, an area that can be quite remote. This is also an area where a number of people have gone missing.

Dwight had a deep interest in archeology and took daily hikes in the mountains behind his house. He was last seen on January 21, 2009, but not reported missing for several days. Law enforcement does not believe foul play was involved in his disappearance, but they cannot explain where he might be located.

Chapter Summary

The disappearance of longtime NPS Ranger Paul Fugate is one of the all-time great mysteries that still haunt the park service. We do hope that Paul's family and friends have resolution to this case.

The disappearance of William Sisco (06/12/94), while prospecting in Happy Valley, and the disappearance of Donald Shellenberger (7/3/94) from Mount Lemmon occur too close together—in location (fifteen miles apart) and time (twenty-one days)—to not be considered related in some way. Although detailed information on each case is not available, the dates and locations are suspiciously similar.

From 1938 to 1967, five boys disappeared—two five-year-olds and two at two years old (one boy's age is unknown)—all in a seven-year span. The disappearance of Paul Fugate changed the demographic of the people missing in Arizona, and the ages increased dramatically. There hasn't been a person reported missing under the age of thirty-two that fits our criteria since 1967. What happened to change this dynamic?

New Mexico

Missing People in New Mexico by Date

Missing Person	Date, Missing•Age•Sex
Larry McGee	06/07/51•7•M
Janet McGee	06/07/51•5•F
Steven Cross	06/07/51•3•M
Albert Cucupa	02/16/60•32•M
	*Missing 411- Eastern U.S.
Ann Riffin	09/13/82•33•F
Emma Tresp	09/08/98•71•F
Melvin Nadel	09/06/09•61•M

Larry McGee, age 7 (Blonde hair)
Janet McGee, age 5
Steven Cross, age 3
Missing: 06/07/51, Santa Fe Ski Basin, Sangre De Cristo Mountains, NM

Two families from Santa Fe drove to the Santa Fe Ski Basin to spend a day picnicking and enjoying the mountain air. The group arrived just before noon and started to set their picnic site.

The area that was chosen for the picnic was at the bottom of the Santa Fe Ski Basin, near ten thousand feet in elevation. The area was not operational for snow skiing, but it was a gorgeous spot because of its extremely rugged terrain and large boulders.

As the families were settling into the picnic area, the three kids—Larry McGee, Janet McGee, and Steven Cross—were running through the area and apparently enjoying the high altitude and cooler air.

Near noon the families realized that they hadn't seen the kids in a while and started to search for them. The search progressively got more frantic as time passed and the children still could not be found. At 3:00 p.m. the families had exhausted all possibilities as to where the children could be, so they went to the ski area and called law enforcement.

New Mexico State Police took control of the search and rescue and immediately requested assistance from the local air force base and other law enforcement jurisdictions. The first night of the search did not produce any evidence. The police set up huge spotlights pointing up into the mountain in hopes that the children would see the lights and walk toward them.

The morning of June 8 arrived with the children still missing, but five hundred searchers had volunteered to look for the kids. Many of the searchers were armed forces personnel from the Kirtland and Sandia bases. All reports indicate that the search was not organized efficiently or defined by a grid pattern. Searchers picked an area and generally walked toward a region to start looking through bushes.

Twenty-eight hours after the kids disappeared, armed forces personnel were over 3½ miles from the location the kids were last seen when they saw a head poke out among a series of downed logs.

One of the children looked up from the logs and called out for assistance. All three kids were found higher in elevation and miles from where they were last seen, yet they were in remarkably good condition. The soldiers stated that it appeared the children were sleeping or resting, and the youngest child was extremely fatigued and tired.

Once the children were brought back to the search headquarters, search personnel and their parents questioned them. A June 8, 1951, article in the *Santa Fe New Mexican* stated that Larry told the press that they had been chased up the mountain by a bear. He also claimed that they ate leaves and all slept together in a hollow log, sometimes drinking water from a stream. (He didn't explain how he knew to eat specific leaves). Larry also made a fascinating remark about why the kids may have been hesitant to immediately make themselves known to searchers: "They had seen some of the searchers, he said, but were afraid to yell because they thought they were big gorillas." For some odd reason, the reporter did not follow up on this statement. Why would the kids be afraid to yell out to searchers unless they had been frightened by something that looked like gorillas?

A doctor was at the search location. He examined the children and said they were slightly dehydrated but in remarkably good condition.

The children in this incident were found approximately six air miles from the location where Melvin Nadel disappeared. The area near the location where the kids were found has many small lakes and sits between 11,000 and 12,000 feet.

Case Summary

This case has many fascinating parts to the overall story. The idea that a bear would chase the kids up the mountain and not catch them does not make sense. If a bear wanted to chase the kids, it would have caught them. The area where the kids were found is like many described in this book—steep, rugged, foreboding areas with many lakes, boulders, and trees. The most perplexing statement made by Larry was about being afraid that the searchers were big gorillas. Why would he say this? I'd also like to know how the kids missed seeing the huge spotlights that lit the mountainside during the night and why they didn't walk towards the lights?

Ann Linda Riffin
Missing: 09/13/82, Highway 3, between Tres Ritos and Mora, NM
Age at disappearance: 33
5'4", 125 lb.

Ann Riffin had a degree in anthropology from the College of William and Mary. She was originally from New Jersey but had lived in Israel. She later moved to New Mexico and obtained a waitress job at a restaurant in Ruidoso. She was an accomplished artist and enjoyed painting landscapes.

In mid-September of 1982, Ann left for a weekend vacation, though it was not known exactly where she was headed. When Ann didn't return to her job and didn't call her parents, they called police and reported her missing.

On September 21, 1982, Ann's vehicle was found stuck in a ditch on a dirt road a short distance from Highway 3. The vehicle was locked, and there did not appear to be any foul play involved. Officers searched the car and determined that the only item missing was Ann's purse. They did find artwork, brushes, and paint, indicating that Ann had been painting landscapes on her trip.

Police found a witness who claimed to have seen Ann getting gas at a station ten miles from where her car was abandoned. The witness said Ann was alone.

It's been almost thirty years since Ann disappeared and police still have no new leads. It is interesting that she disappeared in proximity to Melvin Nadel, profiled below.

Melvin Nadel
Missing: 09/6/09, Elk Mountain, Santa Fe National Forest, NM
Age at disappearance: 61
5'2", 135 lb.

It's sometimes easier for people to understand why someone goes missing when they have significant medical issues, but when the person who disappears is a black belt in tae kwon do, a Pilates instructor, and a longtime hunter, questions about what happened in the woods are bound to be asked.

Melvin Nadel owned and operated Pilates Fitness Plus near downtown Santa Fe. Melvin was a hands-on owner. He not only met people at the door and did the accounting for the business, but also ran many of the classes. Longtime customers of the studio stated that one of the main reasons they enjoyed the studio was the class that Melvin taught.

Melvin's wife, Edna, operated a daycare facility out of their residence. Their daughter, Kristen, was enrolled at the local community college. Kristen, a certified fitness instructor, taught classes at the Pilates studio. The Nadels had moved to Santa Fe in 1991 from their original hometown, Brooklyn, New York.

It's easy to say that a family is tight and enjoys each other, but the Nadels really did. Melvin and Kristen were extremely close, as Melvin had homeschooled Kristen until she went to community college. The family went on vacations together, camped together, and spent significant time at their businesses together.

Melvin was a small man in stature (5'2") but a big man whom his customers loved. Prior to the Pilates studio, Melvin owned a jewelry business in town. While in Santa Fe, he earned his black belt in tae kwon do and started his fitness regime to keep himself healthy. He knew the value of staying healthy, as both his mom and dad had died early in life.

In the first week of September 2009, Melvin and friends decided to go hunting in the Santa Fe National Forest, Pecos Wilderness in the Sangre De Cristo Mountains. Melvin drove his 2001 Jeep up to an area near eleven thousand feet. He was near Pecos, fourteen miles off NM63 and Forest Road 646. The region has extreme desolation and is very rugged, with many exposed boulders and steep cliffs.

Late in the afternoon on September 6, Melvin told his friends that he was going to walk down an adjacent trail fifty to 150 yards away and stay in that area. He had a slight knee injury and didn't want to walk long distances. Melvin's specific type of hunting involved setting up a blind and sitting to wait for game to pass. He was carrying a camouflaged bow with zebra striped arrows and a

.44-caliber pistol. At 4:30 p.m., Melvin Nadel started down the trail, never to return.

His friends notified the state police, and they initiated a massive search. National Guard helicopters, law enforcement canines, horses, volunteers, and all-terrain vehicles swarmed the area and adjacent mountains without finding one trace of Melvin—no bow, no arrows, no gun, no clothing, nothing. The search was hampered just after the disappearance with the dropping of four to five inches of snow.

The canines brought into camp started their search by walking directly down the trail where Melvin stated he was going. At the 150-yard marker, they stopped. This validates that Melvin walked down the trail, but canines don't just stop without justification. The canines would not proceed farther than the 150 yards.

The official state police search for Melvin ended six days after it started. Edna and Kristen rallied all friends, family, and business relationships to keep the search going for almost six weeks. The six-week period is a reasonable time to search for anyone who had a likelihood of being there, but the state police search of only six days seems short for a man who was in superior condition and had the opportunity to survive.

Law enforcement searched Melvin's Jeep and found the items they expected. They could positively state that the only things missing were the bow, arrows, and pistol that he was last seen carrying. The vehicle had not been damaged and law enforcement did not consider foul play as an option in the disappearance.

One year after Melvin Nadel's disappearance, State Police Lt. Eric Garcia stated that the Nadel case remains open and active, and that many leads have been investigated but none have yielded any evidence.

Case Summary

There are several issues in the Nadel case that pop out as unusual. First, Melvin is a fairly short man. Please look at his photo and notice that he has long hair to the shoulders in the back. If Melvin was approached by a predator from the rear, he could have been mistaken for a female hunter—short height, long hair. Maybe this mistake led to his disappearance. I would also refer readers to the height of each of the missing people highlighted in this section; they are all fairly short people.

To be a successful bowhunter, you have to be a stealthy hunter. You must have the ability to hide the human odor, stay camouflaged, and get very close to your prey. Did Melvin inadvertently get too close to something or someone?

We know that Melvin went to the exact spot he had told his friends—150 yards down the trail. Why would a trained canine track exactly 150 yards down a trail and stop? Canines are trained to continue to track the specific odor until it terminates. Odors don't terminate with death or disappearance.

One year after Melvin disappeared, Edna and Kristen filed paperwork in the superior courts of Santa Fe to have Melvin legally declared dead. This is a standard request because the family needed social security benefits and the ability to transfer titles in local properties. The Santa Fe attorney who filed the case used the following logic in requesting the death certificate: "There are only two explanations for Melvin's disappearance: He wandered off, got lost and died of natural causes, exposure or animal attack, or, was abducted, taken to an undisclosed location, killed and his body disposed."

The likelihood that Melvin was attacked by a mountain lion, bear, elk, or some other recognized mammal in New Mexico is nearly zero. If Melvin had been attacked and killed, there would have been a large evidence scene with blood, bones, and tissue. The area was not vacated long enough for animals to remove all the evidence. He would have been found, at least in pieces. The possibility that Melvin was abducted and taken from the scene utilizing standard abduction techniques also seems extremely remote. Melvin was parked on the only road to the summit of Elk Mountain. Melvin was with friends hunting the mountain, and someone would have seen others in the area. There is a general store that many frequent twenty miles from the disappearance. Workers would have seen others in the area. The greatest question is, Why would anyone want to abduct Melvin? Searchers scoured the area where he disappeared for six weeks, and there wasn't any illegal drug factories or grow patches found, so hiding a drug scene didn't happen.

I believe that Melvin was lying low, very low, in his blind. It was getting cold and dark, and he chose to hunt in the late afternoon, a time when animals start to come out. I believe that something surprised Melvin, something unusual, something fatal, and something he couldn't control and didn't expect. Imagine a search, a very thorough search, where Melvin's weapons, clothing, and the supplies he was carrying were not found. How does this happen?

I think there is a common theme that runs through the heart of each of the disappearances highlighted in this section.

Emma Frances Tresp
Missing: 08/31/98 (reported 9/8/98), Forestry Road 63A, Pecos, NM
Age at disappearance: 71
5'6", 120 lb.

Next to the words "world traveler" in the dictionary, there should be a picture of Emma Tresp. Don't let her age fool you; Emma was smart, educated, and knew how to travel anywhere. Even with her worldwide travel experience, something caught Emma by surprise in the New Mexico mountains. The question is, what happened?

Emma Tresp was a retired nursing-home inspector from the state of Arkansas. Once she retired, her life really got started. Emma had the income, ability, and desire to see different parts of the world, which took her to China, New Zealand, Canada, Alaska, and other great places. In 1998, the year she disappeared, Emma traveled to Ecuador and Peru, where she visited Machu Picchu. At seventy-one-years-young, Emma was quite the traveler and eager to take on new adventures.

Emma was a deeply religious woman who enjoyed visiting a Benedictine Monastery in the mountains of New Mexico. At the start of this trip, Emma traveled from her home in Little Rock, Arkansas, to visit her daughter, Lisa, in Stillwater, Oklahoma. Lisa and her mom had a good visit, and on August 31 Emma left for New Mexico in her white, four-door 1997 Honda Civic. It has been established that Emma stopped at a filling station for gas in Santa Rosa, New Mexico, at 3:00 p.m. It is estimated that Emma took a wrong turn to the mountains at around 5:00 p.m. She was traveling on Forest Road 63A near Glorieta Baldy Peak. She had her map lying on the seat next to her when she apparently decided to turn around on the rough dirt road. As she was backing up, the vehicle got stuck on the ledge and couldn't be moved. Emma was nine miles from the small community of La Cueva. There was no cell reception in this area and little vehicular traffic. Emma left her car with the following contents inside:

Blanket
Six-pack of unopened Diet Sprite
Hat
Cookies
$2 in change
Travel map
Suitcase with clothes
Metal thermos

The only item that could be determined missing from the car was her purse.

After Lisa didn't hear from her mom, she called her sister, Rose, who was a nun. Rose called the Benedictine Monastery. It was determined that Emma never arrived, and the family headed for New Mexico to start a search.

On September 13, a local resident saw a posted flyer and remembered seeing Emma's stuck Honda on Forest Road 63A. The resident notified law enforcement.

New Mexico State Police located Emma's car but did not find anything disturbed or any fresh tracks in the area. A search was immediately initiated utilizing National Guard helicopters, SAR teams on foot and on horseback, cadaver dogs, canines, and volunteer searchers. At one point, two hundred searchers were on the scene, but nothing was found.

State police investigators have stated that in August 2008 there were 1,019 active missing person cases in New Mexico. The investigators also stated that they did not believe that Emma was a victim of foul play, but they could not explain where she was located. The Emma Tresp case had a $20,000 reward for her discovery.

This project has given me a fascinating perspective on missing person cases, a perspective that law enforcement would not possess because of their inability to spend excessive time researching cases throughout North America. The cases in New Mexico fit the specific criteria of a cluster. Emma went missing just seven air miles southwest of Melvin Nadel. Imagine the entire state of New Mexico and here we have two cases—that both baffle law enforcement—just seven miles apart. The Ann Riffin case also falls into this cluster because of its proximity to Tresp and Nadel. It's a mind-boggling scenario.

The first inclination is to deduce that someone is driving the backwoods of New Mexico looking for wandering people to abduct. That's craziness. Melvin Nadel was armed (with a bow, arrows, and a pistol); I don't think anyone wants to take on that scenario. Imagine how many miles you'd have to drive to see a seventy-one-year-old woman walking alone on a dirt road—not plausible. Emma was walking on a dirt road she had just driven up to the point of getting her vehicle stuck. The idea that she would have wandered off this road isn't logical. Emma Tresp was an experienced traveler; she knew the road to safety was the road she was walking. She would have followed the road back to the main highway if all had gone well. Emma knew that if she passed out or became ill, the only way to be found would be to stay close to the road—nothing else would work. Well, she wasn't found anywhere—not near the road, in the hills, or the mountains.

I don't believe that Emma voluntarily left the roadway. I'm only guessing that she probably took bottled water with her in her purse when she left walking down the roadway. The answers to this puzzle are somewhere hidden in the mountains, roadways, and adjacent communities. Locals know the obstacles and issues that occur in the mountains, and they have the answers if law enforcement is asking questions. Could it be that a drug runner picked her up, maybe a poacher, maybe a serial killer? Just about anything is possible. The New Mexico State Police investigator who has the Emma Tresp case made this statement: "It's like she vanished off the face of the earth."

Chapter Summary

The disappearances of Ann Riffin, Emma Tresp, and Melvin Nadel all occurred in the first half of September. It's unusual that all three people disappeared in a month that is not known for its harsh weather.

As you continue to read this book, you will see that the clusters of missing follow a pattern.

The adults featured in this chapter could have been mistaken under certain conditions as three women. Considering the month of the disappearances, the proximity in which all three of the victims disappeared, and the physical characteristics of the victims, there are too many similarities for the disappearances not to be related.

Another major oddity with the missing in this chapter is that all six disappeared in the same mountains and all in proximity to each other. All of these people disappeared in the Santa Fe National Forest. If you consider the number of national forests in New Mexico (Carson, Cibola, Gila, Kiowa Lincoln, Santa Fe) and the number of managed wildlife areas (Black Kettle and McClellan Creek Grasslands, Brokeoff Mountain Wilderness, San Andreas National Wildlife Area), you start to get an understanding that there are many areas in New Mexico that are wild and filled with large mammals; yet the Santa Fe National Forest (specifically, the Sangre De Cristo Mountains) is where people disappear. Why?

Comparing the missing in Arizona with the missing in New Mexico, there is one glaring similarity—the 1960s. The demographics of the missing people fitting our criteria changes in the '60s, going from a very young group to an older sect.

UNITED STATES ROCKY MOUNTAINS

Utah

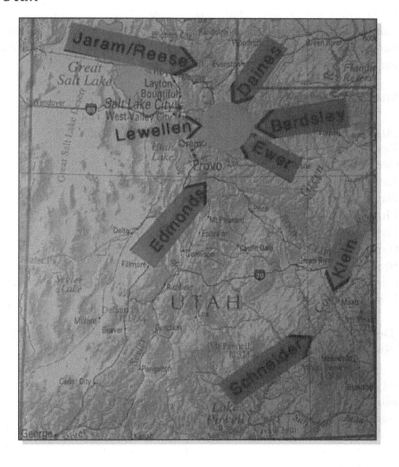

The Uinta Mountains contain the cluster of missing people for the state of Utah. The mountains run from the far northeastern section of the state into Colorado and are east of Salt Lake City near the eastern Utah border.

A majority of the Uinta range is categorized as a wilderness area, and vehicles cannot be driven on the property. Most of the range is also in the Ashley National Forest.

State Highway 15 bisects the center of Utah and is where the major cities are located—Salt Lake, Provo, Orem, Logan, Ogden, Valley City, etc. Every missing case listed in this chapter is located east of Highway 15. There are seven males and one female meeting our criteria in this region.

Missing People in Utah by Date

Missing Person	Date Missing•Age•Sex
Raymond Ewer	08/09/69•19•M
Greg Lewellen*	08/03/73•66•M
Jennifer Klein	05/25/74•3•F
David Jaramillo	06/13/85•21•M
Lloyd Reese	06/13/85•13•M
Daniel Edmonds	08/22/95•22•M
Garrett Bardsley	08/20/04•12•M
Brennan Hawkins	06/17/05•11•M
Kenneth Schneider	10/03/05•78•M
Clinton Daines	10/16/09•35•M

*Details on the disappearance of Greg Lewellen can be found in the "Sheepherder" chapter of *Missing 411: Eastern U.S.*

Raymond Ewer
Missing: 08/06/69, Island Lake, Uinta Mountains, Utah
Age at disappearance: 21

Raymond Ewer, his dad, and two friends traveled from their home in Washington Terrace, Utah, to enjoy a weekend fishing high in the Uinta mountains. The plan was to fish a series of lakes in the area.

The men were fishing Island Lake at noon on August 6 when Raymond got his fishing line tangled. He was returning to camp from the lake when he vanished (very similar to the disappearance of Garrett Bardsley (UT) and Danny Greenwood (AZ)). His father and friends immediately started to search but failed to locate him. After failing to find Raymond, his friends left to call authorities.

The search for Raymond Ewer was uneventful until searchers found a sheepherder in an extremely remote area seven miles north of Island Lake near Hoop Lake. The sheepherder told searchers that he had seen the man Sunday and had given him directions to Island Lake. He offered Raymond food and water, but he only asked for water.

The search for Raymond Ewer was one of the longest in the state of Utah's history—over four weeks. The sheriff exhausted almost every avenue he could imagine looking for Raymond. Canines, motorcycles, horses, aircraft, and ground crews scoured thousands of acres for the man. On September 12, searchers made one last effort to find Raymond. Volunteers scoured the region where Raymond was last seen but again could not locate the man.

Raymond Ewer disappeared approximately twenty miles east of where Garrett Bardsley would disappear thirty-five years later.

Jennifer Lee Klein
Missing: 05/25/74, Colorado River, Moab, Utah
Age at disappearance: 3
3'2", 35 lb.

Jennifer Klein and her family were in a campsite along the Colorado River approximately ten miles north of Moab, Utah. There were several other groups in the nearby campsites and many people in the water and walking the area. Jennifer was playing in the sand near the river. Her father, mother, and brother were all in the immediate area. The father decided to go back to the vehicle to retrieve something when a fight between two dogs broke out. The altercation between the dogs got everyone's attention, and this is when Jennifer disappeared.

Law enforcement was immediately notified and searched the area and river. The parents said they cannot remember anyone in the camp ever being questioned or identified by law enforcement. Many in the area appeared to be transients and will never be identified. A search of the river never found Jennifer and her body never surfaced. The Klein case is still considered an open missing person case in Grand County, Utah.

When you read this book and "Missing 411 Eastern U.S.", you will understand that dogs play a role in the disappearance of many children.

David Mathew Jaramillo
Missing: 06/03/85, East Canyon Reservoir, Salt Lake City, Utah
Age at disappearance: 21
5'8", 160 lb.

David Jaramillo and Lloyd Reese were friends. On June 3, 1985, the boys decided to meet a group of friends at the East Canyon Reservoir in the hills east of Salt Lake City. Sometime during the day's activities, David and Lloyd became separated from the large group and disappeared. Both were last seen in a brown Datsun B210 driven by David.

In May 2010 the Salt Lake City Police Department announced that their cold case unit was reactivating the Reese/Jaramillo because of new and additional evidence. Detective Mike Hamideh stated, "It's the smallest piece of information that could bring closure to these families." The detective also stated that he hoped families and friends who had additional information would come forward. Paul Jaramillo, David's father, was interviewed in May 2010 and stated that he felt the boys either were accidentally killed or something else unfortunate happened to them. The mother of Lloyd Reese, Marsha Clark, stated that there isn't a day that goes by that she doesn't think of Lloyd. At this point there are no formal suspects, and no additional evidence has been made public.

Lloyd M. Reese
Missing: 06/13/85, East Canyon Reservoir, Salt Lake City, Utah
Age at disappearance: 13
5'7", 135 lb.

For details on this case, read the details on David Jaramillo above.

Daniel C. Edmonds Jr.
Missing: 08/22/95, Salem, Utah
Age at disappearance: 22
6'4", 140 lb.

Daniel Edmonds Jr. was last observed at a family member's residence in Salem, Utah. After visiting, Daniel went hiking in the Mount Nebo area south of Salem. It is believed that he was specifically in the Diamond Fork region. His vehicle was found near trails in the area of Mount Nebo. A search of the area failed to find Daniel. Few details are available on this case.

Garrett Bardsley
Missing: 08/20/04, Cuberant Lake, Uinta Mountains, Utah
Age at disappearance: 12
5', 105 lb.

The Garrett Bardsley case ranks in the top ten most unexplainable disappearances I have ever researched.

Kevin Bardsley and his son, Garrett, were camping on a Boy Scout outing at Cuberant Lake in the Uinta Mountains in the Wasatch National Forest of northern Utah. The lake sits in a deep basin at an elevation of approximately 10,200 feet. To the east of the lake is a steep mountain leveling off at eleven thousand feet. On the other side of the mountain is a steep cliff. Mount Marsell is just to the south of the lake and has an elevation of 11,300 feet. Two-thirds of the lake is surrounded by a large mountain, so sits in somewhat of a bowl. The entry and exit point of the lake is to the west, where there are seven other lakes in proximity to Cuberant. This entire region is dotted with hundreds of small lakes with nearby peaks up to twelve thousand feet.

Kevin and Garrett woke early the morning of August 20, 2004, to get a fresh start on the fishing. There was still dew on the ground as Garrett and his dad walked approximately two hundred yards from their campsite to a location at the bank of the lake. As Kevin was rigging the pole for Garrett, Garrett slipped into the water and got his shoes and pants wet. The guys fished for a short while until Garrett stated that they were not catching anything and he would walk back to the camp to change his socks.

Kevin watched as Garrett walked the correct path back to camp until he lost sight of him in the trees. Kevin knew that there would be a group of boys waking up back at camp and Garrett wouldn't be alone. After fifteen to twenty minutes without seeing Garrett, Kevin went back to the camp. Kevin immediately realized that Garrett wasn't in the camp and notified other leaders. He then ran back to the lake calling his son's name. Garrett was never seen again.

The Summit County Sheriff's Office was immediately notified and a massive search was started. It was over a one-hour hike to the closest roadway from the point where Garrett disappeared. Within a short period of time, the sheriff asked for assistance from the FBI.

Searchers found a Nike sock in a field of boulders approximately a half mile from where Garrett was last seen. Garrett's mom identified the sock as belonging to Garrett. The day Garrett disappeared, a storm moved into the area with freezing rain, hail, and snow at higher elevations. This change in weather hampered search operations. Law enforcement officials have stated that there is no evidence that Garrett was abducted, and they believe that he became lost as he headed back to the campsite and later perished from exposure.

There are three other cases of missing boys that have very similar circumstances: Dennis Martin, seven years old, missing June 14, 1969, Great Smoky Mountains National Park, Tennessee; Samuel Boehlke, eight years old, missing October 14, 2006, Crater Lake National Park, Oregon; and Danny Greenwood, Reservation Lake, Mount Baldy, Arizona. In all of these cases, the boys were with their fathers in a national forest/park setting, and there were no females in any of the groups. The boys disappeared into a very remote area, and all of the cases occurred between June and October. The FBI participated in the search for Dennis Martin and Garrett Bardsley, even though they state that they do not participate in searches for missing people (FBI policy). Why they participated in some searches and not others is another mystery that only the local agent in charge can answer. Dennis Martin and Samuel Boelke disappeared in United States National Parks; Garrett Bardsley disappeared in a United States National Forest; Danny Greenwood disappeared in a United States Wilderness Area. The most remote disappearance is Garrett's. A one-hour hike to the nearest road makes the idea of abduction and carrying the victim unlikely, unless the suspect is extremely strong and agile. I would encourage the reader to closely examine each case and absorb what each story tells them. I completed FOIA requests on Samuel Boelke and Dennis Martin and received extensive documents from the NPS on each case. Since both occurred inside a national park, an FOIA request was applicable. Garrett Bardsley's SAR was handled by a local sheriff's department. The FOIA process is not applicable to cities and counties; it only applies to federal agencies.

There are two aspects of the Bardsley case that cause me great concern. First, the father is not a suspect in the case, so eliminate that thought. Garrett was very close to camp when the father lost sight of him. He did lose visual on Garrett when he entered a heavily wooded area. Remember, this lake sits on a small plateau in a half-bowl setting; it's hard to understand how anyone Garrett's age could have been lost when you look at a geological survey map of the region. Half the lake is surrounded by a very steep mountain (he can't climb out that way), and the other half has a steep decline to the Weber River. He would have remembered he hadn't climbed up or down to get to his fishing spot. It's an 800-feet drop over a small mountain down the southwest side of the lake to even get to the point to go down to the river—highly unlikely. First concern: What happened in the forest area to cause Garrett to disappear? This is the lone area in the entire region that offers good cover.

The second issue that causes concern is what the searchers found a half mile from where Garret disappeared: his sock. How would his sock get in the middle of a boulder field? Why would Garrett be in the middle of a boulder field? He would have known he didn't have to cross the field to get to his fishing spot or campsite.

As a closing on the Bardsley case, Kevin has done a fantastic job of funneling his energy by starting a foundation to assist others lost in the woods. He developed a criteria to quickly form search teams, walking in pairs in the woods, etc. Congratulations, Kevin Bardsley!

One thing I have learned from studying the cases of missing boys and girls: You can never take your eyes off your kids when you are in the outdoors—ever! No, this is not pointing a negative finger at Kevin Bardsley. I've been guilty of this with my children. After reading thousands of missing person cases, certain consistencies emerge and certain characteristics about cases become evident. Children disappear in the woods when parents and guardians are not watching them. It's almost as though someone is watching us. When our eyes wander from our kids, they disappear.

Brennan Hawkins
Missing: 06/17/05, 5:30 p.m., Uinta Mountains, Utah
Age at disappearance: 11

The disappearances of Brennan Hawkins and Garret Bardsley have many similarities: location, season, sex, age, and other case facts. Pay close attention to the details of each case. The boys disappeared approximately five miles from each other.

Brennan was with 1,400 other Boy Scouts on a weekend camping trip at the Bear River Boy Scout Camp in the Uinta Mountains of Utah. On Friday, June 17, at approximately 5:30 p.m., Brennan had just climbed a rock-climbing wall and was removing his climbing harness. Other people in the area saw Brennan remove the harness, but that was the last time he was seen.

It had been approximately ten months since Garrett Bardsley disappeared ten miles away at Cuberant Lake. The search for Garrett was very lengthy, but he was never found.

Kevin Bardsley, Garrett's father, responded to the search for Brennan and added additional support for the family.

Searchers set quadrants and a search pattern to find the boy. Most of the search was in an area downhill from where the boy vanished. The search carried on for three days without any significant success. On Tuesday, a searcher was outside the search grids and uphill from where Brennan was last seen when he found the boy standing in an ATV trail. A Fox News story on June 22, 2005, stated the following: "Volunteer Forest Nunley, a 43-year-old house painter from Salt Lake City, was the searcher who found Brennan. Nunley said he came across the boy 'standing in the middle of the trail. He was all muddy and wet.'" Brennan was found near Lily Lake, five miles from the point he was last seen. Later in the same article, SAR Commander and Sheriff Dave Edmonds stated that "Brennan walked straight up a ridge for several miles from the point where he went missing. Contrary to earlier reports, Hawkins did not cross a river and was not wet when found." Hmm, the searcher who had found the boy clearly stated that the boy was found wet. How would Brennan have gotten wet if he was on top of a ridge?

The thousands of newspaper articles I have read in the last several years have shown me that law enforcement and the press try to twist the facts at times to fit the story they want to place in front of the public. I've seen this too many times. I believe that there are more details to this story that need explanation.

Brennan's disappearance mimics many I have researched, especially when it describes the missing person's location when they are found. A June 23 article in the *New Mexican* states, "Brennan does not remember much of the four days he was missing, his parents said. They said they do plan to push him to talk about his time in the woods, but they have learned few answers ... Brennan's mother said he believes he was gone only one or two nights and doesn't remember even going camping or much else because most of it is a blur to him."

I think it is incredibly important for searchers to interview the lost after they are found. We need to understand human behavior of all ages and socioeconomic backgrounds if we are to successfully launch SAR efforts. There is some reason that so many people suppress their memories and don't remember what happened to them while they were lost.

I believe that it's extremely possible that many answers to Garrett Bardsley's disappearance can be found in closely understanding the facts behind Brennan's disappearance. A complete incident debriefing with Brennan is critical to understanding the totality of the event. I would hope when Brennan gets older that he does submit to an extensive interview about his disappearance.

Kenneth R. Schneider
Missing: 10/03/05, near Canyonlands National Park, Utah
Age at disappearance: 78
5'11", 180 lb.

Kenneth Schneider is a successful published author of several fine books, *Autoking vs. Mankind, On The Nature of Cities, Runaway Economy*, and *Forging a More Perfect Union*. He was born in Central Utah and was visiting the canyons in the area after he arrived on his trip from his home in Seattle, Washington. On October 3, 2005, Kenneth was driving his gray '90s Nissan Sentra in Stevens Canyon off Highway 211 near Canyonlands National Park close to Monticello, Utah. A couple of Good Samaritans stopped to help when they saw that Kenneth had gotten his vehicle stuck in a ditch. That same couple returned later and saw that the car was stuck again, but Kenneth wasn't in the area. The couple found a note stating that Kenneth was walking to a ranch eight miles away.

Stevens Canyon is the location where Schneider's vehicle got stuck. The elevation in the valley is six thousand feet, and it is on the fringe of the Manti-La Sal National Forest. This is also the topographic border between the desert and the green forests of the region. This is approximately ten air miles from Monticello but probably forty actual driving miles from the city. Schneider was approximately eight miles from State Highway 211.

Law enforcement started a search for Kenneth, but he was never found. Police were able to contact Kenneth's family and determined that he had a hip condition that prevented him from walking more than a half mile without discomfort. Law enforcement and family members believe that Kenneth became lost or injured and died in the area. The San Juan County Sheriff's Office still holds a case file on Kenneth Schneider.

Clinton Jason Daines
Missing: 10/16/09, Big Mountain Monument, Salt Lake City, Utah
Age at disappearance: 35
5'11", 120 lb.

Clinton Daines is an avid outdoorsman who apparently decided to go deer hunting on opening day 2009. His 2003 Ford Ranger pickup was found by searchers in the Big Monument parking lot in East Canyon. Inside the truck law enforcement found an empty box of 9mm hollow-point shells; they later found he had just purchased a new Glock pistol.

Big Mountain Monument is a majestic sixty-feet-tall statue commemorating the Mormon Trail east of Salt Lake City. The parking lot is at the head of Emigration Canyon, which leads into the mountains at the foot of Pioneer Trail State Park.

A search of the area was performed without finding Clinton. There are few leads in this case.

Colorado

Colorado Missing People

Colorado is the only state with fifty-three peaks towering over fourteen thousand feet. It offers fantastic wildlife viewing, fishing, and hiking. It has large-population zones within a thirty-minute drive of gorgeous forests. Colorado is fortunate to have many of the world's best ski resorts, including Vail, Aspen, Breckenridge, Snowmass, and Beaver Creek. If you enjoy the outdoors, Colorado would be a great state to call home.

This chapter describes some of the most unusual disappearances of people I have ever researched. There are no reasonable explanations for many of these people simply vanishing in areas where there was no place to hide and no roads for an abductor to make an escape.

It is an interesting coincidence that four of the first five people featured in this chapter have a disparity in age of only two years, and then, after a thirty-three-year gap in disappearances, the profile of the missing in Colorado changes significantly.

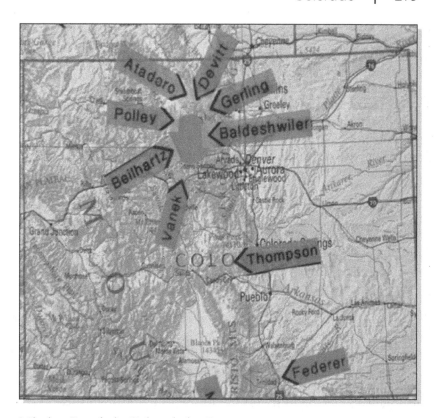

Missing People in Colorado by Date

Missing Person	Date Missing•Age•Sex
Joseph Halpern	08/15/33•22•M
Albert Beilhartz	07/02/38•4•M
Ernest Polley	07/23/43•22•M
David Devitt	10/09/49•21•M
Bruce Gerling	10/09/49•20•M
	33-Year Gap
Robert Baldeshwiler	06/29/82•12•M
Jaryd Atadero	10/02/99•3•M
Teresa Schmidt	09/06/02•53•F.
Michelle Vanek	09/24/05•35•F
Evan Thompson	05/27/06•8•M

Joseph Halpern
Missing: 08/15/33, Taylor Peak, Rocky Mountain National Park, CO
Age at disappearance: 22

Summer is a great time for college students to escape the stress of the academic life and look for a wilderness adventure. That's exactly what twenty-two-year-old Joseph Halpern, along with his parents and a friend, Joseph Gerrick, did in August 1933.

Halpern was a graduate student at the University of Chicago and held a summer job at the Yerkes Observatory in Williams Bay, Wisconsin. He traveled from Williams Bay to meet with the group and establish camp. Gerrick and Halpern discussed which mountain they would climb; they chose Taylor Peak (elevation 13,100 feet) in the Rocky Mountain National Park.

The group camped in Glacier Basin, and the two men decided to make their ascent on the morning of August 15. Halpern got an early start and was the lead climber. He quickly outpaced Gerrick. In a few hours, Gerrick couldn't hear or see his partner. He was getting nervous. He continued to call out for his friend as he made his ascent—no answer. Gerrick decided to descend. He notified park personnel and a search was quickly initiated.

NPS SAR teams were directed by Gerrick and searched the rugged slope where Halpern was last seen. They blanketed the mountain for six days and didn't find one piece of equipment or any evidence of Joseph Halpern. Park officials even checked the sign-in book at the summit of Taylor Peak—no signature. Over 150 searchers participated in the SAR, but nobody could even find the small backpack Halpern was carrying.

It's been almost eighty years since Joseph Halpern disappeared, and nothing has ever been found indicating that he was on Taylor Peak. There are very similar disappearances of climbers on several large peaks in the western United States.

Albert Beilhartz
Missing: 07/02/38, 8:30 a.m., Roaring River, Rocky Mountain National Park, CO
Age at disappearance: 4
Blonde hair

I filed an FOIA request with the Rocky Mountain District of the United States National Park Service for all documents and photographs related to the Albert Beilhartz disappearance. I was advised that all reports for this time period were destroyed.

If there is one case in this book that exemplifies the difficulties, complexities, twists and turns common to missing persons cases, this is it.

The Beilhartzes left their Denver home for a long holiday weekend at Rocky Mountain National Park. The family drove through Estes Park and west through the valley that parallels the Fall River until they arrived at the confluence of the Roaring River. The family then drove northwest on Old Fall River Road, which was normally closed during the winter, to arrive slightly north of the junction of the two rivers and establish their camp on the Roaring River.

The area around the Roaring and Fall rivers is a low basin with an approximate elevation of 8,600 feet, with surrounding mountains rising to over fourteen thousand feet. The region has many small lakes, streams, and rivers, and there are many wild mammals throughout the area.

Early on Saturday morning, July 2, the Beilhartz family had a mountain breakfast and then walked off hiking toward the Roaring River. The family hiked north along the Roaring and was immediately surrounded by beautiful, large, thick pine trees that completely engulfed the valley and the river. This valley has very steep walls on both sides, and the river runs down the center. After approximately thirty minutes of enjoying the scenery, William Beilhartz realized that he hadn't seen his son, Albert, in several minutes. He started to search for the boy. The casual search soon turned frantic as there were few areas that Albert could have escaped to or hid. William eventually ran back to camp and requested assistance from law enforcement officials.

It wasn't long before the NPS had rallied hundreds of volunteers and official staff to search for Albert. One of the first supervisors on the scene made the assumption that the boy had fallen in the river and probably drowned. The NPS summoned four sets of canine tracking teams to search the area in an effort to track scent. What you are about to read is fact, and it exemplifies one of two possibilities for the press: one, they manipulate the news so you only hear what the NPS wants you to hear; or, two, news agencies are very inept. The first story is dated July 5, 1937. The *St. Petersburg Times* reported the following: "The dogs picked up the boy's trail near the spot where he was last seen and followed it for a mile and a half along the banks of the Roaring River to the Junction of the Ypsilon Peak and Lawn Lake Trails. There the hounds seemed to lose the trail." This clue would mean that the boy traveled upstream and uphill against every young child's normal behavior and intuition. Another article dated July 5, 1937, by the *Evening Independent*, reported, "Bloodhounds repeatedly led searching crews to the edge of the riverbank yesterday." This article was followed the next day by more remarks from the NPS stating the boy probably drowned. These are two different articles about the same missing person event: one is right, one is wrong.

The NPS was so concerned that Albert may have drowned, they obtained authority from the Colorado Fish and Game to divert the Roaring River with sand bags and dynamite five beaver dams in an effort to empty the river. They also placed a large screen just before the Fall River to catch the body should it flow downstream. The NPS blew up the beaver dams, diverted the water flow, and emptied the Roaring River. The NPS did not find Albert in the empty riverbank. Around this time the Beilhartzes were getting frustrated with the park service's claims the boy had drowned and started to make their own allegations. They believed their boy had been kidnapped.

It appeared that somebody in government service was starting to listen to the family's concerns. On July 7, a searcher was looking through an abandoned cabin and found what they believed to be a fresh bandage. The searcher remembered that Mrs. Beilhartz had told the NPS that her son was wearing a bandage over his heel because his new boots had caused a blister. The FBI took custody of the evidence and stated they would test the bandage, but they never reported whether or not it belonged to Albert. It was also never understood why the FBI chose to be involved in this case, as there was no direct evidence that the found bandage was Albert's or that he had been abducted, but the FBI chose to be involved.

The day Albert disappeared, a married couple, the Eellses, were walking on a roadway adjacent to Mount Chapin, which is six miles to the west of where Albert went missing. The couple were resting on the side of the mountain completely unaware of the search being conducted thousands of feet below. They saw something very peculiar. The following is from a July 8 article in the afternoon edition of the *Greeley Tribune*: "The Beilhartz child disappeared at 8:00 a.m. (approximately). Eells said he and his wife had walked far up the Old Fall River Road until they became tired. He said that they stopped to rest and then looking far up the mountain (Mount Chapin) side saw a boy sitting on a rock. When the couple climbed to the point near the rock, Eells said that the little boy disappeared. He expressed belief that no child could have reached the spot without assistance."

Mr. Eells drove back to the park after he and his wife realized that a boy was missing. He gave an extensive interview to park administrators and actually took them back to the spot he had seen the boy. The NPS was so convinced by Eells' story that they formed an advanced search team to climb Mount Chapin. An article titled "Search Group For Baby Climb To Devils Nest" in the *Greeley Tribune* morning edition read: "A searching party will be sent at dawn into the rugged Devils Nest region high on the slope of Mount Chapin in an attempt to find a 4½-year-old boy missing since Sunday. The decision to expand the search to this area, six miles from the spot the child was last seen, was reached late today when park officials returned from a trip to the region where a Denver man said he saw at 1:00 p.m. Sunday what he believed was a small child."

Remember, I believe that peaks, valleys, lakes, and rivers get their names for specific reasons. How did Devils Nest get its name?

Searchers combed Mount Chapin but did not find Albert. I am very sad to report that Albert was never found, and few articles about his disappearance ever surfaced after the initial search.

Many of the incidents surrounding Albert's disappearance struck me as very, very odd, and I wanted to learn about the area where he went missing. I continued to plunder through periodicals and reports for weeks trying to understand the area and the local history. I was surprised, but not shocked, by what I learned.

The disappearance of Albert Beilhartz started a series of strange catastrophic events in Rocky Mountain National Park that you will never read about in any official park documents. On July 2, 1938, Albert Beilhartz disappeared. Twenty-nine days later, William Brunie and John Fuller (college students from Iowa) were attempting to climb Long's Peak (14,235 feet) inside the Rocky Mountain National Park and approximately sixteen miles from Mount Chapin. The following is the article from the *Helena Montana Independent* dated August 9, 1938: "John Fuller, 20-year-old college student from Iowa, was killed today climbing Long's Peak, a 14,235-foot mountain in Rocky Mountain National Park. Fuller fell to his death from a rock wall towering above a steeply pitched snowfield. J. Harton Herschler, chief park ranger, said, 'William Brunie of Lincoln, Nebraska, climbed the peak with a companion and reported he saw a man crossing the snowfield and later saw his body cascading over the snow.'"

This is a very strange description of a mountaineering accident. A man is seen in a snowfield and then a man is seen flying over the snow. The article almost makes it appear as though Fuller was thrown or launched out over a ledge and over the snow. The article later stated that this was the first death from mountain climbing at the park since 1935; this wasn't going to be the last in 1938.

Ten days after John Fuller died, Robert Watson (21) was climbing Red Mountain, five miles east of Mount Chapin, when a rockslide killed him.

Five days after Robert Watson died, Rowland Spencer (18) from Kansas City was staying with a group at the YMCA inside the Rocky Mountain National Park. An August 23 article by the Associated Press had the following: "Rowland Spencer, 18 of Kansas City, was killed today in a fall on 'Giants Track Mountain,' a short distance east of the east boundary of the Rocky Mountain National Park."

Readers, if I had made these stories up, you'd say they were too far-fetched. No, the names, locations, and events you just read are facts. How did a mountain get the name "Giants Track Mountain"? I have no idea.

The further I read into the history of many of the high peaks in Rocky Mountain National park, the more I found disturbing trends and deaths. Could mere coincidence explain three deaths and one missing child in a fifty-two-day span? Are "Devils Nest" and "Giants Track Mountain" locations that happen to come into this story by pure coincidence? Something very strange was occurring in the Rocky Mountain National Park in 1938.

Ernest Polley
Missing: 07/23/43, Lindbergh Peak (now known as Lone Eagle Peak), Indian Peaks Wilderness, CO
Age at disappearance: unknown

William Mays (24) and Ernest Polley were on a summer vacation from their jobs at Alcoa Aluminum in Cleveland. The men were alumni from the Colorado School of Mines where both had been graduate students. William was interested in fishing and Ernest was a mountain climber. In July 1943 the men hiked into an area now known as the Indian Peaks Wilderness, a very desolate and foreboding area. There are few trees at higher elevations, and jagged, rough cliffs made climbing the peaks extremely hazardous.

The men made camp at the base of Lindbergh Peak (now known as Lone Eagle Peak). They left their belongings at the campsite, and William left to fish Crater Lake (no, not the Crater Lake in Oregon but an interesting coincidence). Ernest turned his attention to Lone Eagle Peak at the south side of the lake.

Ernest never came back from the mountain. William hiked out to notify authorities. A massive six-day search ensued with supplies being brought into Crater Lake to support the teams on the mountain. The weather rapidly changed during the search and rain hit the area. The only item that searchers found to even indicate any human had ever been on the mountain is a mud and rock basin made to gather water. Searchers located the water basin two thousand feet up the mountain from Crater Lake.

The head ranger working the SAR made a decision on July 29 that the formal search for Ernest Polley would end. The SAR discovered nothing.

Case Summary

It doesn't make sense that Ernest had any involvement making the water basin. At only two thousand feet up from the lake, he should have had sufficient water for his trip. These types of water catches are usually only made when someone is going to be at a location for an extended period of time. The individual that built the basin was someone who was going to frequent the region, not Ernest.

I have seen many photos of Lone Eagle Peak, and it's truly hard to understand how anyone can go missing in that location. There are few areas to hide, not many large boulders, and it has many, many acres of wide-open terrain. It is a real mystery what happened to Ernest Polley. The disappearance of Polley is very similar to the disappearance of Carl Landers, who went missing from Mount Shasta in northern California in similar circumstances and terrain. Many other climbers have gone missing from high peaks while climbing alone under similar circumstances.

David Devitt, age 21
Bruce Gerling, age 20
Missing: 10/09/49, Flattop Mountain, Rocky Mountain National Park, CO

College students in Colorado can enjoy the great outdoors without driving hundreds of miles. Eleven Colorado A&M students decided to go on a big adventure to the Rocky Mountain National Park in October of 1949. The group had decided they would hike a trail over the 12,300-foot Flattop Mountain, making their start point at Grand Lake and ending their trip at Bear Lake.

Everything about the A&M excursion started very well. On Sunday afternoon, for reasons that are not clear, two of the students got separated from the main group—David Devitt of Arvada, Colorado, and Bruce Gerling from Phoenix, Arizona. It wasn't until late Monday afternoon that the others realized the two had not arrived at the designated location. They notified authorities.

As SAR teams were being assembled, the park service was closing the mountain to travelers because a fierce snowstorm was hitting Rocky Mountain Park. Rangers set up a base camp at Bear

Lake, six miles from Estes Park. A search was initiated and almost immediately a call for assistance was made to the army at Camp Carson in Colorado Springs. Fourteen handpicked men specially trained for extreme winter operations responded to the SAR call.

After one arduous week of searching, sometimes searching in unbearable conditions, the chief ranger for Rocky Mountain National Park, Barton Hershaler, met with Lt. E. C. Gulczynski, commander of the dispatched army team. The two men came to the conclusion that they had searched every conceivable location where David and Bruce could have been. Both commanders agreed to terminate the search. They explained that the hands and feet of searchers were frostbitten by the severe cold and strong winds, and they feared that the David and Bruce couldn't have survived the conditions. The leaders also expressed concern for the safety of the SAR teams as another reason to terminate the search.

David and Bruce have never been found.

Robert Baldeshwiler
Missing: 06/29/82, Flattop Mountain, Rocky Mountain National Park, CO
Age at disappearance: 12

Martin and Lois Baldeshwiler left their Lansing, Illinois, home bound for the Rocky Mountains. Once they arrived in Denver, they set their sights on Rocky Mountain National Park just to the north. Martin and Lois were traveling with their twelve-year-old son, Robert, and knew they could partake in physical activities because of Robert's athletic abilities and age.

Once the family arrived at the park, they decided to climb 12,234-foot Flattop Mountain because the trail was very well traveled, easy to follow, and only 1.9 miles from beginning to end. No special abilities are needed to climb the mountain, and the dirt and gravel path is almost perfect for the entire trip. There are some large boulders along the route, but they can be easily navigated.

Soon after the family started their trip, Robert accelerated past his parents and was always in front of the group. The hike didn't have any special incidents. They passed a few hikers going up and down, nothing out of the ordinary. As they got closer to the summit, dark clouds started to loom on the horizon and it appeared a storm may be close. At this point in the trip, Robert was out of the couple's sight. They quickened their pace but still couldn't see their son. A man coming down the mountain was later questioned and confirmed that he had seen the boy hiking to the summit alone and was concerned because a storm was coming. The couple became very concerned when they couldn't find their son and went back down the hill to notify park rangers.

About the time Martin and Lois reported Robert missing, a horrendous rain storm hit the park. Park officials quickly gathered emergency crews and started to search the possible areas. The next six days saw one of the largest searches in the history of Rocky Mountain National Park. Over 250 people participated in the seven-day search; two helicopters were doing flyovers; tracking dogs were brought to the mountain; and over $114,000 dollars were expended looking for Robert. Fifty square miles were blanketed by the park service. At one point searchers were less than ten feet apart as they walked the mountain in a line looking for the boy.

A July 6, 1982, article in the *Telegraph Herald* stated the following: "Officials called off their search for a twelve-year-old Illinois boy missing for a week in Rocky Mountain National Park, saying they are mystified by the lack of clues."

Glen Kaye, the park spokesperson for this SAR, added, "There is absolutely no trace and the search was thorough. There has not been a footprint or piece of clothing—nothing." Glen confirmed that teams had dropped into crevices, holes, behind boulders—every conceivable place a twelve-year-old boy could hide.

An article in the *News and Courier* of July 6, 1982, added the following: "Kaye said searchers were positioned Monday in a narrow band about a half mile wide and planned to traverse an area from the 11,000 feet elevation to about 9,000 feet ... Robert, who was running ahead of his family when he became lost, was heading into a storm, leading officials to speculate he may have sought shelter at lower elevations. It's also more common for young kids to go downhill than uphill." The search was terminated without the NPS finding any shred of evidence that Robert was ever on the mountain.

On July 12, 1982, six days later, hikers on Flattop Mountain saw a bloody visor in a snow bank and reported the find to rangers.

Late in the afternoon, two rangers were sent to investigate the visor and found the body of Robert Baldeshwiler on a steep slope on the mountain. A July 12, 1982, article in the *Lawrence World Journal* stated, "Kaye said the body of Robert Baldeshwiler, 12, lay at an elevation of 11,200 feet on 12,324-feet Flattop Mountain, where the boy disappeared while on a family hiking trip ... The boy was found on a rock in an area that was previously searched ... He may have fallen all the way in one swoop, but since the area was searched before, it's possible the body could have tumbled part way at a later time."

Case Summary

As you read this book you will quickly start to realize that many of these stories have a similar tone. I'll let you develop your own hypothesis at this point, but later I will explain some issues and concerns regarding this SAR.

The NPS stated that they were concentrating their search between 9,000 and 11,000 feet. Knowing the elevations they were working, they must have believed 11,000 feet was the highest probable point that Robert would be located. The NPS (Glen Kaye) stated that they had searched the area where Robert's body was eventually found. OK, but how did the body get there? If you follow the explanation given by Glen, Robert must have fallen after the search was conducted. OK, but how high must he have gone in order to fall *down* to 11,200 feet? How did he get that high? The NPS and SAR teams are considered experts at this type of incident. How could they have made this egregious mistake? Did they make a mistake?

One of the last statements Glen made is the general belief that children, when lost, usually walk downhill. Robert was twelve years old. He knew the parking lot and the safety of his family's car were downhill, not uphill. He knew the comfort of his parents' arms were below him, not above him. It would be very difficult to figure out why Robert ended up higher in elevation than SAR commanders believed he would be located. It would seem prudent to believe he may be lower than the point expected if he turned and ran downhill just as he was running uphill. What would have prompted Robert to continue moving uphill, especially knowing bad weather was on the way? Did something else happen on Flattop Mountain that we don't know about? I do not believe that the helicopters could've missed a bloody piece of clothing against the white backdrop of the snow with Robert's body nearby. The facts almost insinuate that the body was placed in its location after the search.

There are many stories in this book about hikers and climbers who are alone at high elevation and simply vanish. There is no evidence of where they went; they don't leave behind equipment or clues; they simply cannot be found.

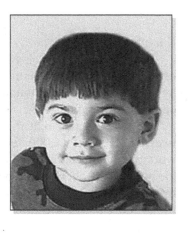

Jaryd Atadero
Missing: 10/02/99, Comanche Peak
Wilderness, CO
Age at disappearance: 3
3'6", 40 lb.

In October of 1999, Allyn Atadero was a physical education teacher in Jefferson County, Colorado. Allyn is the father of a three-year-old boy and six-year-old girl. Allyn owned the Poudre River Resort on the South Fork of Poudre River in Larimer County, Colorado. The resort was approximately fifty miles west of Fort Collins and seventy-five miles northwest of Denver.

During the weekend of October 1–3, 1999, Allyn Atadero's resort was host to a singles-group excursion, the Christian Singles Network. The group was going to have an outdoor excursion at a beautiful resort before winter hit the region. The gorgeous resort sits on Highway 14 and is an easy drive from downtown Denver.

On Saturday the group decided to drive initially to a fish hatchery (This is what was told to Allyn, the group later changed their plans without notifying Jaryd's dad) and then drove on to the Big South Trail that parallels the Poudre River and enters the Comanche Peak Wilderness. Allyn's daughter and son were at the resort with him, and the daughter asked if she could go with the singles and hike the trail. Allyn had taken his daughter on the trails in the past and knew she understood the rules, so he allowed her to go. Jaryd, Allyn's son, saw the group leaving and pleaded with his dad to allow him to go with his sister and the other eleven singles. Allyn later stated that he knew Jaryd had not gone before but also saw the boy really wanted to go with the group. He relented and allowed Jaryd to go. He saw the face of his son as the cars were leaving and remembers Jaryd's smiling face as they left the lodge parking lot.

The singles group first went to the fish hatchery and then drove to and parked near the entrance of the Big South Trail, and a few people took responsibility for watching the kids as they hiked the path (Remember, Allyn never knew his kids were going to the trail). Within a short period of time, Jaryd was running ahead of the group, hiding in the bushes adjacent to the trail and scaring the singles as they walked by. After hiking approximately a mile and a half, one of the people who were supposed to keep track of Jaryd realized that he hadn't seen him in fifteen to twenty-five minutes. It was probably during this time that the boy ran ahead of the group and completely out of their view.

The Big South Trail parallels the Poudre River. On one side of the trail is the river and on the other side are very steep mountain walls. There are big trees with heavy forests in the areas adjacent to the river and many places to hide and be concealed.

Once the singles group realized that Jaryd was missing, they looked throughout the area for the boy. Someone drove back to the resort to tell Allyn that everything was "OK" and Jaryd was "OK," but they just couldn't find him. This started the mechanism for an all-out search for Jaryd. The Larimer County Sheriff's Office, U.S. Forest Service, and other law enforcement agencies responded.

Searchers spoke with two fishermen who were farther down the river in the direction that the group last saw Jaryd. The fishermen stated that they had seen the boy. Apparently, Jaryd approached them and asked, "Are there bears in these woods?" The fisherman didn't think much of the question and didn't see anyone along the river or near the boy. This is the last confirmed sighting of Jaryd Atadero.

The Larimer County Sheriff's Office started the SAR operation for Jaryd and was the lead law enforcement agency on the case. They brought canines in to search the area, but they were unable to find Jaryd's track or his scent. An air force helicopter even joined the search but eventually crashed, injuring several of the five personnel on board. A massive search by over seventy people, canines, helicopters, and planes produced nothing of evidentiary value. There were a few missteps in this case: one being that they found Jaryd's footprints cross the track of a mountain lion. Experts brought into the case confirmed the tracks were made at different times and didn't relate to one another.

After searchers had thoroughly and completely covered every inch of the area they felt Jaryd could be located—with bad weather and winter approaching—the sheriff's office determined they had to forego any further searching. With the news that searchers had not found any evidence that Jaryd was in the area, Allyn asked the sheriff's office to have the FBI join the search. On October 7, 1999, five days after Jaryd disappeared, Larimer Sheriff's Office spokesperson Cindy Gordon stated, "The possibility of an abduction was very slim."

OK, Deputy Gordon said "very slim" but not impossible. The sheriff's office did not want the FBI to join the case because they stated they had no evidence that an abduction occurred; but then again, they didn't have any evidence that it didn't occur. The sheriff stated that the FBI was monitoring the Jaryd Atadero case. Allyn went to his local congressman for assistance in having the FBI join the case because he was convinced that Jaryd was abducted. Again, the FBI wasn't actively involved but was apparently contacted by the congressman.

Allyn became frustrated with the sheriff, stating that there was no evidence to determine where Jaryd may have gone, but they were unwilling to admit to the possibility that Jaryd had been abducted.

After the official search for Jaryd ended, many volunteers and others continued to search the area after the winter snows cleared. The area where Jaryd disappeared was near nine thousand feet in elevation.

On June 10, 2003, almost four years after Jaryd disappeared, hikers were in the area of the original disappearance and found pieces of clothing. The hikers knew about Jaryd's disappearance, so they took some of the clothes but left pieces to identify the location. Larimer County Sheriff's Office sent investigators to the scene. They recovered one pair of pants, inside out with right leg torn off, a pair of tennis shoes, and a pullover coat with tears in it. Photos were taken of the clothes and forwarded to Allyn for review. Allyn confirmed that these were the clothes that Jaryd was wearing the day he disappeared. The clothing was found 550 feet up from the Big South Trail on an extremely steep hillside. The sheriff further stated that it did not appear that there was any blood on any of the recovered clothing.

On June 14, investigators went back into the area and searched for additional evidence of Jaryd's presence. One hundred fifty feet from where the clothing was found, investigators discovered the top of a child's skull and one tooth, but nothing else. Investigators stated that they had to carefully climb on all fours to reach the location where the bone and tooth were found. On June 14 at 5:10 p.m., thedenverchannel.com had the following statement in an article about the recovery of Jaryd Atadero's remains: "Sheriff's officials, who have come under fire recently for not previously searching on foot in the area where Jaryd's clothing was found, contend the boy could not have climbed the slope alone. Campanella said adult investigators had to scramble up the slope on all fours to recover the rest of the boy's clothing." I have just one question for the sheriff: How did Jaryd and his clothes get up the hill if he couldn't have climbed there himself?

There are many issues in the Jaryd Atadero case that remind us of other cases in this book, such as the case of Charles McCullar in Crater Lake. Charles went missing and was found in a remote wilderness; only his skull and small bone fragments were found. Much of his clothing was never found. There is also the case of Garrett Bardsley in Utah. Garret walked away from his dad's position at a lake, attempted to walk back to camp, and disappeared, never to be found. A piece of his clothing was found uphill from the trail he should have taken. Again, it was an unusual place for clothing to be found. There is also the case of Geraldine Huggan from Northern Ontario. The young girl disappeared and few remains were found. The girl's pants were found inside out. No blood was found on the clothes. Bart Schleyer from Yukon disappeared and only small pieces of the man were found. Schleyer's pants were found with no blood on them. These cases have significant similarities that are not normally associated with the recovery of a missing person's remains.

There was another strange statement made by law enforcement in regards to Jaryd's tennis shoes. The boy disappeared in October of 1999, and the clothing was recovered in June of 2003. That would be four winters in the elements. A statement was made that it didn't appear that the tennis shoes had spent an extreme amount of time in the elements. A photo of the shoes was run in several publications, and they still had fairly vibrant colors.

Case Summary

I believe that the Larimer County Sheriff's Office conducted an extensive and comprehensive search for Jaryd Atadero. Knowing the mindset of SAR personnel, they are dedicated, thorough, and attentive to details. I don't believe that the personnel would have missed a location 550 feet off the trail where Jaryd disappeared. If ground searchers had missed the clothes, then I believe the canines would definitely have hit on the scent. It is also in the immediate area of the comprehensive helicopter search.

As in the McCuller, Huggan, Schleyer, and Bardsley cases, the question is how the clothes and remains got to the locations in the condition that they did. As is stated by law enforcement sources, it was nearly impossible for Jaryd to get to the location on the hillside where his remains were found, just as in the McCuller case. How did he get through twenty-foot drifts of snow and end up in the Bybee Creek drainage (Crater Lake, Oregon)?

It almost appears as though Jaryd's remains were placed in the recovery location at some point near the time the discovery was made. If the tennis shoes were not in the elements for four winters, then someone placed them out in the open where they were recovered. Allyn Atadero believed that his son was abducted, as there was no evidence he was on the trail where he disappeared. Allyn was so sure his son was abducted that he asked Congress and the FBI for assistance. Well, maybe he was correct.

The tooth that was recovered from the hillside was evaluated by a forensic dentist and positively identified as Jaryd's. I never read one article that attempted to explain what animal would completely devour every bone in Jaryd's body except what was left. Where are the rest of the remains?

Allyn and Arlyn Atadero wrote a book about the Jaryd Atadero missing person case, *Missing: The Jaryd Atadero Story*. It's worth a read. My personal prayers are with the Atadero family.

Authors Note: The Jaryd Atadero disappearance is one of the cases highlighted in our movie, "Missing 411." Please refer to our website for additional details, www.canammissing.com

Teresa Schmidt
Missing: 09/06/02, Deckers, CO
Age at disappearance: 53
5'2", 100 lb.

The Lost Valley Guest Ranch is located approximately twelve miles west of Deckers, Colorado, and approximately forty miles northwest of Colorado Springs. The ranch has over fifteen buildings, a swimming pool, a main lodge, and horse stables. The four-diamond resort sits in a beautiful valley just west of Cheesman Reservoir. The ranch has been owned for over fifty years by the Foster family and is now owned and operated by Bob and Karen Foster. The facility has catered to the wealthy for many years, and at over $250 per night, you need to have some cash to stay there.

During the first week in September of 2002, Lost Valley Guest Ranch was hosting a medical convention. Among the guests were Doctor Wiltz Wagner and his wife, Teresa Schmidt, from Avon, Indiana. Wiltz was a professor at Indiana University specializing in physiology and biophysics. Teresa was a social worker and author and very successful in her professional practice. Wiltz was going to attend the various seminars at the convention, and Teresa was going to visit the grounds, see the stables, and enjoy the mountain landscape. Teresa knew the area. She had been at the ranch before a huge fire hit the region on June 8, 2002. It was the largest fire at that point in Colorado's history and caused 40 million dollars in damage to the 137,000 acres that it charred. The fire skirted the Lost Valley resort but destroyed much of the foliage around the ranch's perimeter.

Teresa hadn't hiked the area since the fire ravaged the grounds just over two months earlier. On Friday afternoon of September 6, Teresa told her husband that she was going on a hike. She was going to take a water bottle and some snacks and head east toward the Overlook Trail, which leads to a view of Cheesman Lake. Teresa was known to take these types of hikes and had a great appreciation of the outdoors.

Teresa was last seen at approximately 3:00 p.m. on a trail leading toward the rocky point that overlooks Cheesman Lake. This point is quite visible on a Google Earth Map and is just northeast of the ranch. When Teresa had not returned by 7:00 p.m., her husband reported her missing to the staff.

Jefferson County Sheriff's deputies initially organized the search for Teresa, but then Alpine Search and Rescue did a majority of the actual search, with the assistance of canines, helicopters, motorcycles, and horses. The terrain in the area where Teresa disappeared is not that rugged, and it did not have significant ground cover because of the fire. You would encounter significant ground cover traveling east toward the reservoir, but little on the valley floor.

The search only produced one clue as to Teresa even being in the area. The searchers found one of her footprints on each side of the ridge near the overlook, but that is it. Jim Shires from the Jefferson County Sheriff's Department made the following statement referring to the search: "There was nothing, not a water bottle, not a candy wrapper." The search effort also brought five different canine teams to the spot Teresa was last seen. Dogs were not able to pick up a viable scent trail or refused to search.

The search was hampered by heavy rain Sunday night. A flash flood advisory was in effect until 5:00 a.m. Tuesday for the entire region. All aircraft were grounded from Sunday night until Tuesday morning. Searchers stated that the inclement weather obliterated any opportunity to find tracks belonging to Teresa.

The search for Teresa Schmidt was officially terminated late in the afternoon of September 12. The search encompassed four days, nearly one hundred volunteers, three helicopters, five search dogs, and nine agencies. This entire effort to find Teresa only produced two footprints.

Case Summary

Teresa Schmidt's case was included in this chapter for a variety of reasons. The guest ranch sits at approximately 7,600 feet in elevation. The overlook is about a half mile from the ranch and has a peak elevation of 8,400 feet. The overlook is one of only two rocky knobs to the east of the ranch, but there is an entire boulder field as you go west. Cheesman Lake is one mile east of the overlook and sits at an elevation of 6,900 feet.

The disappearance of Teresa occurred at an entirely different type of topography than the other missing people described in this chapter. The mountains where Teresa disappeared are much smaller and gentler than the mountains where most people have vanished in Colorado. There is also a difference in that Teresa was in an area that was recently ravaged by a horrendous fire. The fire left very little ground cover to hide something or someone.

Bad weather obliterated any opportunity to find Teresa. If you have been in an area scorched by fire, you know that ash on the ground is a great conductor of tracks. The torrential rains that hit the area just after Teresa disappeared contributed to the angst of the searchers and were one of the major factors that contributed to Teresa not being found.

Teresa knew the area where she was hiking. She had food and water. If she had been attacked by wild animals, remnants of her body would have been visible during low air flights, and dogs would have picked up the scent, even after torrential rains. I don't believe that any known predator attacked Teresa. There are elk in the area, but elk don't eat or abduct people. In high-elevation searches, there is always the possibility that an avalanche obliterated and entombed a body, but not in this case as the hills and mountains are much too gentle to generate a ground movement such as this.

Looking at the list of missing people who have disappeared in Colorado in the last seventy years, I think it's a little unusual that the last two missing adults are the only two missing women on the entire list. Something atypical happened to Teresa Schmidt, and I pray for her family.

Michelle Vanek
Missing: 09/24/05, Mount of the Holy Cross, Eagle County, CO
Age at disappearance: 35
Blonde hair

Michelle Vanek was a married mother of four and a triathlete in superb physical condition. By 2005, a family friend named Eric Sawyer had climbed thirty-eight of Colorado's fifty-three mountains with elevations over fourteen thousand feet, but he still had not conquered Mount of the Holy Cross. Michelle had always told Eric that she wished to climb one of the easier mountains when he was available to accompany her.

On September 24, 2005, they started their journey to climb Mount of the Holy Cross at the Half Moon Campground in Eagle County. They were going to take a route to the summit and be back before darkness hit the area. Both hikers brought warm clothing, food and water. Michelle also brought a pair of ski poles that she would use as walking sticks.

Eric later told authorities that the pair had realized they were on the wrong trail midway into the hike and switched directions. At thirteen thousand feet, both hikers complained of headaches, a common ailment at high altitudes. Mount of the Holy Cross has an elevation of 14,005 feet, and during the hike to the summit, Michelle was consistently sixty feet behind Eric. Four hundred feet below the summit, she told him she couldn't go on. She said she was out of water, tired, and wanted to rest. Eric claims he told Michelle they could return to their cars at that time, but Michelle told him to make the summit. He gave her direction on where they could meet farther down the mountain if she got the energy, or she could wait there. It was 1:30 p.m.

At 1:42 p.m. Eric made the summit. There were others at the spot taking photos and signing the logbook. Eric took photos for others, and they took photos of him. He called his wife and said he had to hurry to get back to Michelle. It was estimated that Eric was on the summit for five minutes. He proceeded down the mountain but didn't see Michelle. He went on different trails and backtracked in different directions, but he never saw her. Eric even asked others on the trail if they had seen Michelle. Nobody had seen her descending. Eric continued to descend on Half Moon Trail until he got back to the campground, where he notified authorities.

The search for Michelle Vanek is known in Colorado as the biggest search in the state's history. However, the SAR did not begin smoothly. The second day of the search was greatly hindered by torrential rains that hit the mountain. The Vail Mountain Search and Rescue Team was the primary response team. They were supported by seven hundred searchers. People were combing the mountain like they were searching for a small bag, but they were searching for a grown woman. The searchers looked in some places even a child couldn't hide.

Tim Cochrane was the commander of the Vail SAR team. In an interview on October 1, 2005, by the *Vail News*, he stated, "It's truly a mystery as to where Michelle is. That's probably the most baffling thing. We've put five search dogs where we know she was, and they haven't found anything."

There was only one odd report given to the newspaper in the article cited above: "'Hikers on the mountain Sept. 24 have also told searchers they saw a "shape" below the summit—that could have been Vanek—when her friend reached the top,' Cochrane said."

Authorities interviewed Michelle Vanek's husband, Ben. He stated that Eric Sawyer was a longtime friend of the family, and he is fully certain that he'd do nothing to harm his wife.

Case Summary

It doesn't seem reasonable that Eric Sawyer would have harmed Michelle on Mount of the Holy Cross. There were a number of hikers on the mountain that cold September day, and he would never have known when the next one was coming around the corner. Also, everyone in both families knew he was with Michelle, and it would make no sense to harm her.

Michelle had a small backpack and two ski poles. Where are they? The mountain was absolutely saturated with searchers, helicopters, and dogs, but nothing was found. I know a little about canines and tracking. They do find people. I've witnessed dozens of successful searches. Why wouldn't a canine pick up the scent of a woman in the specific location where she once was?

I've seen many photos of this mountain; it is much like the other mountains in Colorado where others have disappeared. There are no trees, some large boulders, and some dangerous cliffs and drops. I am fully convinced that the Vail SAR team covered all possible locations where Michelle may have fallen. I doubt she is there.

It concerns me that witnesses said they saw a "shape." That's not a usual description that's used when we talk about people. When they said shape, what did they mean? How many shapes can there be on a trail at thirteen thousand feet? Did that shape play some role in Michelle's disappearance?

I do not believe that Michelle Vanek died of natural causes on Mount of the Holy Cross. Michelle was in great physical condition—maybe not acclimatized to an altitude of fourteen thousand feet, but for a thirty-five-year-old woman, she was healthy. Something catastrophic happened to Michelle Vanek, something that none of us could have probably survived.

Evan Thompson
Missing: 05/27/06, northwest of Canon City, CO
Age at disappearance: 8

Evan Thompson was a mentally disabled eight-year-old boy on an outing with a group of students and teachers from his school for disabled-learning children. The group was at a campground just northwest of Canon City, Colorado, at an elevation of 7,200-foot. On Saturday morning, May 27, 2006, a teacher finished feeding Evan and told him to wait for the group to clean up. It was while Evan was waiting that he disappeared.

Once the camp realized Evan was missing, everyone started to call his name and search. It wasn't long before the sheriff's department and state police were at the camping facility searching for the boy. Search teams were called from throughout Colorado and brought bloodhounds, airplanes, helicopters, and ground teams.

Searchers believed they found footprints from the boy during the first two days of the search, but they did not have luck finding him.

During the middle of the fourth day of searching, one of the searchers thought they heard something. The searcher called Evan's name and he responded. The boy was found in a cave over five miles from the location where he disappeared. He was in good condition but had some scratches on his body and was missing one shoe. He was taken to a local hospital and found to be in very good condition, considering he was in the woods for four days.

Searchers and school officials tried to question Evan about his ordeal, but he seemed unable to recall specific details. He did tell them that one night he slept in a tree, one night under a log, and one night in a cave. He also told them that the day he disappeared, a crow flew up next to him and he followed it from camp.

Searchers stated that from the prints they found, they estimated Evan walked over eleven miles in the four days he was missing.

Case Summary

The book *Lost Person Behavior* by Robert Koester states on page 140 that children seven to nine years old will be found in a distance of less than 4½ miles in a dry climate 95 percent of the time. Evan was found five miles away but had walked eleven miles.

In a very odd twist to this story, the air force had utilized FLIR during their search for Evan. If Evan had been in a cave or under a log or in a cave, FLIR would not have seen him.

Wyoming

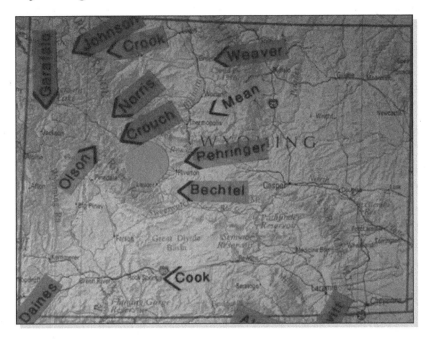

Wyoming is one of the most diverse states in North America when you look at its topography. The highs and lows in elevation are extreme, and this makes the SAR of missing people complicated, expensive, and technically challenging. If people are missing at ten thousand feet, the challenges of getting aircraft into the area or ferrying searchers to the region becomes more expensive and dangerous. It's also extremely fatiguing for the rescuers.

There is something within the missing person phenomenon that searchers, researchers, law enforcement and government officials do not understand and/or will not publically address, maybe they don't even realize it exists. Why do some rural regions have one group of missing people—males or females? It is usually very slanted toward one sex and a segmented age bracket.

Wyoming, however, has an equal number of men and women missing. Three of the women I have chosen to write about went missing in the same general area. I know that many will claim that these women were the victims of a serial abductor, which is possible. Fran Weaver went missing in a region that is extremely remote and has little or no traffic in the winter because of road conditions, making it very doubtful that a serial killer would go to those extremes to kidnap anyone in that location. I think it would be much easier to stay on the perimeter of a city and take someone when nobody was looking.

A vast majority of serial killers/abductors have historically shown that they work alone and are usually loners when they commit their crimes. They don't tell others of their crimes, and it's usually a secret they attempt to conceal for a lifetime. If someone goes missing on a rural trail, there would be many complications for a serial abductor to overcome if they wanted to take custody of the victim. How would they move the victim on a trail? How would they conceal their own identity to other hikers and law enforcement? These areas are lightly traveled and locals usually know who is moving through the area. Many hikers carry firearms; how would they overcome that issue? What would they do with the body if the victim refused to succumb?

The victims I identify in Wyoming have never been found, except one. If a serial abductor did engage someone on a trail and killed them, they would be unable to move the body a considerable distance. The suspect would have to bury the body close to the crime scene. Law enforcement has FLIR on most helicopters when performing an SAR; this has the ability to see radiant heat coming from anything, even bodies in graves. This scenario does not make it feasible to use the standard paradigm to explain what happened to these people.

Wyoming Missing People by Date

Missing Person	Date Missing•Age•Sex
Dewey Cook*	03/02/42•25•M
Janet Federer	09/29/48•6•F
Frank Norris	09/21/49•46•M
Fran Weaver	02/01/60•56•F
Vanita Crook	05/03/61•25•F

Lynn Olson	06/28/63•16•F
Tom Garafalo	11/25/65•28•M
Frank Mean*	04/21/66•55•M
Dennis Johnson	07/12/66•8•M
	23-Year Gap
Kathleen Pehringer	04/17/89•41F
Amy Bechtel	07/24/97•24•F
David Crouch	09/07/97•27•M

*Details on the disappearances of Dewey Cook, and Frank Mean can be found in the chapter "Sheepherders," *Book #2, Missing 411: Eastern United States.*

Janet Federer
Missing: 09/29/48, 1:00 p.m., ten miles north of Cheyenne, WY
Age at disappearance: 6

Mr. and Mrs. Clarence Federer and their family lived on a ranch ten miles north of Cheyenne, Wyoming. On September 29, 1948, six-year-old Janet was playing in the family's yard with her two dogs. Sometime near 1:00 p.m., the family realized that Janet had disappeared and they started to search their property.

Cheyenne sits five miles north of the Colorado border near the eastern side of the state. The area ten miles north of Cheyenne is predominantly ranches and farms in a fairly flat topography. Pole Creek Reservoir sits just to the east, along with other small lakes in the vicinity.

As searchers started to scour the property, the Federers were shocked that they couldn't immediately see or find little Janet. Late on the first night, the family was extremely nervous, and the sheriff and state highway patrol brought in additional resources for the following day. Late on the first night, one of the dogs that left with Janet returned to the residence without the girl. The dog would not leave the confines of the Federer property, even at the prompting of her parents—strange behavior for a dog that had just lost its best friend.

The next morning, local ranchers, farmers, and eight hundred people from a local armed forces base participated in the search. One rancher got into his plane to search the plains from the sky. At approximately 9:00 a.m., Jack Strong was flying ten miles north of

Janet's residence and thought he saw a large dog in a creek bed. Jack landed his plane on the prairie and walked to the creek. He found Janet lying against the creek bed, alive, with her dog nearby. Strong flew the girl back to her ranch and then to the hospital in Cheyenne.

A photo of Janet ran in the October 1, 1948, edition of the *Milwaukee Journal*. The photo shows a young girl with eyes that are almost bulging out of their sockets in a complete stare. She has large boils on her forehead and an extreme number of scratches on her cheeks. She appears in shock. Doctors stated that Janet was suffering from extreme bruising, scratches, and exposure.

Case Summary

There are several factors in this case that are very unusual. The book *Lost Person Behavior* by Robert Koester states that a child four to six years old will be found, if lost on flat ground, 95 percent of the time less than 4.1 miles from the point where they disappeared. Janet was found over two and half times as far. Like many children who are found, Janet was found with scratches on her face. Jack Strong attempted to question Janet about her disappearance; he stated that she didn't say anything.

Eight hundred searchers didn't believe Janet could have traveled ten miles in twenty hours; for this reason, they were not in the area where she was found. It's hard to imagine that a six-year-old girl could travel a half mile per hour for twenty hours nonstop.

Frank Norris
Missing: 09/21/49, Gros Ventre, northwest of Pinedale, WY
Age at disappearance: 46

Frank Norris and his wife traveled from their home in Shoshoni to Gros Ventre on a hunting trip. They booked the trip at Falers Hunting Camp, which is located at the head of Gros Ventre River. The couple rented two horses and made the twelve-mile ride to Grizzly Basin, a location that is surrounded by small lakes and deep valleys at the ten thousand foot elevation. Once at the basin, the couple established their base camp and made their daily trips.

On Wednesday, September 21, Frank went out alone for the day while his wife stayed at camp. He never came back. Mrs. Norris rode back to Faler's and said she needed help to locate her husband.

The sheriff was called and a search team from Faler's road off in search for Frank.

The Faler search team located their rented horse walking back toward their main camp alone. The horse was found with its reins tied together, and Frank's gloves were stuffed in the opening below the saddle horn. His rifle was found in its scabbard with a full magazine. The search team briefed Lester Faler and Mrs. Norris of what they found. Both Lester and Mrs. Norris validated that Frank never dismounted and tied his reins; he always let them hang loose so the horse would not run off. Mrs. Norris told Sheriff Olin Emory that her husband had a weak lung and rarely dismounted to walk any significant distance.

Frank was reported missing in Teton County, even though the Faler camp is in Sublette County.

I sat with a group of law enforcement friends, and we talked through the Frank Norris case. First, Frank had a medical condition; he would not and could not walk far. He had a regular practice, which all knew, where he would not tie the horse reins together before dismounting. His gun was still in the scabbard and the magazine was full. Let's look at the reasonable possibilities of what happened.

Frank could have shot an animal, gotten to it, and had an argument in the field with another hunter, who killed and buried him in the wild. Scenarios similar to this happen more often than many know, but this isn't what happened with Frank. His gun was found with a full magazine and not fired. The gun was still in the scabbard and recovered by searchers. If Frank had been killed by a serial killer or just an angry person, the chances that they would have taken his firearm are fairly good. It is a prized possession.

Maybe Frank dismounted to use the bathroom (again, a scenario that we do not believe occurred). Frank's wife and the Falers stated that Frank would never tie the reins together and dismount the horse, ever, so discount this option.

It is possible that Frank was riding the horse without his gloves on when he was knocked to the ground by a branch, accidentally hit by a stray bullet, or victimized in some other manner and mortally hit the ground. In counsel with guides and fish-and-game officials, it is extremely rare that a wild animal would attack a rider on a horse; a horse has a pretty good radar when danger is present. If Frank was reluctant to leave the comfort of the horse, maybe this could have happened; though you'd think the horse would have some type of injury secondary to Frank's. None was noted.

The standard scenarios in which hunters and hikers go missing and are later found don't fit the Norris case. As I've searched through hundreds of horse-related missing cases, Frank's case is not as unique as I first thought. There are dozens and dozens of missing people in North America who have disappeared under similar bizarre and unexplainable circumstances. Why hasn't the press addressed these facts for the public? Why has the press allowed local, state and federal law enforcement to list people as "dead" or deceased" when there is no evidence they are dead? It's a very easy way to wipe their slate clean, claim there is no issue, and ignore a continuing problem that is plaguing the North American wilderness. These people are listed as deceased and their bodies are never found.

An extensive archival search revealed several articles on Frank Norris and his disappearance. The last article I could find was in the *Billings Gazette*, December 7, 1949, with the following headline: "Four Wyoming Hunters Lose Lives in Season." As I browsed the article, I found Frank's name and presumed they found his body. The reality of the article and what I have discovered during my research on missing people should be of concern to the public. The article stated, "He disappeared in the Grizzly Basin sector of Gros Ventre Country north of Pinedale September 21 and has not been seen since." This is all the article stated about Frank. It went on to describe three other hunters that had been killed by gunfire. Again, the article stated four Wyoming hunters lost their lives, but there is no proof that Norris is dead. He is still missing.

The act of declaring someone dead while missing in the wild is a slippery slope and is much more common than the public understands. It is a method for local sheriff, state or federal law enforcement to eliminate a missing person statistic and terminate any other expenses associated with the case. It is also a method to eliminate any possibility that there may be an issue with ongoing disappearances in that jurisdiction. With the advent of the Internet and mandatory reporting of missing children, any opportunity that law enforcement may have of eliminating a long list of missing people on their Web site will be taken advantage of. The best I can determine is that Frank Norris has never been found, and he is one of six people missing in the mountain range that runs northwest from near Lander to Teton National Park. You will not find this information on any Web site or database. Where have these people gone?

Fran Weaver
Missing: 02/01/60, twenty-five miles northwest of Cody, WY
Age at disappearance: 56
Owner of Goff Creek Lodge (now named Creekside Lodge) at Yellowstone Cody, WY

Fran Weaver had recently become the owner of Goff Creek Lodge, ten miles east of the east entrance to Yellowstone Park. John Goff, a hunting guide, trapper, and personal friend of Theodore Roosevelt, founded the lodge in 1912. Letters between Roosevelt and Goff are still on site at the lodge.

In January and February of 1960, Fran was staying with a friend, Olive Fell. Olive was a local artist who had made friends with Fran upon her recent purchase of the lodge. Olive's cabin was twenty-five miles northwest of Cody and approximately fifteen miles from the Goff Lodge.

Sometime during the day of February 1, 1960, Fran left her cabin and went for a hike. When she didn't return for dinner, Olive became concerned and called law enforcement. Sheriff Harley Kinkade and a contingent of deputies scoured the North Fork Mountains for Fran, but no trace was found. They then switched their focus and decided that she might have gone to her own lodge. They started to search the Goff Lodge area. The lodge sits near Highway 20 along the river at an elevation of six thousand feet. An extensive search of the area around the ranch was unsuccessful. As a coincidence, the Goff Creek Lodge is extremely close to the location where Vanita Crook disappeared.

Law enforcement officials described Fran Weaver as tall and slender, with auburn hair and blue eyes. They stated that she came to Cody from Baton Rouge, Louisiana. Fran's husband, Art Weaver, traveled to Cody and assisted in the futile search.

I found four newspaper articles about Fran Weaver and none indicated that she was ever found; however, she is not listed on any database as a missing person.

The Goff Lodge is still open but operating under a different name.

Vanita Crook
Missing: 05/03/61, Kitty Creek, WY (forty-five miles west of Cody)
Age at disappearance: 25

For some cases I've researched, information is scarce and the reality of what occurred is hard to determine. This is one of those cases. I was conducting a historical archive search of Wyoming missing people cases when I found out about Vanita Crook. There was one article in one newspaper and nothing more. She is not listed as missing on any database and there are no articles indicating they found her.

On May 3, 1962, the *Billings Gazette* ran a story with the headline: "No Trace Found, Cody Area Woman Missing For Year." The article states that Vanita was sitting in a car in the mountains forty miles north of Cody. She had traveled with her parents to their rural cabin at Kitty Creek for a weekend of relaxation. The parents walked to the cabin and carried items inside while she waited in the car. During the time that Mr. and Mrs. Erwin Crook were gone, Vanita vanished. The parents could not find the girl and contacted the sheriff's office.

Vanita wore glasses approximately 50 percent of the time. Her glasses were found in the backseat of the car. A massive search throughout the mountains failed to produce any trace of Vanita.

Kitty Creek is in a very isolated region of far northern Wyoming. It is forty-five miles west of Cody and nine miles east of the eastern entrance to Yellowstone National Park. It is just inside the northwestern fringe of the Washakie Wilderness Area. The creek is just south of Highway 20 at an elevation of 8,800 feet.

Vacation homes in rural areas are havens for crime. I've known many rural deputies who have taken countless burglary reports from families who have been gone from their homes for months, come for the weekend, and discover a burglary. This exact scenario happened to my family three times when they owned a vacation home in Lake Tahoe. On one occasion they came through the front door, found the back sliding door open and a warm pot of beans on the range. Anyone owning a rural home could accidentally trap a suspect in the house, especially if there is only one way in and one way out.

Could Vanita's parents have accidentally frightened a subject that was staying near the house when they arrived? They might have arrived and gone into the home while a suspect was hiding in the bushes. Vanita was still in the car; maybe she was forcibly taken. This scenario presents many issues, the least of which is the strength necessary to carry someone away against their will. If the victim fights, the average person will be drained of energy very quickly and would not be able to carry anyone for any significant period of time.

Vanita wasn't an athlete, hiker, or someone who regularly engaged in outdoor activity. The idea that she voluntarily walked into the wilderness is ludicrous. Vanita Crook's disappearance must have haunted her parents for the rest of their lives. There is no mention of what they did with their cabin after her disappearance, but it is doubtful that they ever had a "normal" vacation there again.

Lynn Dianne Olson
Missing: 06/28/63, sixteen miles north of Pinedale, WY
Age at disappearance: 16

Lynn Olson and her twin brother lived with their mother in Salt Lake City, Utah. Their father was a ranch hand in Pinedale, Wyoming. The kids were staying at their grandparents' dude ranch on Green River Lakes, north of Pinedale. Stanley Decker had owned the dude ranch for a number of years, and the kids had an opportunity to have fun at the ranch and spend time near their father. This is an absolutely gorgeous area with large, green, open meadows coupled with huge cliffs and deep valleys. The area to the west has a long, angling ridgeline that terminates near the lakes, while to the east are hundreds of small lakes on a large plateau. This area could be on a postcard for the Wyoming tourism bureau; it is that gorgeous.

On June 28 Lynn took a walk down near the river that borders the wilderness. The elevation in this area is 8,500 feet, and the area is spotted with countless small lakes and creeks. Lynn didn't return, and the grandparents called authorities for help.

Sublette County Sheriff Morris Horton brought in divers to search the lakes and rivers in the immediate area. Lynn was only wearing light summer clothes. For two days after Lynn disappeared, it snowed in the area, making it difficult to locate tracks and maintain a scent trail for canines.

On July 29, family members were still scouring the area for clues when they found a pile of her clothes amongst the trees two hundred yards from the river. This was a very odd find that was difficult to explain. Family members believed that these were the clothes that Lynn was wearing the day she disappeared. Law enforcement never developed any viable clues as to what happened to Lynn.

The location of Lynn's disappearance is in an extremely remote part of the Bridger National Forest. A review of U.S. Geological Survey maps of the region show more small lakes than you can count. There are mountains and lakes with names like Bear and Sheep, indicators that the region has a significant amount of wildlife. There was no blood trail or evidence that Lynn was taken by a mountain lion or grizzly bear. Nobody believed that Lynn walked naked into the woods, and it is even less likely that she attempted to walk out of the ranch due to its remote location. The real question is why Lynn would have taken her clothes off. Did something or someone force the clothes off? Did she have a second set of clothes that she changed into (very, very doubtful)? It's been over forty-five years since Lynn disappeared, and she still hasn't surfaced.

As you go further into this book, you will read about missing people who are found without the clothes they were wearing when they disappeared. Some SAR personnel state that missing people remove their clothes at certain times, while others state that people suffering hypothermia strip off their clothes, something not understood. In the case of Lynn Olson, her clothes were removed where she disappeared. Again, the area is so remote that the idea of a serial predator waiting with a vehicle to abduct her seems impossible.

The Lynn Olson case is another instance where the missing does not appear on any database. If it wasn't for an extensive and time-consuming archival search, you would never know about the disappearance of Lynn Olson, a true Wyoming mystery.

Tom Garafalo
Missing: 11/25/65, Lozier Hill, thirty miles north of Jackson, WY
Age at disappearance: 28

Tom Garafalo was a biologist for the State of Wyoming Fish and Game Department. He lived in Laramie and loved the outdoors. On Thursday, November 25, 1965, Tom made his way to Lozier Hill on the east side of Grand Teton National Park for an elk hunt. The area around the hill is filled with lakes and rivers, and the elevation varies between 7,000 and 7,500 feet. Tom had only planned to hunt for two hours on Thursday, so it was assumed that he didn't carry a lot of equipment.

Once it was determined that Tom was missing, the State Fish and Game Department sent airplanes to search for him and his vehicle. The vehicle was found Saturday and an extensive area search started on Sunday. Teton County Sheriff Carl Roice led the search and indicated that there was eighteen to twenty inches of snow in the area. Searchers were unable to utilize their snowshoes because of the deep powder. Carl stated that if Tom had remained in the Lozier Hill area since Thursday, the chances of him being alive were very slim. He stated that evening temperatures had fallen to fifteen degrees or colder.

I only located one article about Tom Garafalo. There were no follow-up articles and nothing indicating he was ever found.

Dennis Johnson
Missing: 07/12/66, 1:30 p.m., northeast of Canyon Junction, Yel-lowstone National Park, WY
Clothing: Tan pants, boots, red long-sleeve shirt
Age at disappearance: 8
Blonde hair, brown eyes, 3'8", 60 lb.

Prior to writing the narrative for Dennis Johnson's disappear-ance, I filed a freedom of Information Act request to the National Park Service for all documents related to the boy's disappearance. Contrary to some requests I have made, the park service fully com-plied and sent me the entire case file on the event.

Mr. and Mrs. William Johnson had made an arduous journey from their home in Inyokern, California, to Yellowstone National Park. The Johnsons had three daughters and an eight-year-old son, Dennis. Mr. Johnson was a Naval Ordnance employee in Kern County and enjoyed the outdoors.

On July 12, 1966, the family made a short trip from Canyon Junction just a few miles northeast and stopped at a campground to picnic at approximately noon. Once they stopped, seven-year-old Mary Johnson exited the vehicle and helped the family set up their lunch table. It was at this point that Mr. Johnson told the kids to see if they could catch a squirrel. Mary and Dennis ran up an adjacent hill in attempt to find a varmint.

Not long after the kids ran off, Dennis returned but Mary did not. Mr. Johnson told Dennis to go one way and he'd go the other way to find her. Mr. Johnson soon found Mary (she was found by another camper and taken to a local ranger station and brought back to camp) and then hiked back the other direction to tell Dennis. Mr. Johnson couldn't find his son. This was at approximately 1:30 p.m. (I think it's an important fact that Mary was found quite a distance from the Johnsons' picnic site and then returned to the area. What happened to Mary may shed light on what exactly happened to Den-nis, but there is no interview with Mary about the specifics of her disappearance.) The Johnsons looked for their son with the assis-tance of others in the area until 4:00 p.m. and then notified the NPS.

The area where Dennis disappeared is near a region called "The Grand Canyon of Yellowstone," where a river runs through a deep canyon at the far eastern end of the park, approximately fifteen miles south of the Montana border. There are mountains just to the north of the spot where the family stopped; these mountains are very large and rugged. Dunraven Pass would be the vehicular route that someone would take to exit the park and traverse this mountain range. The boy disappeared at an elevation of 7,800 feet.

The National Park Service dedicated one hundred employees for two weeks in the search for Dennis. The day after Dennis disappeared, searchers were working late into the day when at 6:55 p.m. they found a makeshift lean-to one half mile from where Dennis was last seen. This observation was noted on page one of the NPS report dated August 8, 1966. What made the structure, or who was living in the structure, we will never know. The NPS didn't address it in the report. There was also a shelter found during the search for Derrick Engbretson (Crater Lake, OR), also eight years old. This shelter was never explained as to who built it and who was occupying it.

The park service utilized a helicopter, bloodhounds, and tracking experts. The search did have an unusual twist in that the searchers could never find any of Dennis's shoe prints. As part of the official investigation, the NPS interviewed all family members. On July 18, 1966, a park official interviewed Mary Johnson. Mary recounted what happened when the family arrived at the picnic site, how their dad told them to catch squirrels, and how she and Dennis ran up the hill. Mary made this statement: "We were both running on top of the hill. We were trying to catch a squirrel but we didn't find one." She also said that they found a lot of holes but no squirrels. Mary last saw her brother as she was running up the hill. The last page of the interview had this paragraph: "Daddy came back and Denny was lost and we ate. Then all the squirrels and chipmunks came back but I didn't want to catch them because they might bite my hand. . We didn't see any squirrels in the woods." In Yellowstone, there are chipmunks and squirrels everywhere. It seems very odd that Mary and Dennis didn't see any on the hill or in the woods. After her father returned and Dennis was gone, the squirrels and chipmunks returned. What changed in the area that caused the squirrels and chipmunks to return?

After one week of searching, the National Park Service notified the FBI that Dennis was missing and there was a possibility of abduction. There are few details available about the FBI involvement, other than they were notified, an indication that the NPS was nervous about this case. A July 6, 1967, article in the *Modesto Bee* had a statement from one of the searchers: "It was nearly as if he [Dennis] had been snatched from the face of the earth." No name was attributed to the statement.

The formal search for Dennis lasted two weeks, but family members brought in friends and additional family to search for a month, never finding any evidence of Dennis. I did find articles years after Dennis disappeared indicating that the boy was never found, but there is no notation in any database that he was listed as a missing person. This shows another mistake by the NPS and another instance of a missing boy in a national park that they don't want you to know about.

Kathleen Pehringer
Missing: 04/17/89, Riverton, WY
Age at disappearance: 41
5'2", 120 lb.

Authorities state that Kathleen Pehringer was last seen at her residence in Riverton, twenty miles northeast of Lander, Wyoming. Riverton sits within the confines of the Wind River Indian Reservation, yet it is an incorporated city in Fremont County. Law enforcement theorizes that Kathleen left her home willingly with someone, as there were no indicators of a struggle in her residence. They believe that foul play was later involved.

Pehringer lived approximately thirty miles from where Bechtel and Wagner (below) disappeared.

Amy Bechtel
Missing: 07/24/97, Shoshone National Forest, Lander, WY
Age at disappearance: 24
5'6", 115 lb.

Amy Bechtel was a graduate of the University of Wyoming. She did not have children and shared a small apartment in Lander with her husband, Steve. They both worked at a local sporting goods store. Amy was described by friends as shy, reserved, and goal oriented. Her hobbies included rock climbing and photography, and she hoped to someday be an Olympic marathoner.

Amy and Steve had recently purchased a house and were in the process of buying items to furnish it. The couple was slowly moving boxes into the residence. On July 24, 1997, Amy left her apartment at 9:30 a.m. to do a variety of tasks related to the new home. Amy was last seen at 2:30 p.m. in a photo shop in Lander.

Amy was a member of a local health club, where she exercised on a regular basis. The club had scheduled a 10K run on the outskirts of Lander. The route for the race ran along Loop Road in the Shoshone National Forest. Law enforcement officials believe that Amy left the photo shop, went to the race location, and exited her car to check the route or run the course.

At 4:30 p.m. Steve arrived back at their home and started to move boxes into their new residence. He was consumed with the task for several hours. At 10:30 p.m. Steve became concerned that Amy hadn't returned, so he called law enforcement. Officials conducted an extensive search for Amy and her Toyota station wagon. Searchers found Amy's car abandoned along Loop Road in the mountains adjacent to the racecourse. Amy's sunglasses and daily list were found in the car. Her wallet was missing.

Law enforcement focused their attention on Steve, as would be normal in any spousal disappearance. Steve cooperated with the investigation until he was made a suspect; he then got an attorney and refused to talk. Again, there may be information about this case that law enforcement is privy to that the public does not know, but these were newlyweds. They worked together and just recently bought a house. It doesn't make sense that Steve would go all the way out to where Amy was jogging to kill her. He could have vacationed with her anywhere and had her disappear. Doing it that close to home doesn't make sense, but then again most killers don't use good judgment. I personally don't see Steve as a suspect in this case.

Six years after Amy disappeared, a Timex Ironman watch, similar to Amy's, was found by an elk hunter near the Middle Fork of the Popo Agie River that runs parallel to Loop Road, where witnesses had possibly seen Amy running.

There is one main aspect to this case that should be focused upon. The watch that was recovered could easily be tested for Amy's DNA, but it doesn't appear this has been done. If the watch was in the riverbed, as the hunter described, this would not have been the route that Amy was running; she was on the roadway. If someone is going to abduct someone along a roadway, it has to be quick so there are no witnesses. It would be possible for two individuals to pull up next to Amy on the road, open the passenger door, and drag her into the vehicle. This possibility would not account for the watch in the riverbed. As a tribute to Amy, the 10K run was named the "Amy Bechtel Hill Climb."

If Amy's watch was in the riverbed, Amy must have been in the riverbed. Why or how anyone could have dragged her into that area seems almost unbelievable. She was a strong athlete; she would have put up a major fight. Witnesses would have seen the fight from the roadway and could have easily seen into the river area. It's a very perplexing situation how the watch got into the riverbed. If you looked at a map and drew a line from where Amy could have been on the roadway jogging to the point where the watch was located, could Amy be somewhere up into the hills past where the watch was located, was she taken into the wild? If Amy was taken into the forest, the assailant was big, strong, fast, and had a high level of endurance.

The idea that Amy took her wallet with her while she ran is not unusual to me. When I've jogged in remote areas where a car

252 | Missing 411-Western U.S. & Canada

burglary could occur with no witnesses, I have taken my valuables with me. It is surprising that she didn't drop the wallet if a forced abduction did occur.

Another Lander woman went missing in 2005. Ann Wagner, fifty-two years old, was reported missing in the newspapers. Greg Wagner, Ann's husband, reported her missing to authorities, saying that she left a note indicating she was going to Ocean Lake, twelve miles northwest of Riverton on Loop Road. On September 25, 2005, a hiker spotted Ann's 1998 Tahoe parked a few hundred yards off Loop Road. Police stated that they conducted a search and found the body of Ann Wagner. They did not release the location of the body or the cause of death. Ann and Amy's disappearances had the common elements that they were both alone, both disappeared on Loop Road, both disappeared in the Shoshone National Forest, both of their names started with *A*, and their first names only had three letters.

To compound the story about Ann and Amy, there is a third woman who went missing in the same general area. Kathleen Pehringer lived approximately twenty miles from the other two women.

After the initial search for Amy started to wind down, twenty-five FBI agents from Denver and other parts of Wyoming came to Lander to assist in the investigation. What makes the FBI involvement puzzling is that they claim they do not investigate "missing" people. A point in fact, the only federal violation that the FBI may partake in this type of investigation is if the victim was kidnapped and transported across state lines, or a crime occurs and a local jurisdiction specifically asks them for assistance. There are a handful of missing people cases (Charles McCullar, Crater Lake, OR, as an example) in which relatives requested FBI involvement but were refused. There is obviously much more to these disappearances than the public knows about and much more to understand about why the FBI sometimes does or doesn't assist in an investigation.

One last idea to focus on Amy's watch. The Timex was found in the riverbed. As you read further in the book, you will notice that many victims are found in or near a riverbed. If a serial predator wanted to hide their tracks, the rocks in a riverbed are the best place to conceal that portion of their identity.

David M. Crouch
Missing: 09/07/97, Island Lake, Bridger Wilderness, WY
Age at disappearance: 27

David Crouch was the son of Gloria and William Crouch of Chester, Maryland. He graduated from high school in 1988 and eventually owned and operated the Bike Doctor in Stevensville, Maryland. He was known to everyone as an avid outdoorsman, to the point that he actually did a hike on his honeymoon with his wife, Donna. He did not have children.

In September of 1997, David ventured to Wyoming with friends to do some hiking and fishing. On September 7, David got separated from his friends near Island Lake at an elevation of 10,500 feet. His friends did an extensive search but could not find him.

The days after David disappeared, the region was hit by heavy rains that hindered search dogs ability to follow scent. The local sheriff had search and rescue crews ferried into the location by a local helicopter company because the search location was so remote. The sheriff stated that they had the area confined to one square mile where they thought David would be located. The sheriff stated that the area is "extremely rugged with canyons and drop-offs in dense timber."

There was one article that I could find about David's disappearance, and no additional information could be located. He does not appear in any public database as a missing person.

Idaho

Idaho and Eastern Washington Missing People

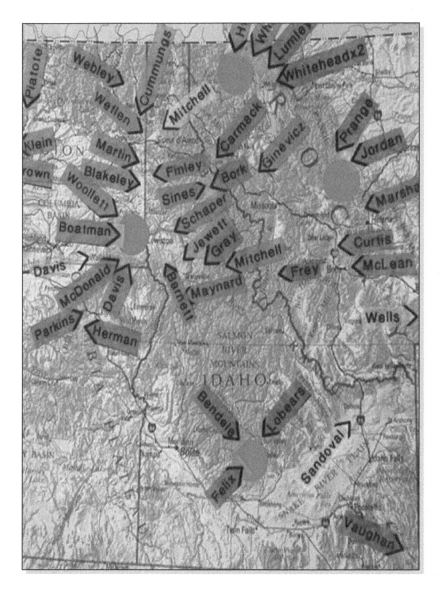

Idaho and Eastern Washington Missing Person List by Date

Missing Person	Date Missing•Age•Sex
James Vaughan	08/20/1883•18 mos.•M
J. Mitchell	01/11/1909•NA•M
Emmet Mitchell	07/10/31•50•M
Frank Lobears	06/25/33•7•M
Donald McDonald	12/15/49•17•M
Bobby Boatman	10/14/51•14•M
Catherine P. Maynard	01/19/53•38•F
Rose Jewett	08/11/57•95•F
Christine Woollett	05/12/66•2•F
Lowell Smith	10/05/68•60•M
Louis Sandoval	09/06/69•66•M
Gayla C. Schaper	06/29/79•28•F
Richard Ray Barnett	08/31/82•2•M
Julie Ann Weflen	09/16/87•28•F
Tina Marie Finley	03/07/88•25•F
Brian Sines	11/22/91•29•M
Ruben David Felix	02/23/97•2•M
Ronald S. Gray	09/19/08•62•M
Avery B. Blakeley	03/26/09•2•M

Details on the disappearances of the following people can be found in *book #2, Missing 411: Eastern United States* under the corresponding chapter.
J. Mitchell, "Sheepherder"
Emmet Mitchell, "Sheepherder"
Rose Jewett, "Berry Picker"
Louis Sandoval, "Sheepherder"

James Vaughan
Missing: 08/20/1883, Gentile Valley, Idaho
Age at disappearance: 18 months
    This story could also be included in the state of Utah section. The location of this occurrence was in the far southeastern section of Idaho in proximity to disappearances in northeast Utah.

If I fabricated this story and presented it as fact, the majority of you would laugh and say that I should have a better imagination. Well, on August 26, 1883, the *Salt Lake Tribune* published a story titled, "Carried off by Bear, An 18-month-old Child Taken into the Mountains but Found Alive and Well the Next Day."

The article states that a mother was working at her house in the Gentile Valley of southeast Idaho just northwest of Bear Lake. As the woman was doing the family wash, she suddenly realized her son, James, was missing. She immediately searched the area but could not find her eighteen-month-old boy. The mother ran to a neighbor's house and made a plea for assistance. Seventeen neighbors responded and started to look for tracks.

The article states that late on that first afternoon some of the men found the tracks of "a huge bear." The men followed the tracks through the canyons and valleys toward Bear Lake. As evening started to arrive and they still hadn't found the boy, the men returned to their homes and waited till morning.

Before dawn the next morning, three men left to return to the area where they had last seen tracks. At 10:00 a.m. Ed Goslin spotted James "curled up in a bunch of weeds and grass in the bushes sound asleep with his little tattered and torn dress thrown over his head, while close by, beside the sleeping child, was the warm bed of what must have been a very large bear, which had abandoned its captive on approach of the men in search." James did not have his shoes on, and he had a slight scratch on one foot.

The child had been carried four miles through valleys and over some very rough terrain and thick brush.

Case Summary

If I hadn't read the original article, I'm not sure I would have given this a second thought. That said, I have heard a very similar story told multiple times. I have consulted with bear experts, and they categorically claim this can never happen. They claim that the bear will eat the child, or maybe drop the child and flee, but not coddle and keep the child warm all night.

The scenario as it's described does cause me to ask several questions. The article states that the bear had to have gone through heavy brush to reach the location where the child was found. Why didn't the child have extensive scratches and bruises from the brush? The bear would have to carry the child in its mouth, which would make James close to the ground and susceptible to scratches. If the bear was carrying the child, where are bite marks that must have been inflicted? Why wouldn't the clothes he was wearing be torn to shreds by the bite marks that the bear must have inflicted?

I believe that something very, very unusual happened in Gentile Valley in August of 1883, and we still haven't heard the entire story.

Frank Lobears (Son)
Missing: 06/25/33, Chamberlain Basin, Idaho
Age at disappearance: 7 years

Frank Lobears' father owned two mining claims, four miles apart, approximately 165 miles north of McCall, Idaho. The claims are in rugged country that still had snow in late June of 1933. The closest ranger station to the Lobears' claims is the Big Creek Ranger Station.

On June 25, 1933, the seven-year-old son of Frank Lobears put on snowshoes and started the four-mile trek across the snow to visit his mother at the other mining claim. It appears Frank didn't know his son had left and then didn't realize his son never arrived at the other claim until Tuesday, June 27.

Searchers from both mines immediately started the search for the young boy. Approximately two miles from the point the boy was last seen, searchers found two snowshoes that the boy had apparently removed. At that location the prints in the snow stopped and he went to hard ground. Searchers could not find any additional tracks anywhere.

Ten days after the Lobears boy disappeared, and an unbelievable fifteen miles of tracking through the bush and ground, searchers found his handkerchief in the desolate headwaters of Hand Creek. The Hand Creek site is approximately six air miles from the origin of the boy's trek.

On July 6 Idaho Governor Ross stated, "It looks as if we never will find the boy." State airplanes, ground troops, volunteers, law enforcement officers and almost every other search mechanism available in 1933 were part of the attempt to find the boy. On July 7, 1933, the search for Frank Lobears' son was terminated.

Remember the fact that the handkerchief was found in a creek bed. Many of the people who disappear are found in or near creek beds.

Donald McDonald
Missing: 12/15/49, Blacksnake Ridge, Walla Walla, WA
Age at disappearance: 17

Hunting elk in the Blue Mountains of southeast Washington in the middle of winter is not an easy task, but this is what Jack Farquharson (21) and his friend Donald McDonald (17) decided to do in December of 1949. Both men were raised in the greater Walla Walla area and had substantial hunting experience.

Both guys were hunting a ridgeline called Blacksnake Ridge. It was cold and the weather was about to change drastically. Jack was leading the pair and spotted a nice-sized elk and shot it. The two boys started to track the wounded animal. Jack concentrated on tracking the blood and prints in the snow. Jack eventually found the dead animal and then turned to speak with Donald, but he was gone. Jack called Donald's name several times, but there was no answer. He walked back through their tracks, trying to retrace their path, but eventually lost them in the heavy snow.

Jack gutted the elk and brought it back to the camp that he and Donald had set up. The next two days, Jack searched for his friend without finding any trace of him. On Saturday morning, half frozen, Jack Farquharson stumbled into the Walla Walla County Sheriff's Office and reported his hunting partner missing.

The county sheriff, local ranchers, friends, and relatives searched for a week for Donald but couldn't locate the hunter. They didn't find his rifle or his clothes—not one item to confirm that Donald was anywhere in the Blacksnake Ridge area. Snowstorms had hit the area the day Donald went missing, and this hampered search efforts and the ability of trackers to follow a path. It seemed that there was little luck in finding Donald alive.

There were a few old and abandoned cabins in the Blue Mountains that Donald may have utilized for shelter. Eventually all were located and checked, but there was no evidence they had recently been used. The search for Donald was abandoned after one week of heavy storms.

In June of 1950, there was another search for Donald. People felt that after the snow melted there would be a greater chance to recover his body. A three-day search led by Sheriff A. A. Shick produced nothing to confirm Donald was in the area.

It has now been over sixty years since Donald McDonald disappeared, and the reality of his disappearance is hard to understand. It is true that bodies rot and eventually go back to the ground, but clothes and rifles sometimes stay years and even decades, especially rifles. Nothing belonging to Donald McDonald has ever been found.

Bobby Boatman
Missing: 10/14/51, Godman Spring, Walla Walla, WA
Age at disappearance: 14

As you read the accounts depicting the facts behind the disappearance of Bobby Boatman, I want you to think about the disappearance of Donald McDonald. The facts behind each disappearance are remarkably similar. Even though they happened in different counties, both happened in the Blue Mountains of southeast Washington and within two years of each other.

An October 16, 1961, article in the *Walla Walla Bulletin* stated: "Bobby left here Saturday morning with two older men and was last seen on a ridge Sunday morning near Godman Springs, 30 miles southeast of Dayton. His companions spent the day searching for him."

The morning following Bobby's disappearance, his friends reported him missing. That first night snow started falling hard in the mountains.

Deputy sheriffs, ranchers, and volunteers assisted in the search for Bobby. Authorities stated that they were optimistic they would find Bobby alive because of his background as a Boy Scout and his survival skills. The weather was so odd that it prompted District Ranger Homer Oft to make the following statement on December 21, 1949, to the *Bulletin*: "Freakish weather conditions blotted out communications with the 125 searchers who plowed through waist deep snow in sub-freezing temperatures looking for the youth."

A seven-day search for Bobby was unsuccessful.

It was almost five years to the exact day since he disappeared that law enforcement had their first break in the Bobby Boatman disappearance. On October 9, 1956, hunters in the Blue Mountains found a rifle and a red cap. The items were found near Godman Springs by hunters Billy Watson, Robert Bailey, Albert Bailey, and Jess Black. The rifle was a .30-caliber Remington. Both items were turned over to the sheriff. Sheriff E. E. "Duke" Warwick who took the rifle to a friend of the Boatmans', who confirmed the rifle was Bobby's. It was later confirmed that the red cap was also Bobby's. An October 17, 1956, article in the *Walla Walla Bulletin* stated: "The red baseball cap of Boatman was discovered in a bush with the rifle nearby, as though he might have dropped both items and taken off running, the Watson party told Warwick. The covered portion of the cap was still identifiable as having been red."

On October 12, 1956, Sheriff Warwick took a team back into the area where Bobby's rifle was found in an effort to locate the body. An article in the October 20 *Lewiston Morning Tribune* reported the following: "Bones and clothing in the area believed to be those of a teenage hunter who vanished five years ago were found in the Blue Mountains Thursday under suspicious-stirring circumstances." Sheriff Warwick identified the remains as Bobby Boatman. The incredible part of the find is what is described next: "Deputy Sheriff Herschel Bowman, who was at the scene, said evidence indicated the boy's body had been placed under tree roots and covered with dirt, then later pulled from the shallow grave by animals. The bones were partially covered with dirt and debris about 100 yards from where hunters found Boatman's rifle and cap."

This was a very lucky find for the sheriff and his men. If it weren't for hunters coming forward with what they had found, the chances of Bobby ever being recovered would have been minimal. One of the last paragraphs in the article is probably one of the most disturbing statements by a law enforcement officer I have ever read: "Sheriff Warwick said that on the basis of the evidence at hand, we don't know if there was foul play in the case. We will look into the possibility." This is disturbing because of other statements made by the sheriff's office just three days earlier. On October 17, 1956, Deputy Sheriff Billy Burton of Walla Walla County had explained to the media that in 1952 a knife and its sheath and a rope that Bobby Boatman used as a belt were found on a sandbar in Box Canyon. This little tidbit adds a lot to the investigation and should have been directly addressed as a major clue.

I could not find any article or report from the Walla Walla sheriff or coroner indicating the cause of death for Bobby Boatman.

Case Summary

In thirty-plus years of being an investigator, detective, and researcher, and reading thousands of missing person cases, I have never heard of anyone ever being buried under tree roots.

Hunters who found Bobby's cap and rifle said they believed it looked like they were dropped during Bobby's flight from something, something deadly. Bobby was killed and buried in a highly unique manner—under a tree. Tree roots offer a major barrier to anyone wanting to find the body or retrieve it. I don't think anyone in law enforcement would ever think of digging up trees to find a body. Over time tree roots will completely encase a body.

Bobby's knife, sheath, and rope belt were found in a creek bed a great distance from the body. Someone or something took the items off Bobby's waist and carried them from the scene and eventually left them near a creek..

The facts of this case do not add up to a calculated killing. If you are going to make the effort of concealing the body by burying it under a tree, why not also bury the rifle and cap? Why would you leave the rifle and red cap lying in an area where they could easily be seen? Why would you take the knife, sheath, and rope and leave them in an area where they could be retrieved?

Bears and mountain lions would not take a knife and sheath and carry it to another location a great distance away. These animals would leave everything where they found it. I have never heard of any animal burying anything under a tree stump.

The location of Bobby's body makes me greatly suspect that the body of Donald McDonald could be buried in a similar manner. They disappeared in too close of proximity to each other and the dates are too close to be ignored. If Donald was also buried under tree roots, it's understandable why his body has never been recovered.

Another similarity is that Bobby's knife and sheath were found in a creek bed. The last similarity between the Boatman and Mc-Donald cases: both young men disappeared when they were on a ridgeline, as was reported by their friends.

Catherine Painter Maynard
Missing: 01/19/53, White Bird, Idaho
Age at disappearance: 38

Operating a cattle ranch is a difficult task for any man, but how about a single thirty-eight-year-old woman operating on the edge of the Nez Perce National Forest? Catherine Painter Maynard was not your typical city female. She was living on and running a fully operational cattle ranch twelve miles east of White Bird on Skookumchuck Creek. Catherine had her mom living with her, running the household.

On January 12, 1953, Catherine realized that a few of her cattle had gone missing. Catherine took her cow pony and rode off into the wilds to look for her cattle. Late that afternoon snow started to fall and Catherine had not returned. Catherine's mother became very concerned and called other ranchers in the area to assist in a search.

On Wednesday three searchers found Catherine's body sprawled in the snow with no pony in the area. Searchers found a very peculiar site. A January 23, 1953, article in the *Lewiston Morning Tribune* included the following in bold: "When Mrs. Maynard left home Monday she was wearing felt boots under her overshoes. When she finally collapsed in the snow, she had removed both overshoes and one of the felt boots."

Her body was found on Banner Ridge twelve miles east of White Bird. Searchers found Catherine's pony tied to a tree two miles from her body. The mortician who did the autopsy, Jesse Robertson, stated that Catherine had suffered from "prolonged confusion preceding exhaustion." Jesse stated on January 22 in the *Spokane Daily Chronicle*, "Death was due to exhaustion."

Case Summary

This is another case that completely defies logic. We will never know what exactly killed Catherine Maynard, but it was not exhaustion. She was on a ridgeline and she lived in the area. She was less than two miles from her ranch and two miles from her pony; I doubt she was lost. How she got to the location where she was found is the million-dollar question. I do not believe that Catherine would have walked miles without her pony, especially in inclement weather.

The weather had started to turn bad the first night she was missing. I don't believe that Catherine would be taking off her shoes while it was snowing. This is one of the many instances when journalists try to justify a very unusual circumstance to calm community concern. I believe the issue of Catherine's shoes being printed in bold in the newspaper shows there was concern for this fact in the local area.

Many people may completely overlook the issue that brought Catherine out that night. She was looking for missing cattle. We need to ask ourselves where those cattle were and who or what took them.

Christine Woollett
Missing: 05/12/66, 8:00 p.m., Spokane, WA
Age at disappearance: 2

Mr. and Mrs. Jack Woollett lived in a nice home approximately one thousand yards from the Spokane River. The home sat uphill from the river and had a nice view of the city from its rural location. The area around the residence was thick with large pine trees and scrubs.

In the early evening hours of May 12, 1966, the Woolletts left to work their building maintenance job in the city. Their daughter, Christine, stayed at their residence with her babysitter.

At approximately 8:00 p.m., Christine was allowed outside wearing a large coat. This was the last time anyone saw Christine Woollett. After the babysitter was unable to find Christine, she called the sheriff, who enlisted the assistance of off-duty firefighters, police officers, and his own sheriff's department deputies to search for the two-year-old girl. The local river was dragged and everything in the surrounding hills was combed for evidence of the girl.

May 13 brought about two very strange incidents that were reported by searchers. At approximately 3:00 a.m., searchers were still out in the forest looking for Christine when they reported hearing a child's cry coming out of the darkness, (*Spokane Daily Chronicle*, May 13, 1966). Then, at 7:30 a.m., another searcher reported hearing what he described as a moan from what sounded like a child coming from the desolate hillside near where he was searching. The Gonzaga University student said he couldn't tell the exact direction, but a massive search of both areas was completed without finding any evidence of Christine.

A May 14 article in the *Spokane Daily Chronicle* included the following statement from Sheriff Reilly: "Reilly said there is always a slim possibility the child may have been abducted." The sheriff later stated that he felt the girl drowned in the river, but he didn't have any evidence to support his belief.

On May 16, the three-day search for Christine Woollett was terminated. The sheriff stated that he would occasionally be checking the river and the nearby Long Lake and Lake Spokane, but felt there was nothing else his department could do.

Case Summary

This is another case in which searchers give up the search and start to claim abduction, then change paths and claim she drowned in a river. They were obviously frustrated by the lack of evidence. A three-day search for a two-year-old girl is not enough time to adequately address all aspects of a disappearance and search.

I find it very unusual for search teams to report sounds of a crying or moaning child coming from the forest. SAR teams must have been shocked and concerned when they heard those sounds and were unable to locate their source. If those sounds did come from Christine, I believe the teams would have found her (if she was in the woods voluntarily). The question is, what made the sounds in the woods?

Lowell Smith
Missing: 10/5/68, Pilot Knob, Grangeville, Idaho
Age at disappearance: 60

It's a rare occasion when a former professional athlete makes the news for being lost in the wild, but that is exactly what happened on October 5, 1968. Lowell Smith was a former Green Bay Packers football player. Lowell had an excellent job in Fernley, Nevada, where he was the superintendent of the Fernley United Serra Mining and Milling Company.

In early October of 1968, Lowell traveled to an area called Pilot Knob nineteen miles east of Grangeville, Idaho. Pilot Knob is known as a great hunting area in the fall and is in the northern section of the Nez Perce National Forest.

Idaho County Sheriff Gene Fuzzell conducted a historic five-day search for Lowell. Two helicopters were utilized in the search along with a massive ground team. On October 9, ground teams happened onto Lowell's camp in the Lightning Creek drainage. This area is thick with old-growth trees and significant ground cover. The team found the brand of cigarettes that Lowell smoked, along with ammunition, food, and evidence that Lowell had been there at least two days. Another item they found at the camp caused serious concern—Lowell's rifle. A hunter would never leave their rifle in camp and wander from the immediate area. Never.

Lowell was a very influential figure in Nevada. His family had two senators call the Idaho governor and ask for the search for Lowell to continue. The Idaho governor got their National Guard to assist in the search for two additional weeks. A total of three weeks was spent searching the area where Lowell's camp was found. Lowell was never located and no other evidence was ever discovered.

Case Summary

It's hard to imagine that hundreds of National Guard members, spending weeks searching an identified area around a campsite, cannot find a missing hunter. It would appear that Lowell was nowhere in the area close to the campsite. He was a very experienced hunter and would never leave the camp area without his rifle. If Lowell knew never to leave without his rifle, and his body wasn't found anywhere near the camp, what forced him to leave?

Gayla Christine Schaper
Missing: 06/29/79, Moscow, Idaho
Age at disappearance: 28
5'8", 135 lb.

Ken and Gayla Schaper owned Dutchboy Dairy, located east of Moscow on the Troy Highway. Moscow is less than one mile from the Washington border.

On June 29 at approximately 7:00 p.m., Ken dropped Gayla at their pasture on Lenville Road southeast of Moscow in gently rolling hills that are filled with farms and scattered homes. At 7:30 p.m. Ken returned for his wife but she was gone.

Ken was considered a suspect in Gayla's disappearance until he took a polygraph and passed. There was complexity in this case involving an individual near the pasture where Gayla was working. According to news sources, law enforcement had some belief that this neighbor may have been involved in the disappearance, but no arrests have been made.

The pasture and surrounding area were thoroughly searched the night Gayla disappeared, but nothing was ever found indicating where she might be. People of interest involved in the investigation have passed away, and evidence in the case is slowly passing with time. Ken Schaper still lives in the area. This is still an open case.

Richard Ray Barnett
Missing: 08/31/82, Grangeville, Idaho
Age at disappearance: 2
3', 32 lb.

A summer vacation to Grandpa and Grandma's house is something many of us enjoyed as youngsters. It was a time to get away from the parents, see a new area, and have the grandparents cater to us. I'm sure that Richard "Rickey" Barnett felt the same way when he left his mother's house and went to stay with his grandparents seven miles north of Grangeville, Idaho. Grangeville is in the eastern portion of Idaho near the center of the state. It sits on the northern edge of the Nez Perce National Forest but is mostly gentle rolling hills with farms and ranches.

Waldo and Martha McCoard owned the Hillcrest Farms, a very successful dairy farm in rolling hills north of Grangeville. Jim

McCoard was their son and was divorced from Rickey's mom, Judy Barnett. Judy allowed Rickey to spend time on the grandparents' farm and experience a different side of life.

On August 31, 1982, Rickey got up early with his grandparents and went onto to the ranch to do chores. The farm was a big operation with employees. The grandparents were in the chicken barn preparing for a shipment, and employees were preparing the cows for the day. Rickey was last seen at 7:00 a.m. near the chicken barn. At 10:00 a.m. the grandparents realized he was missing. After searching for thirty minutes, they called the sheriff's department.

The dairy farm is at the end of a half-mile road that comes off the highway. There is no other reason to be on this road unless you are there to see the McCoards. Everyone on the ranch knows when someone comes down the McCoards' road.

By the end of the day, over two hundred people were searching the grounds and surrounding hills for Rickey. The McCoards' pastor from the LDS church was the primary liaison for the family, and he helped with the search efforts. The four-day search would be one of the most intense searches the Idaho County Sheriff's Department had ever undertaken.

Kathy Hedberg, a reporter for the *Tribune*, wrote a series of articles about the disappearance of Rickey. I was able to interview Kathy by phone about the events. She stated that it was a very large search operation. She was with a canine team that heard an apple had been found in a small valley with a creek. There were small bite marks in the apple. This wild apple was placed on top of a large boulder in the creek. Kathy went with the SAR people and found the apple. The sheriff's team decided a small animal had bitten the apple, and they didn't think it was a viable lead. Kathy also stated that a canine appeared to pick up Rickey's scent. The dog tracked it to a fence line on the farm and then stopped. The search team didn't quite know what to make of the canine stopping and not going farther than the fence.

Kathy stated that in the last thirty years since Rickey disappeared, there have been two primary theories about what happened to the boy. The original theory was that the grandmother played some role in taking the boy off the farm and gave him to someone to get him away from her stepdaughter. The grandmother later passed a polygraph test and was completely exonerated of any involvement.

The second and most recent theory deals with a ranch hand who left sometime after Rickey disappeared. Law enforcement hasn't been able to contact the man since the disappearance.

Kathy said that the sheriff did not believe that a stranger would drive up the McCoards' road and abduct the boy because of the isolation of the ranch.

The Idaho sheriff thoroughly searched the McCoards' ranch for four days. The search included helicopters, airplanes, canines, volunteers' horses, and hundreds of interested and willing city folks. On September 7, 1982, Sheriff R. W. Walkup made the following statement to the *Tribune*: "God knows we've done everything we can. If we had a trace, we'd keep going, but we haven't had a clue, not a footprint, not a piece of clothing, not a sound, nothing." The search was officially terminated, but the case is still alive today. The case file has been passed through three detectives (as each retired, a new detective got the report).

Julie Ann Weflen
Missing: 09/16/87, fifteen miles north of Spokane, WA
Age at disappearance: 28
5'2", 100 lb.

You usually don't expect people to be abducted while they are working at a remote power plant, but that is exactly what happened to Julie Weflen. Julie was an employee of Bonneville Power Authority, and her job was to energize power equipment, read meters, and keep transformers operational. On September 16, 1987, Julie was working at the Power Authority. At 2:30 p.m. she signed in to the Springhill substation fifteen miles north of Spokane. It was estimated that she was there for one hour. Something happened at approximately 3:30 p.m. and Julie disappeared.

The exact location of the substation is where Four Mound and Coulee Hite roads meet northwest of Spokane, less than one mile from Riverside State Park. Nine Mile Reservoir is less than one mile east of the substation. The Springhill substation is in a rocky, desolate area without towns. It is on a small, dirt side street where a passing driver may not even notice anyone there.

Detectives stated that they found Julie's hardhat and sunglasses on the ground near her van. There were drag marks on the ground near the van and the vehicle was unlocked. Authorities guessed that Julie was overpowered by two people; this was based on her strength and the evidence at the scene.

There are four women missing from the greater Spokane area under suspicious circumstances, per law enforcement sources. I would have readers look at the photos of Julie Weflen and Tina Finley (case details below) and notice the similar dark complexion and attractive features of the two women. The cases in this section all occurred in proximity to the Idaho border.

Tina Marie Finley
Missing: 03/07/88, Plummer, Idaho
Age at disappearance: 25
5'6", 135 lb.

Tina Finley was at a bar the night she disappeared. Near the end of the night, Tina had a male friend drive her back to the area of her residence on an American Indian Reservation. He said he dropped her at a dirt road near the residence and left. She was never seen again. It was raining very heavy when Tina was dropped off.

Tina's purse, ID, and shoes were found on the side of the road in the area where she was dropped off. Authorities found other property belonging to Tina in an abandoned house ten miles south near the city of De Smet.

Besides the original search for Tina, a second search was conducted in early April 1988, two miles south of Plummer along Highway 95, but no new evidence was found. The friend who dropped Tina off has passed a polygraph test and is not a suspect. The FBI has entered this case.

Brian Sines
Missing: 11/22/91, southeast of Clarkia, Idaho
Age at disappearance: 29

Brian Sines was an employee of the Potlach Lumber Mill in St. Maries, Idaho. He had a day off of work and decided to go to the mountains south of Clarkia on a hunting trip. Brian failed to arrive at work Monday morning, so friends and relatives went to the area he was hunting, where they found his truck. A February 27, 1992, article in the *Spokane Chronicle* reported the following: "They found Sines' pickup parked in the middle of a forest service road as if he had stopped suddenly and jumped out to chase a deer. Searchers followed his tracks up a ridge but lost them on the other side."

The writer of the article obviously made an assumption that Brian was chasing a deer. I say that he saw something that attracted his attention to the point that he stopped in the middle of the road and left his truck. Once his friends found the truck, they brought in search dogs to pick up a scent. The dogs followed a trail up a ridgeline and then stopped. Searchers scoured the area but could not locate Brian.

Nothing happened in the Brian Sines case until a water-measuring team went into the wilderness to measure the snowpack on February 25, 1992. The team found a bone and pieces of bone near the bottom of a ridgeline and notified law enforcement.

Shoshone County Sheriff's Office responded to the location and found keys, credit cards, and clothing that was later identified as belonging to Brian Sines. Searchers found an intact clavicle, one arm bone, and one leg bone, but many pieces of bone were scattered across and down the ridge. There was some thoughts that Brian may have fallen, but no bones were found broken. Bones were found in pieces, but that was attributed to animals.

The coroner made a determination that Brian died of exposure—a very bold statement. Brian was only five miles from his truck, which seems odd. If he did bolt from the truck to chase something, it would seem odd that he'd travel five miles knowing his truck was blocking a forest service road. I would understand a short chase and maybe firing a few rounds if he saw something. The idea that he stayed with whatever he was chasing for five miles, equaling at least an hour chase, seems very unusual. It's possible Brian died somewhere else and was carried to the ridge, but we will never know.

Ruben David Felix
Missing: 02/23/97, Shoshone, Idaho
Age at disappearance: 2
2'6", 32 lb.

Shoshone is approximately seventy miles south of Sun Valley and is near the center of Idaho. This case is included in this section because it matches other cases in the state of two-year-olds missing from home yards.

Ruben Felix was with his father at the family ranch on the outskirts of Shoshone. His dad states that he momentarily left the boy in their front yard drinking from a bottle. When he returned the boy had vanished.

Detectives initially believed that Ruben might have drowned in a nearby river. Multiple searches of the river failed to produce Ruben's body. Other officials affiliated with the case believe that Ruben may have been abducted, but no evidence to support either theory has been found.

Readers need to recognize the similarities between the three cases of missing two-year-olds (Barnett, Blakeley, and Felix) from rural yards throughout western Idaho. Investigators cannot ignore the similarities among these disappearances.

Ronald S. Gray
Missing: 09/19/08, Nez Perce National Forest, Idaho
Age at disappearance: 62

If anyone could live in the outdoors and survive brutal conditions, it was Ronald Gray. Ronald had a military background with tours of Vietnam where he had to eat bugs and snakes to survive. When he came back from the war, he became a local police officer in Massachusetts, and then spent the majority of his career as a Massachusetts State Trooper, where he eventually retired after twenty-six years.

Ronald loved the outdoors and had made two previous trips to the same area of Idaho to hunt elk and deer. He knew the landscape and he trusted the hunting guides who established his camp. Gray was the type of hunter who enjoyed the challenges of hunting alone, which is what he did on September 19, 2008. He had met with the hunting guides, who told him where they stashed extra supplies in the woods. He carried a global positioning unit to find the supplies and establish his exact location at any time. Ronald told the guide service that he would meet them on September 23, a date he never kept.

One of the largest searches in the history of the Nez Perce National Forest was undertaken for Ronald Gray. Even members from the state police in Massachusetts came to Idaho to assist in the search. Helicopters, horses, and ground teams scoured the area, but nothing was found. There was a rumor that he had made a radio call that he had hurt his knee, but this was never confirmed.

A large section of the 8,500 square miles of the Nez Perce was searched for two weeks. Again, nothing was found. On October 15, 2008, the search for Ronald Gray was terminated. Since the termination, hundreds of hunters and searchers have continued to look for Ronald, but they have never found any of his property or Ronald.

Avery Barnett Blakeley
Missing: 03/26/09, Malden, WA
Age at disappearance: 2
2'8", 27 lb.

Malden, Washington, sits approximately ten miles west of the Idaho state line and is included in this section because of the proximity to numerous missing people along the Idaho-Washington border.

Avery Blakeley's mother was helping her sister move from a residence. While the women were moving, Avery was momentarily left alone in the yard. It was during this short period that Avery disappeared. He was last seen at 12:30 p.m., and it is guessed that he disappeared at 1:30 p.m.

Nearby Pine Creek was flowing very high in March 2009, and some believed the young boy fell into the creek and perished. The creek during the spring months is just large enough that it would be unsafe to cross. During summer months the creek could be easily traversed. The Spokane County sheriff brought divers and a fast-water recovery team to the area. They searched for the boy for twenty-four hours but did not find him. Searchers did find one of Avery's slippers on the bank near the creek.

On April 10, the sheriff returned to the scene with canines and cadaver dogs. The team searched the ten miles downstream from the residence but could not locate the body.

It is quite surprising that the sheriff only performed the original search for twenty-four hours and then quit. It is also surprising that the sheriff's office did not return during the summer to thoroughly search the creek with a cadaver dog.

This missing person case is still open.

Chapter Summary

There are several unusual cases in Idaho. There are a few very odd coincidences when you refer to the list of missing.

The three two-year-old boys from Idaho—Blakeley, Felix, and Barnett—went missing under very similar conditions. It seems odd that all three of these boys were exactly two years old and all disappeared from a rural home or ranch. At first glance their disappearances may seem random, but I don't think they are. In 1883, a child eighteen months old goes missing; fifty years later a seven-year-old goes missing; thirty-three years later a two-year-old goes missing; and then sixteen years after that another two-year-old disappears. All of the children who disappeared have a number of adults between them who also went missing. The last two youngsters on the list were two years old, and their disappearances happened twelve years apart. A total of four two-year-olds disappeared in a span of forty-three years, with no other youngsters missing during that time span in this region—very, very odd.

Montana

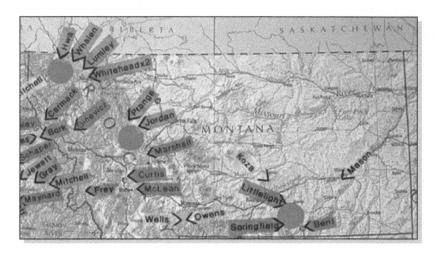

The incidents cited in this chapter will shock some people. These stories prove that truth is stranger than fiction. If I wrote these in a fictional account of camping in the mountains, readers would laugh and say "impossible." Unfortunately, these are true stories that happened in remote areas of Montana.

Montana Missing Persons by Date

Missing Person	Date, Missing•Age•Sex
Alexis Bork	11/7/1896•NA•M
Jack Wells*	11/05/1901•NA•M
Joseph Whitehead	08/24/24•29•M
William Whitehead	08/24/24•32•M
Frederick Lumley	08/13/34•NA•M
Al Owens*	11/07/45•71•M
John Koza*	04/26/50•50-60•M
Patty Ann Mclean	07/04/53•3•F
Ida May Curtis	07/04/55•2•F
Mary Gay Bent	07/13/58•5•F
Lawrence E. Prange	08/14/58•20•M

William Carmack	07/22/59•55•M
Arthur Jordan	11/08/59•59•M
Fritz Frey	11/14/60•65•M
20-Year Gap	
Megan Ginevicz	04/30/80•2•F
Nyleen Kay Marshall	06/25/83•4•F
Patrick T. Whalen	11/02/00•33•M
Robert Springfield	09/19/04•49•M
Yi-Jien Hwa	08/11/08•27•M
Wyatt Little Light	12/23/08•2•M

*Details on the disappearances of the following individuals can be found in the chapter "Sheepherders" in *Book #2, Missing 411: Eastern United States*:
Jack Wells
Al Owens
John Koza

Alexis Bork
Missing: 11/07/1896, Flathead Mountains, MT
Age at disappearance: unknown
    I could only find one article on this incident, a November 10, 1896, news brief in the *New York Times*. The article states that Alexis Bork was a preacher, and he had gone with a hunting party on November 5 to the Flathead Mountains outside of Troy, Montana. He went hunting with a group on a Thursday and returned, but he went out again alone on Saturday and did not return.
    On Sunday a search team was organized to locate Reverend Bork. Here is what the article stated: "Several miles from the camp the searchers found blood on the snow and later came to a place where it was evident that a terrible struggle had taken place. A trail in the snow led some distance to a point where the body of the young minister was found mangled, torn and frozen. It was evident that Bork had been attacked and overcome by some animal, which afterward dragged the body to the spot where it was found."

Case Summary

This is a highly unusual case because bears in Montana are hibernating by mid-November. It's obvious from the article that the writers and sources in Montana had no idea what could have killed the preacher, and the article didn't make any mention that he had been consumed.

Joseph Whitehead, age 29
William Whitehead, age 22
Missing: 08/25/24, Glacier National Park, MT

If anyone were going to pick two brilliant young men to write about, it would be the Whiteheads. Joseph was a graduate of the Lewis Institute and a former lieutenant in the Army Ordnance Division. At the time of his disappearance, he was an engineer for Universal Battery in Chicago. Joseph's brother, William, was a twenty-two-year-old student at the Massachusetts Institute of Technology (MIT) and was set to graduate the following year.

The brothers left their mother's home in Chicago on August 21, 1924. As they traveled west across the United States, they wrote their mother daily about their adventures. The boys arrived at the Lewis Hotel inside Glacier National Park on August 24. The boys sent their mother a card from the hotel on the day they arrived. That was the last time Mrs. Dora Whitehead ever heard from her two sons.

The Whiteheads had told friends that they were going to hike from the hotel to Granite Park, an area near the center of Glacier National Park. The route that the boys would have taken is adjacent to Lake McDonald, which is near the hotel. The lake was searched and all paths near the shoreline were checked. At that time the park was busy with tourists, and if someone were injured close to a trail, others would hear their cries for help. Nobody reported anyone in distress.

The journey to Granite Park is long. They would pass Lake McDonald and cross the divide, where they would have to continue on foot toward the east side of the park. After not receiving further correspondence, the boys' mother called the NPS and asked for a search. The park complied.

The National Park Service continued to be prompted by officials in government to not give up the search for the Whiteheads. It was obvious from the communications circulating in the media that these two men needed to be found. The Whiteheads were both highly educated, in very good physical condition, and had common sense. They shouldn't have disappeared.

A few short days after Dora Whitehead alerted the park, Glacier National Park stated that they would utilize all available rangers, volunteers, and other government workers in a systematic search of every possible location where the Whiteheads could be.

The NPS searched for six weeks and found nothing. Dora Whitehead wasn't satisfied with the search and contacted President Calvin Coolidge to ask for more assistance. The FBI was assigned the case and pursued many clues, but all led nowhere and everything was deemed "not credible."

On March 14, 1925, the Whitehead family distributed 25,000 posters of the men, explaining the circumstances and offering a reward. Nothing of value ever came from the poster effort.

On August 19, 1925, Dora Whitehead and her daughter traveled to Glacier National Park and were briefed by the park superintendent on the efforts to find her sons. The park service explained that the black bears living in the area at the time were not dangerous and that they did not believe animals were involved in the disappearance. An article in the *Chicago Daily Tribune* on August 19 stated, "Mountaineers with whom they [Dora Whitehead and her daughter] talked were convinced that the two had met with violence."

Case Summary

It is a very rare occurrence that two intelligent and grown men go missing in a national park together. Almost ninety years later, the Whiteheads still haven't been found and there are no leads. These men were in excellent physical condition and were ready to make the journey they had planned. There are no notes in anything I've read that weather played a role in their disappearance.

Whatever happened to Joseph and William could happen to anyone, and that is a scary thought.

Frederick H. Lumley
Missing: 08/13/34, Glacier National Park, MT
Age at disappearance: 27

Dr. Frederick Lumley was a professor at Ohio State University and had traveled to Glacier National Park to hike the gorgeous terrain. Frederick left his baggage at the Glacier Hotel and started his hike. The last time anyone saw the professor was August 13, when he was seen leaving Goat Camp.

Frederick never returned to pick up his luggage, and a search was organized. Searchers interviewed hikers and determined the last confirmed sighting was when he left the Goat Camp area. Park officials theorized that Frederick was going to travel either around or over Mount Cleveland the day that he was last seen.

Park officials organized a huge search but could not find any evidence. Mount Cleveland was checked, but none of his equipment could be found at the base or on the mountain. The twelve-day search for Frederick culminated without finding the professor or his equipment. He was classified by the park service as "missing and presumed dead." You will not find Dr. Frederick Lumley on any missing person database or listed as missing on any ledger or list the park service may maintain.

The NPS's statement, "Missing and presumed dead," is a convenient method for them to wash their hands of a missing person and not note them as missing on an ongoing basis. The reality of this statement is that there is still a person missing and nobody is looking for him. Nobody will know that Frederick disappeared in a specific area of the park because a missing person report is not open and active. The case was closed.

Patty Ann Mclean
Missing: 07/04/53, 2:30 p.m., fifteen miles northeast of Butte, MT
Age at disappearance: 3

Mr. and Mrs. William Mclean traveled fifteen miles northeast from their home in Butte to a campground in the Deer Lodge National Forest for a Fourth of July picnic. The McLean's had two boys and three girls in their family.

It was approximately 2:30 p.m. on the Fourth and the family was playing ball when they realized that little Patty Ann had wandered off. The four other children and the parents all participated in yelling and searching the picnic grounds for the small girl. It wasn't long into the search that the parents enlisted the assistance of the U.S. Forest Service, who called the local sheriff's department. Within hours there were hundreds of people searching for Patty Ann.

The first night of the search was unsuccessful but searchers continued to search the heavily wooded and swampy area for the toddler. The local sheriff had brought in bloodhounds, but they failed to find the girl.

At approximately noon on July 5, some searchers focused on the area near the picnic site while a few others wandered deep into the forest to a rocky cliff. In an unbelievable stroke of luck, three searchers were climbing up a rock ledge and found the girl on a rock halfway up a cliff. Patty Ann was missing one shoe but was in good condition considering it had gotten down to forty-three degrees the night before.

In another unbelievable aspect of this case, Patty Ann was found over eight miles from the location where she disappeared. In the book *Lost Person Behavior* by Robert Koester, he states that a missing three-year-old will be found less than 5.6 miles from the point last seen in 95 percent of searches. Patty Ann was found 2.4 miles outside the 5.6-mile mark and up a "sheer rock cliff" (*Long Beach Independent*, July 6, 1953).

Patty Ann was interviewed after she went to the hospital. She said she slept under a log, indicating that she wasn't on the cliff at night. She also said she had seen "little cows" (*Interlaker*, July 6, 1953).

Case Summary

This is another case where a small girl disappears in the forest from a family event where other small children are present. It is hard to believe that a three-year-old could walk eight miles in twenty-three hours and then climb a sheer rock cliff. What did Patty Ann mean when she stated that she had seen "little cows"?

Ida May Curtis
Missing: 07/04/55, Kootenai National Forest, Libby, MT
Age at disappearance: 2

Mortimer Curtis was a logger employed by Leigh Creek Camp in the Kootenai National Forest. Mortimer worked in the camp with his dad, Curtis. The Fourth of July weekend brought families to the camp to spend time with their husbands and fathers. The families placed tents on the perimeter of the camp and spent the weekend playing with the other children and loggers. It was a way for the logging company to keep their men in camp, yet allow for social time with the families.

At approximately 1:30 p.m. on July 4, Ida May Curtis and her nine-year-old brother, Cecil, walked off the camp grounds. Cecil told the family that Ida May had seen something in the forest near the clearing where they were standing. The kids returned to the camp and were playing around the tent when they claim that a bear entered the tent and then left hopping on three legs carrying Ida May. They stated that the bear ran into the woods with the little girl. Curtis confirmed that he thought he saw a bear just about that time running through a creek, and it appeared to be carrying something. He stated that he tried to chase the creature but could not keep up.

The children told Ida May's mother what they observed, and she looked in the tent. She couldn't find Ida May. She ran into the woods and didn't see anything. The authorities were quickly notified and a massive search was immediately initiated. Almost 250 searchers from as far away as Spokane responded to search for the little girl.

The mother was interviewed and confirmed there was no way her daughter would leave the immediate area of the other children unless she was taken.

Just after Ida May disappeared, a fierce rain hit the area, followed by a snowstorm. The storm greatly hindered search efforts because tracks and scent had been washed away.

On July 5 at approximately 4:30 p.m., searchers found Ida May alive. The girl was found nearly three hundred yards from where she originally disappeared. She showed her parents where she was held by a mother bear (her words). It was a crude shelter on the opposite side of the creek from the campground. The shelter was

282 | Missing 411-Western U.S. & Canada

made of cedar slashings. A July 5, 1955, article in the *Spokane Daily Chronicle* stated, "The girl was found, huddled in a crude shelter of cedar slashings, which were too heavy for her to lift." This indicates that Ida May could not have made the shelter. If they were too heavy for Ida May to lift, then how could a bear lift them?

Doctors examined Ida May and found her to be in perfect condition—no scratches, no bite marks, and no effects from exposure to the elements.

Case Summary

This is a fascinating abduction to study because there are many more facts that we don't know. I have yet to ever find a credible story where a child is held captive by a bear overnight, comforted, and then released unharmed the next morning. Maybe the children were stretching the truth when they described what they saw when Ida May was abducted (we don't know); but Curtis's statement that he saw a three-legged animal running and carrying something when Ida May disappeared has to be believed. That said, many questions come to mind. How did Ida May live through a snowy night without getting cold and suffering from exposure? How did she cross the creek without getting soaked? How can a bear grab a child and not leave teeth or claw marks? Why would Ida May lie about what happened when other children and her grandfather confirmed her story?

More fascinating aspects of this case include statements made by Lincoln County Sheriff Ray Frost after the girl was found. He made several statements to the media claiming that Ida May was never taken by a bear; she just wandered off. When the media representative said that this isn't what the family reported, Sheriff Frost stated, "I don't see why they keep saying that … I think I'll go out and talk with the parents again." Why would the sheriff make a special trip to speak to parents who had just gone through a traumatic ordeal unless he wanted to stop the story?

Another odd fact: the camp the loggers were occupying at Leigh Creek had been occupied for many months. It seems extremely odd that the weekend children arrive at the camp a bear supposedly walks into a tent, picks up a child, and hops away on three legs, outrunning a man trying to catch them. It seems almost impossible. When bears are confronted, they usually get angry and stand their ground. They don't flee, especially while holding something as large as a two-year-old girl. It also seems almost impossible for a bear to hold a child in its arm and run on three feet without injuring or dropping the child. Remember, the bear had to cross a creek to get to the location where they supposedly spent the night.

Yet another part of this story that seems impossible is that the bear grabbed the girl, took her to its den, and then comforted her through the night. A bear might take a child to its den to eat her, but not to comfort her.

I believe something took Ida May and comforted her through the night. The real question is, what grabbed her?

The final element of this story that needs to be discussed is the den made of cedar slashings. There are two other cases in which young boys disappeared and a crude shelter was found nearby—Dennis Johnson in Yellowstone National Park, and Derrick Engbretson in Crater Lake National park. The boys were never found, and whatever made the shelter was never identified.

Mary Gay Bent
Missing: 07/13/58, 3:00 p.m., Sage Creek Campground, MT
Age at disappearance: 5
Blonde hair
Disability
The Bent family had driven to the Sage Creek Campground to celebrate the fifth birthday of Mary Gay. There were other friends and family that came to the picnic. Mary had twin brothers, John and Arthur (7), and a one-year-old brother named Fred. Mary had the appearance of someone with a disability, as her left arm and shoulder were heavily bandaged after an extensive bone marrow transfer to accelerate growth in her arm.

At approximately 3:00 p.m. the day of the picnic, Mary asked her mom if she could walk the twenty feet to the restroom. Her mom said that was fine. Mary didn't come back. Family and friends immediately started to call for the girl and ran throughout the area looking for Mary, but there was no trace of her. The family started searching less than five minutes after she went to the bathroom. They knew she couldn't have gone very far.

The Bents called the USFS and the local sheriff. The call for assistance also brought the state police and bloodhounds from the Montana State Prison. Forty officers spent the entire first night searching for the girl without finding any evidence. Rescuers were searching in almost impossible conditions because it was raining very hard. Bloodhounds were not successful in finding Mary. The area where Mary disappeared is in a small valley with Sage Creek flowing down the center. Sage Creek has trout, and the surrounding mountains are large and tall.

There were several different groups of searchers in the field. On July 14, one searcher was alone one thousand feet up the mountain from the campsite and thought he saw a clump lying on the ground below a large pine tree. As the searcher approached the tree, he saw a large coat with its hood pulled up over the head of the body. It was 2:00 p.m. when the searcher pulled the hood back and found Mary Gay Bent asleep two miles from the campsite and a remarkable one thousand feet higher in elevation (at seven thousand feet). The girl was among large tress and thick vegetation. Her arm with the bandage was not injured.

Mary didn't explain much about her ordeal other than to say that she had gone back and forth from where she was found and the campsite where she disappeared, almost implying that she knew where the campsite was but didn't return. She was asked how she stayed dry in the driving rainstorm; the girl stated that she slept under a log.

Case Summary

It's hard to understand how anyone can get lost walking twenty feet to a restroom, especially when they know their parents are within yelling distance. It's equally hard to decipher what the girl meant when she stated that she had been going back and forth throughout the night. How could she have gone back and forth throughout the night without getting soaked from the heavy rain? I do think it's important to note that this is another child that claimed they slept under a log, I'm not sure that this is intuitive for a small kid.

Lawrence Eugene Prange
Missing: 08/14/58, Seeley Lake, MT
Age at disappearance: 20
One of the oldest rules when visiting the great outdoors is to never hike alone. This is the rule that Lawrence Prange broke when he visited the area of Seeley Lake on August 10, 1958.

Lawrence was from Lake Villa, Illinois, and always enjoyed the outdoors. His interest in wildlife led him to study to be a wildlife technician at University of Montana at Missoula. Lawrence found an old wooden cabin behind the university that he made his home. Lawrence's girlfriend, Susan Heck, was a fellow student. Lawrence enjoyed all parts of the wild and that included hunting. The trip to the Seeley Lake region was intended to be a hunt for mountain goats. Lawrence had made a trip to this region before, and he would again take as his companion his German shepherd, Queen.

Lawrence entered the wilderness carrying a backpack with two rifles, and Queen carried her own backpack with supplies. Lawrence was due out of the Mission Range on August 14, and he had agreed to contact his parents and girlfriend when he returned. He never made those calls. The alarm was sounded and Mr. and Mrs. Prange headed for Montana. Sue Heck headed for the search center.

Searchers utilized helicopters, men on horseback, specialty trackers, and even brought in canines in the hopes of luring out Prange's dog. After more than a month of searching, the SAR teams had found nothing. On September 20, an SAR team riding the range saw Queen running wildly through the brush. She was seen on the northwest side of Lindbergh Lake. The area around Lindbergh is very lush with thick vegetation. There is ample water in the area for all wildlife. SAR teams could not get near Queen because she was too jumpy and nervous. The location where teams spotted Queen was more than three miles from the primary search location at Rocky Heights.

The SAR team returned to the base and asked Lawrence's girlfriend to accompany them in an attempt to retrieve Queen. Sue

Heck was the only person who could get close to Queen. The dog eventually calmed down and followed the teams back to base camp.

After a day of calming the dog and feeding her, searchers took Queen to the top of one of the primary peaks they believed Lawrence had hunted. Queen wanted nothing to do with even being on the mountain and wanted to get out of the area. Searchers carefully examined Queen and did not find any wounds on her indicating that she may have been in a fight with an animal. Lawrence's parents and his girlfriend were quite puzzled by the fact that Queen's backpack had been removed as it was something that needed human intervention to take off, searchers never found this or any of Lawrence's equipment. Teams theorized that whatever happened to Lawrence must have occurred while he had his equipment on his back because they never found his campsite.

Case Summary

There is something about the general Seeley Lake region that doesn't bode well for hikers and hunters traveling alone.

I've tracked dozens of cases in which hikers and hunters have died and the canine companion is sitting next to the corpse refusing to leave. This is the only case I've ever seen where the canine was running loose in the wild and the hunter is never found. It would almost seem as if Queen was deathly afraid of the circumstances surrounding Lawrence's disappearance and wanted nothing to do with whatever may have happened. Even if Lawrence was murdered, you'd expect the dog to go back to the corpse.

Lawrence may have been well armed, but as searchers, his girlfriend, and parents stated, both of his rifles were kept in his backpack. If the rifles were not readily available, Lawrence could have been jumped by something and never had a chance to defend himself.

Three miles east of where Queen was located is the timberline region, where you'd expect a goat or sheep hunter to set up camp. The area is dotted with dozens of small lakes, which makes this a very difficult area to search. Almost in the middle of this beauty is Lucifer Lake. With a name like that, I wouldn't like to camp there.

On September 24 the search for Lawrence was over. His parents went to his cabin in Pattee Canyon and collected his belongings. Sue Heck returned to the university and resumed her studies to become a wildlife technician. The Pranges went back to Illinois without ever knowing what happened to their son. Queen went back to Illinois with the Pranges. Oh, if only that dog could talk.

William Carmack
Missing: 07/22/59, Thompson Peak, Superior, MT
Age at disappearance: 55

The story of how supply packer William Carmack originally disappeared is intertwined with the disappearance of his boss, the owner of a sheepherding company in Superior, Montana. Both stories are equally bizarre and defy conventional explanation.

William worked for the Faure and Servell Sheepherding Company for almost three years. His job was to lead a supply train of horses and mules through the Lolo National Forest to the site of the sheep. This was a fairly uneventful job for those three years until, on or near July 21, 1959, something so bizarre happened that the county sheriff stated that he couldn't understand what happened.

The sheep camp was approximately fifteen miles from Superior, Montana. William loaded four horses and two mules with supplies. He headed into the wilderness with his rifle for a ride to the camp.

The sheep company knew that William was en route to their location and expected him sometime near July 22. He never arrived. Walter Eastman was a sheepherder at the camp, and he rode into town to report William missing. He rode the trail that William should have been on and never saw the pack or his supplies.

Sheriff Francis Tamietti was a veteran of searching for missing people. He quickly organized a search party, and they started to arrive at the base camp.

Sheriff Tamietti and Ranger O. J. Esterl eventually found a two-mile stretch of scattered supplies extending along a ridgeline. Equipment was littered everywhere. After a continued search, several of the pack animals were found tangled in their bridles and ropes. Some saddle packs were twisted and "some partly torn off" (*Tri City Herald*, July 26, 1959). Further up the hill, searchers found that the lead horse had been tied to a tree and had struggled to get free. Searchers stated that the ground in the area was very hard and they could not see tracks. They also stated that none of the animals appeared to have injuries inflicted by a bear or mountain lion. Searchers eventually found William's rifle in the dirt on a hillside, not on a trail. There was dirt in the barrel, but the gun had not been fired. They conducted an extensive search of the area but could not find William.

In a very surreal coincidence, as searchers were still looking for Carmack, the owner of the sheepherding company, Joe Servel, went missing from his camp. The sheriff and rangers had two simultaneous searches going for two people from the same company at two different but close locations. The co-owner of the sheepherding company, John Faure, stated that Joe was last seen at their camp fifteen miles from Superior, Montana.

After searching for almost four full days, William's body was found on a trail in the Bitterroot Mountains. Searchers stated that it appeared he had died of natural causes but no confirmation was given. I could not find any other information on William.

Two days after William's body was located, searchers found Joe Servel wandering seventeen miles from the Lost Gulch area. Joe was not wearing shoes or socks. An article appeared on July 29, 1959, in the *Robesonian* stating the following:

"The 67-year-old co-owner of a Washington sheep company was found wandering barefoot in a rocky western Montana canyon Tuesday. Joe Servel of Yakima had been missing since Saturday in the rugged area where one of his pack train operators was found dead three days ago. Sheriff Francis Tamietti said Servel couldn't explain how he had wandered away from his mountain camp. Suffering from shock and exposure, he was taken to a Superior hospital."

Case Summary

Let's discuss William and his body before the location of his equipment and horses. It took searchers an additional two days to locate William after they found his equipment strewn for two miles along a ridgeline. It appears someone tried to rope his horse to a tree, as it is described that the horse tried to escape. William had been operating a supply train for three years, and he was a very experienced woodsman. Mountain men know not to go anywhere without their firearm. That is a lifeline. William was found dead on a trail nowhere near the equipment, rifle, or horses. The rifle was found on the side of a hill with dirt in the barrel, as though it had been thrown. Who tied up William's horse? Someone did. We know that William wouldn't have done that. He would have ridden the horse. Searchers stated that the animals did not have any injuries consistent with bears or mountain lions. Something spooked the pack train so much that it nearly killed the horses and mules and did kill Carmack. I know something about mules: they are very smart and they are not afraid of much. They will stick around and fight rather than flee, they are much different then a horse. They can easily kill a mountain lion and probably take on a large bear. Whatever happened to that pack train was highly unusual and must have frightened the horses and mules nearly to death.

I'm not one to believe in coincidences, especially in the wilds of North America. To believe that the disappearances of Joe Servel and William Carmack are not intertwined would not be rational. How the disappearances came to happen is unknown. When Joe was interviewed about how he wandered away from camp and didn't have shoes, he couldn't answer and apparently didn't know. How could that happen? This man lived in the woods. He knew that mountain like you know your street. Something happened to Joe that either scared him so bad that he had temporary amnesia or something worse happened. We will never know. If Servel had been missing for days and found deceased without shoes, some would claim it was caused by hypothermia, dismiss that notion in this case. I also believe that this case should serve to exemplify the fact that for some unknown reason, in some instances, missing people strip their clothing and that clothing is never found.

Arthur Dillon Jordan
Missing: 11/08/59, Seeley Lake, MT
Age at disappearance: 59

On October 23, 1959, Arthur Jordan left the Teepee Lodge just east of Kalispell, Montana, and headed for Seeley Lake for a month of elk hunting. Arthur was a conscientious husband and called his wife regularly. The couple talked about the hunting and when his wife should expect another call. That next call never came, and his wife reported Arthur missing on November 8, 1959. Snow had hammered the Seeley Lake area just prior to November 8, and it toppled phone lines in the area. Missoula County Sheriff's Office sent twenty-six men into the Seeley Lake area to search for Arthur, even though weather and ground conditions were treacherous. After two weeks of extensive searching, deputies located Arthur's pickup and camp. Inside the pickup they found his .30-06 rifle and a hunting jacket. A November 25, 1959, article in the *Daily Interlake* stated, "Thirty-four searchers tracked through the snow-covered Seeley Lake country. They found remains of an elk with one quarter missing." A follow-up article written April 12, 1960, stated, "Jordan's camp was found intact last fall with guns, clothes, ammunition, and a freshly butchered elk."

After several starts and stops and an additional spring search, Arthur Jordan was never found.

Case Summary

What can we surmise from this story? Something serious happened to Arthur Jordan. Grizzly bears are hibernating during the month of November. If they did attack Arthur, there would have been a bloody scene, which was never found. Arthur did not leave the confines of camp voluntarily, or he would have taken his coat and rifle (both were found in his truck). The real question is what happened to the quarter of elk that was missing from the camp? Did whoever took Arthur take the elk? Why would someone take a quarter of the elk? Why not take the entire animal? If someone was bold enough to take an elk and Arthur, why not take his valuables? Whoever or whatever took Arthur had to have an unbelievable ability to survive in the wild, as conditions at the time were treacherous.

I did contact Missoula County Sheriff Carl Ibsen. Sheriff Ibsen was extremely interested in tracking down the reports related to this incident and gave the case to a sergeant. After several email exchanges, the sergeant was unable to locate the Missoula County Sheriff's reports in the incident.

Fritz Frey
Missing: 11/14/60, Lolo, MT
Age at disappearance: 65

Fritz Frey was a Missoula rancher who enjoyed the outdoors, specifically hunting. On November 14, 1960, Fritz went to the Petty Creek Wilderness and Johns Creek on a hunting excursion. The elevation in the area is between 4,000-5,200 feet. Supposedly, Fritz was last seen on the West Fork of Petty Creek, but some believe he may have gone to the Johns Creek area. The Petty Creek Wilderness is approximately twenty miles west of Missoula.

A large search party led by Missoula County Sheriff William Walker spent several days searching various drainages but failed to find any clues. Search efforts were continually hampered by snow flurries that hit the area when Fritz disappeared.

In June of 1961, Sheriff Walker again formed a search team of nearly one hundred people and scoured the area where Fritz disappeared. Professional trackers, smoke jumpers from the federal fire service, and law enforcement professionals all participated in the weekend search but again failed to find any trace of Fritz.

I could not find any news clippings indicating Fritz was ever found.

Megan Ginevicz
Missing: 04/30/80, St. Ignatius, MT
Age at disappearance: 2
2'1", 25 lb.

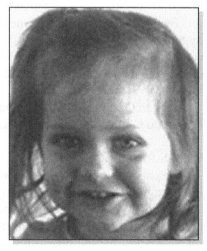

Dona Smith is Megan Ginevicz's mother. She divorced her husband in April of 1980. Dona was employed as a nanny for a family at their remote residence in a valley on the outskirts of St. Ignatius. Dona and Megan enjoyed the lifestyle and tranquility that came with the location. There was only one road to the residence.

On April 30, 1980, Dona put Megan in their unfenced yard to play while she quickly did a few chores in the house. She returned to the yard and couldn't find Megan. She knew nobody had driven up their road because she would have seen and heard them. She searched the area around the house but couldn't find her daughter. She called law enforcement and they were soon on the scene.

The area of Megan's residence is typical of the Montana Mountains—large trees with lots of open range and significant wildlife. It is approximately twenty miles northwest of Seeley Lake, twenty miles north of Missoula, and twenty miles south of Flathead Lake. Lake County Sheriff Glenn Frame supervised the case and searched the area by horseback, four-wheel drive, on foot, and by air, all without finding one trace of Megan. Neighbors were interviewed and confirmed that no vehicles had driven up the valley road, thus making it doubtful that a serial predator in a vehicle took her. The sheriff originally thought Megan may have fallen into a swift-moving creek or river and drowned, but searchers failed to find her body. There was also speculation that a grizzly bear had taken her. Again, no evidence of this was ever found.

Megan's father, William Ginevicz, lived in Colorado at the time. He went to the scene to assist in the search. William believed his daughter was abducted and clearly stated this to the media.

Even though Megan disappeared in late April, the area was hit by a heavy snowstorm hours after her disappearance, a very strange coincidence that repeatedly occurs when people go missing. The storm, which lasted ten days, hindered searchers ability to track and look for evidence.

Megan Ginevicz is listed at the National Center for Missing and Exploited Children as missing and a victim of non-family abduction.

Case Summary

Megan's case isn't unique when you look at other children missing in rural areas that are seemingly under their parents' domain and control when they go missing. I know it isn't rational to think a serial predator is lurking in the outskirts of a ranch, farm, or a national forest waiting for the opportunity to take children, but that is what the evidence supports and that is how Megan's case is classified in the national database.

Megan was a two-year-old girl. How far could she really walk until she got tired? It doesn't make sense that Megan walked away under her own power. Also, her mother knew the dangers of living in the area. Megan was left outside a short period of time. Someone had to be watching for the right time to take the child in order to disappear without leaving a trace of evidence. The real question is how the predator got into the area undetected, and why would they go to these extremes to take a child. The area around the residence was remote and rugged. The idea that someone got away with Megan and didn't leave a scent trail for law enforcement seems odd. However, this is a recurring theme in a majority of the stories in this book.

Nyleen Kay Marshall
Missing: 06/25/83, Maupin Creek, Helena National Forest, Clancy, MT
Age at disappearance: 4

Nyleen Marshall was with her family on a picnic in the Maupin Creek area in the Elkhorn Mountains of Montana. Nyleen was playing with other children and at one point ran ahead of the group. When the kids got to the point where she was last seen, she was gone. Nyleen disappeared at approximately 4:00 p.m. at a location not far from her residence in Clancy.

Local authorities initiated a massive inch-by-inch search of the area around the creek and adjacent trails, but nothing was found.

The FBI became involved in the case early in its inception. Over the course of the last three decades, several leads have been developed that Nyleen may be alive and living with another family. Nothing has ever been confirmed about what happened in the woods on June 25, 1983. The family and law enforcement believe Nyleen was abducted.

There are several stories in this book in which children are walking ahead of their family on a trail, or walking alone on a trail, when they disappear and are never found.

Patrick Whalen
Missing: 11/02/00, Atlantic Creek Backcountry Campground, Glacier National Park, MT
Age at disappearance: 33
6', 160 lb., blonde hair, hazel eyes
Note: I submitted an extensive Freedom of Information Act request with the National Park Service for all documents related to the disappearance and investigation associated with Patrick Whalen. I received over one hundred pages of documents, reports, and photographs that cost several hundred dollars in fees. There were many other documents that the NPS refused to furnish, claiming privacy issues.

Some people are meant to travel, and Patrick Whalen was one of those people. He didn't stay long in many places, but it was obvious that he loved the outdoors. Patrick especially loved the land in Glacier National Park and lands owned by the Blackfeet Native American Reservation. Patrick had numerous encounters with rangers and park officials in the year before he disappeared, but there was never any hint that something was wrong.

In early November of 2000, Patrick's father contacted U.S. park officials explaining that he hadn't heard from his son and was worried that something may be wrong. The park had not had recent contact with Patrick but stated they would keep his name on file.

On November 2, 2000, while driving his truck on U.S. Highway 89 near Kiowa Junction, Patrick hit a deer. Witnesses in the area saw Patrick put a pillow under the deer's head, place a blanket over it, and then leave food near its mouth. It appears Patrick abandoned the truck and left to backpack into Glacier National Park. It is unclear from the reports if the truck was in operating condition. The truck was towed by orders of local police, and it was impounded on November 3, 2000.

There was no activity regarding Patrick Whalen in any of the NPS reports until May 10, 2001, when Patrick's father contacted the park service again. He reiterated he had not heard from his son in months and believed he may be somewhere in the park.

On May 27, 2001, national park ranger Michelle Madland was on a routine patrol hike with a former park employee in the Atlantic Creek Campground. She filed incident report number 010079 explaining what she saw in the campground. She stated that she found abandoned backpacking equipment in a campsite. She stated that she found a tent that was partially falling down but had obviously been there throughout the winter. It was a blue, REI brand tent that had all zippers closed and no tears in the fabric. The tent was sealed. Michelle looked inside the tent and found everything you'd expect in a tent when someone was sleeping inside, except nobody was there. The ranger found a pair of boots, a wool hat, mittens, a pack, underwear, shorts and other clothing, toiletries, a stove, food, a water bottle, a water filtration system, and a commercial driver's license belonging to Patrick Whalen. The most unusual find in the tent was an empty Buck knife case.

Michelle and her co-worker took photos of the site and then hung the food from ropes so bears would not get to it. She clearly stated in her report that it did not appear that bears or other animals had ransacked the campground. She couldn't establish radio contact with the communications center in Glacier National Park, so they hiked out of the area and contacted backcountry rangers assigned to the region.

On May 28, additional rangers converged on the campsite and started an inside-out search that consisted of an extensive investigation of the site and a comprehensive search. Also on May 28, rangers found out that Patrick's truck had been towed six months earlier and was still being held by a local tow company. Investigators went to the tow yard and searched the truck for clues.

On May 30, cadaver dogs arrived at the Atlantic Creek Campground and searched for any indicators that a human body was in the area. After several hours of searching, the dog handler said he was convinced there was not a body anywhere in the area.

Case summary

The disappearance of Patrick Whalen and the subsequent investigation stimulates more questions than answers. I scoured every sentence of the reports I was given, and I never saw one line indicating that Patrick's equipment or vehicle were dusted for fingerprints. The original ranger at the scene found an empty wine bottle in the area and stated that she threw it out. Puzzling. This is evidence and may have contained fingerprints or DNA of someone Patrick was with when he disappeared.

The description that Michelle Madland gave of the tent and the inside contents gave me the impression that someone was sleeping or staying inside when something happened outside. I suspect he got up to investigate, taking the knife for protection. (At this time people could not carry firearms in national parks, though that has since changed). Patrick didn't have time to put his shoes on, but he did grab the knife, explaining the empty sheath. He left behind everything he'd need if he had taken a hike (water bottle, filter, maps, boots, etc.). It would appear that Patrick walked outside his tent to investigate something in the middle of the night and never returned. The area he was camping was known to have many mosquitoes thus the finding of the tent zipped up isn't unusual. If Patrick got up in the middle of the night, he probably zipped the tent to keep bugs out. He wasn't expecting to travel far because he didn't put his boots on.

I want everyone to think through this case clearly. If Patrick was attacked by a wild animal, there would be hair, blood and a scene of a battle for life, this wasn't found. Rangers searched a large area around the tent and Patrick was never found, why?

Robert "Bugsy" Springfield
Missing: 09/19/04, Bighorn Mountains, MT
Age at disappearance: 49

The Crow Indian Reservation is located in the southeastern section of Montana. The reservation is in the Bighorn Mountains, a very steep and rough area known for its big game and big mountains.

On September 19, 2004, Robert Springfield and his son, Colton (13), and his adopted son, Brent Brooks, went to Black Canyon to hunt elk. Robert was wearing heavy winter clothing and was armed with a bow and arrows. The two kids were assisting Robert by attempting to herd the elk down the valley.

Robert was unemployed in 2004 because of an injury sustained on an oil well. The Springfield's were living in Casper, Wyoming, and made the trip to the Bighorns specifically for elk hunting. Robert and his family were members of the Crow Nation Indian Reservation, and they were hunting on ground owned by the tribe.

Late in the afternoon on September 19, after hunting, Robert did not come back to the prearranged spot where he had agreed to meet his two sons. The kids waited until after dark and still had not seen their dad. The boys notified authorities and a search began. The Bighorn County Sheriff's Office and members of the tribe searched the area where Robert was thought to be, but nothing was found. A FLIR-equipped helicopter was brought into the valley and did low flyovers in an effort to locate Robert. The area had many steep canyons with dense foliage and many caves. Robert was not found. The family made several trips to the area and searched by themselves but still could not locate Robert. The BIA (Bureau of Indian Affairs) and county sheriff also brought in canines and searchers on horseback, but nothing was found.

In October 2005 a hunter was in the Black Canyon area had heard a crow screeching. The bird was loud and was incessantly screeching even in the presence of the hunter. The hunter walked to the tree where the crow was sitting. Below the tree lay human remains.

The hunter led authorities to the scene and later told news teams that he found a partial skull, a femur, and a neatly rolled up men's belt next to the skull. Two boots neatly sat next to the skull and femur. There was a men's coat on the ground that had a small tear in the back, and a wallet was found that contained money. The only items that were missing were Robert's bow and arrows.

The Bighorn County sheriff and the BIA were brought to the scene and decided the FBI should be summoned. The FBI came to the scene and took possession of the body parts. The remains were sent to the FBI identification section in Quantico, Virginia.

Veronica Springfield, Robert's wife, was given conflicting information about her husband's cause of death. She said she was originally told that he could have been shot, but that was later recanted when she was told that a tree might have fallen on him.

Veronica also stated that the location where her husband's body parts were found was directly above the camp where much of the search efforts were centered. She couldn't believe the body parts were there when the search was being conducted because she believes searchers would have found her husband.

Two years after Robert's body parts were recovered, the FBI still retained the remains. The FBI stated that they had to put Robert's DNA in a federal database and that they were backlogged and couldn't ship the body parts until it was completed. The family later filed a federal lawsuit against the FBI. On March 3, 2009, the *Tulsa Native American Times* ran an article about the plight of the Springfield's and their efforts to get Robert's body home. The article stated the following about the lawsuit: "The complaint also alleges Springfield died under suspicious circumstances and that the FBI failed to investigate his disappearance. After the body was found, the FBI failed to investigate to positively identify the remains in a timely manner even though there was compelling evidence for the identification, the complaint said."

Case Summary

I'm at least pleased that someone somewhere realized that Robert's death was suspicious and unusual and should have been investigated.

Robert's case is another in a long line of cases described in this book that have a very unusual conclusion. Only a partial skull and femur were found; where are the rest of his bones? His belt is found "neatly" rolled up next to the bones. Who did that? His boots are stacked neatly next to the bones. Who placed them there? How did Robert get the tear in the back of his jacket? Where are his bow and arrows?

If someone came across a bow and arrows lying next to bones, maybe they would steal the weapon. But you'd think they would also call authorities and allow the family to recover the remains. If someone were going to steal the bow and arrows, you'd think they would also empty his wallet of cash.

This is also one of many cases in which the remains are found in an area that had been previously searched. The remains are found so close to the SAR command post that the family believes they would have found the body. One law enforcement source stated that Robert may have died because a tree fell on him. If that's true, who rolled his belt and stacked his boots?

A continuing theme that cannot be easily explained regarding many of the bodies recovered across North America is the absence of large bones.

I've asked several law enforcement friends why the FBI kept Robert's body for two years. Nobody has given me a cogent explanation. The BIA and Bighorn County Sheriff's Office obviously felt something very unusual happened because they called for FBI assistance. The reality of what happened to Robert Springfield will probably never be known.

It has to be noted as highly unusual that a screeching crow is what led a hunter to Robert's remains.

Yi-Jien Hwa
Missing: 08/11/08, Sperry Glacier, Glacier National Park, MT
Age at disappearance: 27
6', 170 lb.

Hiking alone in any wilderness is not recommended and can be dangerous. Something unknown happened to Yi-Jien Hwa when he left for a multi-week hike across Glacier National Park, alone. He had planned on walking one hundred miles per week across the spine of the Continental Divide, traveling from Sperry Glacier to Kintla Lake. The lake is approximately one mile south of the Canadian border. It sits at 4,500 feet elevation and lies just below the ominous Starvation Ridge.

Yi-Jien is a six-foot-tall Malaysian male with a medium build. He was studying in a seminary school in Kentucky and spent his spare time hiking throughout the U.S. He had completed several long hikes at the Great Smoky Mountain National Park, the Appalachian

Trail, Hawaii, and the Red River Gorge. Family and friends have described Yi-Jien as extremely smart, in fantastic physical condition, meticulous, resourceful, and a lover of the outdoors.

Yi-Jien departed for his hike on August 11 and was to call his family at his first major stop on August 19. He never made that first call. Yi-Jien's mother, Kim Guat, knew something was seriously wrong. Kim notified the NPS and they immediately started a search.

The NPS committed significant resources to the search for Yi-Jien. They had warned him against hiking the path he had chosen because of the dangers involved and the passes he was traveling through. Finding him would be a very difficult task because Yi-Jien had not been seen in over a week, and they had no idea where he might be.

The possibilities of what may have happened to Yi-Jien were all explored. They did not find any location where a grizzly bear attacked and left the remains of a body. They looked in and around glaciers and cliffs but could not find a body. The park service brought in canines, but they never picked up a scent. This case is still open and active.

Wyatt Cole Little Light
Missing: 12/23/08, Fort Smith, MT
Age at disappearance: 1 month
1'7", 15 lb.

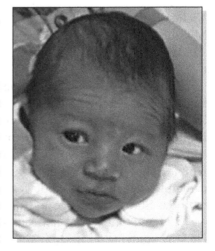

In December 2008, Wyatt Little Light and his parents were approximately two miles from Fort Smith, Montana. Wyatt's father was very familiar with the area they were visiting, as it was one of his hunting grounds. In early January 2009, the family's grandmother passed away, and it was noticed that the Little Light family did not attend the funeral. Family members knew that something was wrong, and they informed law enforcement that Teddy, Juliet, and Wyatt were missing.

BIA officers were alerted by family members of possible locations to search for the Little Light family. Agents found the family's 1996 Chevrolet pickup six miles up Grapevine Road near the highway outside of Fort Smith. There was snow on the ground when the truck was found. Officers searched the area but found nothing of evidentiary value.

In May 2009, after the snow had cleared, authorities went back to the area where they found the Little Lights' vehicle. Approximately two miles from the truck, along a ridgeline, authorities found the scattered remains of Teddy and Juliet Little Light. There were just fragmented remains with clothing from a man and a woman. Authorities combed the area but never found the remains of Wyatt. They found children's clothing in the area but didn't find any remains.

The possible explanations for finding the parents and not Wyatt are almost endless. There is the possibility that Wyatt was completely consumed by animals in the area, but I doubt that because bears are hibernating in this area in December. If Wyatt was consumed, his clothing would have been ripped to shreds and covered with blood and tissue. This wasn't the case. What happened to Wyatt Cole Little Light may never be known.

There is a consistent oddity in many cases in this book: victims are found on ridges. I don't believe that this is a normal location where people would succumb to the elements. I believe that most people would seek shelter before perishing, not stand out on a windy ridge.

Chapter Summary

It's obvious from reading this chapter there are many unusual events that have occurred in Montana. There is nothing more unusual and coincidental than the disappearances of the three girls, all in the month of July, listed below.

Missing Person•Age	Date, Time Missing
Patty Ann Mclean•3	07/04/53, 2:30 p.m.
Ida May Curtis•2	07/04/55, 6:00 p.m.
Mary Gay Bent•5	07/13/58, 3:00 p.m.

Ida May disappears two years to the day from when Patty Ann disappears. Ida May is claimed to have been taken by a bear and held in a small den. Patty Ann is found eight miles from her point of disappearance up a sheer rock cliff. Patty Ann and Mary Gay both stated that they had slept under a log—a remarkable coincidence.

All girls were taken within a five-year time frame, and all were taken between 2:30 and 6:00 p.m. They were the first females to have gone missing in Montana; the next female didn't disappear until 1980. It's also odd that the people who disappeared earlier than these girls and after these girls were all much older than them. This is a definite cluster. The next cluster of missing girls occurs after a twenty-year gap of disappearances, with Megan Ginevicz and Nyleen Kay Marshall going missing in a three-year time span. Again, much older people go missing before and after them.

Do you believe in coincidences?

CANADA

Alberta

The highly unusual disappearances of Bacsu, Owens, and Stewart in Hinton, Alberta, give this region a very uncomfortable feeling. All three women disappeared in a rural setting, and all were alone. Just east of Hinton two men, Nodeland and Neale, went missing under unusual circumstances.

In my years of research, I have never seen a mountain range that has taken more people than the Canadian Rockies between Jasper and Crowsnest Pass. Eleven people are missing from these mountains, all with varying circumstances, but several share the common element of hiking or climbing. This area is known throughout the world for its diverse wildlife viewing opportunities, and it is phenomenal. The area immediately around Canmore, Alberta, has a cluster of four people missing, which seems highly unusual considering the population of the cities in the immediate area and the specific people who have disappeared there.

One specific case, that of Tom Howell, reminds me of many cases of missing people in North America. Tom was a very experienced hunter, knew his area, brought ample supplies, came prepared, and simply vanished. He was hunting alone, and therein lies one major element in almost every hunter disappearance. It seems that Tom Howell shouldn't have disappeared, and they should have found his body.

Alberta Missing Person List by Date

Missing Person	Date Missing•Age•Sex
Lorraine Smith	09/02/50•2•F
Louis Blair*	08/05/56•26•M
Elizabeth Cardwell	09/16/73•31•F
Edward Arcand	06/08/75•27•M

Howard Booth	07/17/77•49•M
James Caraley	07/18/79•22•M
Steve Maclaren	06/30/81•25•M
Shelly Bacsu	05/03/83•16•F
Sharel Haresym	09/04/84•35•F
Edward Ludwig	05/30/86•27•M
Lillian Owens	06/28/91•46•F
Donald Belliveau	01/27/95•28•M
Rhonda Runningbird	03/26/95•25•F
Knut Thielemann	08/04/95•22•M
Melvin Hoel	03/12/97•64•M
Tom Howell	09/12/05•46•M
Wai Fan	09/28/05•43•M
Stephanie Stewart	08/26/06•70•F
Robert Neale	05/02/07•77•M

*Details on the disappearances of Louis Blair can be found in the "Farmers" chapter of book #2, *Missing 411: Eastern United States.*

Lorraine Smith
Missing: 09/02/50, 5:00 p.m., Lake Edith, Jasper National Park, Alberta
Age at disappearance: 2

Mr. and Mrs. Eric Smith left their Edmonton residence on Saturday, September 2, 1950, with their twins, Lorne and Lorraine, and headed for Edith Lake inside Jasper National Park. The ride was slightly over two hundred miles and covers some of the most beautiful terrain in the province. Highway 16 also bisects several of the areas between Edmonton and the park, where many of the missing people in this chapter have vanished.

The family arrived late in the afternoon and headed for the southern area of the lake to establish their camp. They were there to meet a church group that was going to spend the weekend together. Soon after the Smiths arrived, they noticed that Lorraine had disappeared. A frantic search started and the family enlisted the aid of others in the area. Everyone soon realized that two-year-old

Lorraine was nowhere to be found, and the RCMP (Royal Canadian Mounted Police) were notified.

Edith Lake sits at the bottom of a valley that contains more than twenty small lakes and a river. The lake is a popular spot on the fringe of the wilderness approximately three miles from the Jasper Park Lodge. Heavy woods surround the valley and a 7,500-foot mountain looms just to the southeast with a ridgeline that starts near the water.

Within two days the RCMP had two hundred people searching for Lorraine. They also brought in canine search teams, airplanes, water rescue teams, and horseback mounted patrols.

On September 5 the RCMP received reports that blood was found on a ridge near Signal Mountain just southeast of the lake. They sent a team and a physician to check on the report, but details as to what they found were not available. It was on this day that an additional thirty trained searchers were brought into the park from the Canadian Northwest Air Command.

Searchers combed an area in thick woods five miles from Edith Lake. It wasn't clear why they were searching that location, but it was reported that game wardens shot a bear in the area; however, they confirmed that no remains of Lorraine were found in the bear.

A September 7 article in the *Calgary Herald* expressed the frustration of searchers: "A belief continued among some searchers that the child might not be in the area. Police are investigating the possibilities of abduction or an accidental death, where persons responsible may have removed the body."

After several days searchers did something quite intelligent: they brought Lorraine's twin brother into the forest to see how quickly and efficiently he could move on the ground. The article stated that they were surprised how easily he made his way through the forest. An RCAF helicopter flew the area in hopes of spotting Lorraine.

On September 8 the RCMP officially terminated the search. The police so strongly believed she was abducted that they were stopping vehicles at border crossings to search for the girl.

The search included over one thousand searchers who covered thirty-six square miles of forest. It was documented as the greatest civilian search in the history of Alberta. The search commander stated that he did not believe Lorraine had been consumed by an animal because no traces of clothing or blood were found. In fact, the search didn't find any evidence of Lorraine.

Case Summary

The response of SAR commanders is typical and understandable after an unsuccessful mission. If they cannot find evidence that the girl was in the area, they will immediately start to believe that the girl was abducted and taken from the area. A six-day search for a two-year-old girl seems too short for a search in this day and age, but maybe not for 1950. There are many people missing from this mountain range in Alberta.

Elizabeth Marguerite Cardwell
Missing: 09/16/73, Canmore, Alberta
Age at disappearance: 31
5'5", 126 lb.

There are conflicting reports about what happened to Elizabeth Cardwell. However, there is no doubt that she was last seen on September 16, 1973. Her vehicle was found in an area known as Dead Man's Flat, twelve miles east of Canmore. The vehicle was in a desolate location and most of her personal effects and keys were found inside. There are rumors that she was going to attempt suicide, and that she had bought a rifle and went to that location with that specific purpose. Law enforcement officials conducted an extensive two-day search of the area and found nothing to indicate Elizabeth or the firearm were ever there.

Elizabeth was employed by various businesses in the Calgary area, and she possessed a valid pilot's license. This is still an active missing person case.

Edward Joseph Arcand
Missing: 06/08/75, Crowsnest Pass, Alberta
Age at disappearance: 27
5'8", 139 lb.

Edward Arcand was a resident of Coleman, Alberta, when he left town in his 1969 Ford Falcon station wagon. Thirty-seven days after Edward went missing, his vehicle was found abandoned fifty miles north of Coleman on Highway 940. Law enforcement officials are investigating Edward's disappearance, but few clues are being released to the public.

Howard William Booth
Missing: 07/17/77, forty-four miles north of Coleman, Alberta
Age at disappearance: 49
5'6", 145 lb.

Specific details behind the Howard Booth case are not easy to find. It is not known exactly where Howard was prior to the finding of his truck. The vehicle was located on Highway 940, forty-four miles north of Coleman. This highway was a rough dirt road in 1977 and probably rarely used. The location is quite scenic and beautiful.

Twenty-five months prior to Howard Booth disappearing, Edward Arcand (above) also disappeared from the Coleman area within six miles of Booth.

James Christopher Caraley
Missing: 07/18/79, Columbia Ice Fields, Jasper, Alberta
Age at disappearance: 22
5'10", 163 lb.

James Caraley was a hiker and climber. He enjoyed the outdoors. He parked his vehicle in the Columbia Ice Fields parking lot and notified friends that he was going to attempt to climb Mount Andromeda, located directly in front of the parking lot.

Mount Andromeda and Mount Athabasca sit next to each other and are part of the same continuous mountain. Both of the summits are approximately 10,500 feet. Andromeda has a fairly easy route up the southeastern side, but it is not known which direction James went. There were extensive searches by law enforcement, but they were unable to find any evidence of James's whereabouts. His case is still listed on Canadian Web sites as an active missing person case.

Steve Thomas Maclaren
Missing: 06/30/81, Capital Trail Crew Camp, Kananaskis, Alberta
Age at disappearance: 25
5'9", 154 lb.

In June 1981 Steve Maclaren was working on a trail crew at the Capital Camp near Kananaskis, Alberta. This is the entry point for the Canadian Rockies off of Highway 1, directly west of Calgary. This is a very picturesque area with remote regions just beyond the highway.

Steve was working on the crew in the wild when he disappeared. Searchers scoured the region for over a week and never found a trace of Steve. There are few details on where he might be located.

Shelly Anne Bacsu
Missing: 05/03/83, Hinton, Alberta
Age at disappearance: 16
5', 90 lb.

Hinton hides several dark secrets, and the whereabouts of Shelly Bacsu is one. Shelly was last observed walking down Highway 16 toward Highway 40 in Hinton. There was a documentary made about the Bacsu case. There are supposed to be witnesses who saw Shelly abducted by up to three men in a van. The RCMP of Alberta and British Columbia are investigating up to fifteen women who have been abducted on a highway or adjacent roadway. Shelly's case is the furthest east and may not be related to the other fourteen cases, which have been named the Highway of Tears cases. Canada formed a special law enforcement task force to investigate the highway cases, and they are still working on leads. There are no named suspects.

Sharel Vance Haresym
Missing: 09/04/84, Bentley, Alberta
Age at disappearance: 35
6', 222 lb.

Sharel Haresym was supposed to be en route to the Twin Lakes Campground five miles west of Red Deer near Gull and Sylvan lakes. The landscape in this area is filled with hundreds of small family farms. Sharel was traveling approximately forty miles from an area south of Breton to the campground. He never arrived and was never seen again.

Edward Konrad Ludwig
Missing: 05/30/86, Lake Minnewanka, Alberta
Age at disappearance: 27
6'3", 194 lb.

Edward Ludwig was on a rafting trip on Lake Minnewanka, approximately five miles from Banff, Alberta when he vanished. This is a gorgeous body of water surrounded by tall peaks with limited access as you wind your way around the shoreline. There is easy access at the western end but no access as you make your way to the back end of the lake. This area is known for its abundance of wildlife. There are few clues as to where or how Ludwig disappeared.

Lillian Owens
Missing: 06/28/91, Hinton, Alberta
Age at disappearance: 46
4'11", 115 lb.

Lillian Owens was last seen by her husband when she left her house to pay bills at a local bank. Sometime during her trip to the bank, she disappeared. After an extensive search, law enforcement found her vehicle on a rural road near the Athabasca River. Once her vehicle was found, police conducted an extensive search of the river and surrounding fields without finding any trace of Lillian.

According to the 2009 Canadian census, Hinton had a population of 9,825 and a land area of ten square miles. Hinton is known as the gateway to Jasper National Park. It sits in the Athabasca River Valley 176 miles west of Edmonton. The elevation of the city is 3,291 feet and it gets significant snowfall.

Donald Jean Belliveau
Missing: 01/27/95, Columbia Ice Fields, Jasper, Alberta
Age at disappearance: 28
5'11", 182 lb.

Donald Belliveau left Calgary in his vehicle en route to the mountains for hiking. His path took him across the plains to the mountains and onto the Columbia Ice Fields. The ice fields are a major tourist attraction with a visitor center and special transport buses that can take visitors out onto the ice. Visitors pay a small fee and are driven in huge buggies onto the glacier. They are given a presentation and allowed to ask questions about the geological features of the region.

This is also a jump-off point for many hikers and climbers, who head into the backcountry.

Donald's vehicle was located in the parking lot of the glacier, and it is presumed he hiked into the mountains and never returned. Searchers spent a week looking in the backcountry, and pilots searched from the sky. No trace of Donald was ever found.

Rhonda Laureen Runningbird
Missing: 03/26/95, Swan Lake Recreation Area, Rocky Mountain House, Alberta
Age at disappearance: 25
5'5", 145 lb.

Rhonda Runningbird, her husband, their eighteen-month-old baby, and her husband's aunt drove into the Swan Lake Recreation Area for hunting. The truck supposedly got stuck in the mud and the husband hiked into the bush to get help. The closest residence or business was approximately thirty miles away.

Darkness hit the area, and the aunt states that it was at this point that Rhonda also left to get help. Rhonda was supposedly in bad health. Relatives state that Rhonda wore a kidney colostomy bag and was scheduled for surgery five days after she was reported missing. Relatives do not believe that Rhonda could have walked far because of her condition. Early the following morning, Rhonda's husband returned to the truck. The aunt and the husband were stranded an additional night with the baby and still had not seen

Rhonda. Another truck eventually came by, and the husband used the driver's cell phone to call a relative to obtain assistance.

The husband and the aunt eventually got home and reported Rhonda missing. After an exhaustive search, law enforcement stated that they found an unused colostomy bag, a set of Rhonda's clothing that she may have been wearing, and eyeglasses. Law enforcement officials did not believe that Rhonda could have survived the elements. They called off the search several days later.

It is presumed that Rhonda died in the wild, but she is still listed as missing. How did Rhonda's clothing become removed from her body?

Knut Thielemann
Missing: 08/04/95, Athabasca Falls, Jasper, Alberta
Age at disappearance: 22
6', 154 lb.

Knut Thielemann was vacationing in the area of Athabasca Falls on the Athabasca River near Jasper, Alberta. On August 4, 1995, he was walking somewhere near the falls when he disappeared.

The Athabasca River starts in the Rockies and flows east through Hinton toward Edson. The falls are approximately eighty feet high and have a beautiful backdrop against the huge mountains of the Rockies. The falls are not known for their height, as it's the sheer volume of water that flows through the pass that makes it gorgeous to view. The waterfall itself is considered a class five because of its height and associated danger.

Knut is still listed in Canada as a missing person.

Melvin Paul Hoel
Missing: 03/12/97, Cataract Creek, west of Longview, Alberta
Age at disappearance: 64
5'5", 146 lb.

In March of 1997, Melvin Hoel was somewhere in the Cataract Creek area west of Longview along Highway 40. His exact whereabouts during this time are not known, and he could not be located. This region is located at the base of the eastern side of the Canadian Rocky Mountains and has significant wildlife. It is very desolate in this area.

Approximately one year after Melvin went missing, his father died in a nursing home in Lethbridge. There are no other relatives.

Tom Howell
Missing: 09/12/05, Limestone Mountain, Caroline, Alberta
Age at disappearance: 46

Tom Howell was an avid outdoorsman and bowhunter. In September 2005 he went sheep and moose hunting near Limestone Mountain outside of Caroline, Alberta. The mountain is approximately thirty miles southwest of Rocky Mountain House. The summit of the mountain is 6,200 feet and is part of an extended ridgeline running north to south.

Tom's boss filed the missing person report, and several days later RCMP found Tom's truck near the mountain on Forestry Trunk Road. Tom had parked his truck and apparently taken his ATV, loaded with equipment, to drive closer to his hunting location.

SAR personnel found Tom's covered ATV at the base of Limestone Mountain. They dropped a ground crew at the location, who performed an extensive search of the region but found nothing. At his truck, they did find receipts for one hundred dollars' worth of groceries he had purchased prior to his hunt.

Bowhunters are quite different from hunters who use firearms. Bowhunters must use stealth, quiet, and surprise to get their trophy. The hunter must sneak within a very close shooting range to get a quality shot. Part of that stealthy behavior also means that they may surprise predatory animals, which is sometimes dangerous. In Tom's instance it is very surprising they did not find his pack, bow, clothes, campsite—nothing. He completely disappeared. Tom's family was told by SAR that the area is so rough and dangerous that they made a decision not to participate in the search.

Wai Fan
Missing: 09/28/05, Mount Temple, Lake Louise, Alberta
Age at disappearance: 43
5'8", 170 lb.

Investigators believe that Wai Fan was attempting to climb to the summit of 10,500-foot Mount Temple, located just two miles south of Lake Louise. This is in a gorgeous area of the Canadian Rockies. There are numerous large mammals that roam the countryside, but hiking in the area is very common.

Extensive ground and air searches for Wai failed to find any evidence of his location.

Stephanie Stewart
Missing: 08/26/06, Athabasca Fire Lookout, Hinton, Alberta
Age at disappearance: 70
5'2", 105 lb.

Of the thousands of missing person reports I have read, the case of Stephanie Stewart is one of the most puzzling. The facts surrounding her disappearance defy common sense and will cause great concern for any fire lookout attendant anywhere in the world.

Stephanie was an eighteen-year veteran of the Alberta Natural Resources Group that maintains a vigil at 128 lookouts across the province. For thirteen years Stephanie called the Athabasca Lookout her seasonal home. Twenty-five miles east of Hinton, the lookout is perched on a ridge with a commanding view of the surrounding valleys. There is a remote and desolate road that leads from the valley floor to the cabin and adjacent lookout where Stephanie worked and lived.

The lookout residence is a beautiful one-story log cabin that anyone would be proud to call home. Directly adjacent to the cabin is a forty-foot-tall lookout that is no easy climb. The lookout has something similar to a modified ladder inside a cage that makes its way to the top. The description of this climb should help explain that Stephanie was no normal seventy-year-old lady—she was fit! Stephanie had recently completed a climb and summiting of Mount Kilimanjaro in Tanzania. She may have been a small woman, but Stephanie Stewart would not have been an easy target for abduction.

Attendants at lookout towers are required to call their command center three times per day to report their status. Stephanie was extremely diligent on her calls, and when she missed three in one day, a supervisor was sent to check on her.

On August 26, 2006, a supervisor drove to Stephanie's cabin and found a very unusual scene. There was a pot of water on the stove, with the stove burning. The supervisor noticed that her two pillows, blanket, and sheet were missing. The supervisor found her truck parked where it usually was, but Stephanie was nowhere on the grounds. Within hours, twelve law enforcement officials were on the scene; within twenty-four hours, hundreds were at the tower. What followed was one of the largest searches ever undertaken in the Alberta forests. Almost every resource available to search was utilized—canines, helicopters, planes, vehicles, and citizens. Everyone wanted to find Stephanie.

Stephanie has one daughter, Lorie. Lorie gave an interview to the press and stated that her mom was "an old pro at tower work." According to Lorie, Stephanie was "well known in the community of Hinton."

Police have stated that they are handling Stephanie's case as a homicide in an effort to keep resources working the abduction. One of the investigators assigned to comment on the case, Sergeant Taniguchi, stated, "We have been led to believe that Stephanie was likely attacked by a human being." The union that represents the lookout attendants issued a $20,000 reward for Stephanie or clues about her disappearance.

On August 27, 2009, RCMP stated that they had no clues in Stephanie's disappearance.

Subsequent to Stephanie disappearing, the resource department that manages the lookouts removed all directional signs that indicated how to drive to the lookouts. They have also placed locking gates at the roadway entrances to all lookouts throughout the province.

There are several elements to Stephanie's disappearance that don't make sense when dealing with a predator abducting a victim. When criminals plan a major crime, one of their main concerns is having multiple routes to leave the area. They do not want to be seen, heard, or later recognized with their vehicle in the area. In the Stewart case, there is one long and lonely road to the lookout. There is no way for a predator to know if someone is going to drive up the road and interrupt the crime, or observe the suspect as they are leaving the scene with the victim. Anyone with any sense could see that this is a very, very risky abduction and subsequent escape. This is a dirt road without significant traffic. Anyone driving to the lookout would leave tire marks, especially the last vehicle in. The RCMP should know the type and size of tire that was last visiting Stephanie, and that would be a major clue as to the type of vehicle that visited, but the RCMP has not commented on this.

If the RCMP had a significant clue that a vehicle had participated in the abduction, it is extremely doubtful they would expend thousands of dollars in flight time for helicopters and airplanes to search the vast openness that surrounds the lookout. I also don't think they would have placed hundreds of people on the ground in this area.

Stephanie was in great shape for a seventy-year-old woman, but with the advent of FLIR on helicopters, they can fly over any area and see radiant heat coming from a body. If Stephanie had been abducted and was being forced to hike out, she would have been seen. She also would have been seen by satellites that the government could utilize in a search. Yes, the Canadian and United States governments do have the ability to direct a satellite camera into a specific area and monitor the area to a degree so finite they can read a license plate from space.

Did the Alberta Sustainable Resource Department really believe that Stephanie walked out of that area? Sergeant Taniguchi stated that the RCMP believed she was attacked by a human being. That's an odd choice of words. Why would the sergeant state she was attacked and not abducted? Were there clues at the scene that Stephanie may have been assaulted or worse? I can guarantee that the RCMP has interviewed the family members of Stephanie at length. The RCMP would want to know if she was concerned for her safety, if she had problems with someone in the recent past, or if there were something about the lookout tower and that surrounding area that had caused her concern. Maybe she had witnessed illegal drug activity, another type of crime, or maybe this was a completely random act (doubtful).

Two other women—Shelly Bacsu, 16, 1983; and Lillian Owens, 46, 1991—disappeared from the Hinton area. It may be pure coincidence, but notice the ages of the victims. The victims ages increase with time: 16 in 1983; 46 in 1991; 70 in 2009. Is this a coincidence or is their rationale to the increasing ages? It is very odd for a small community such as Hinton to have three women disappear in a twenty-three-year period—all in remote and rural areas.

Robert Samuel Neale
Missing: 05/02/07, Peers, Alberta
Age at disappearance: 77
5'8", 170 lb.

Robert Neale was the owner of a ranch/farm near Peers, Alberta. His residence sat close to the Macleod River and at the foothills on the eastern side of the Canadian Rockies. The topography in this area is fairly flat, with some slight elevation increase as you travel west.

It is believed that Neale was working on his ranch and either walked off or somehow disappeared in the immediate vicinity. This case sounds very similar to other ranchers and farmers you will read about in their respective chapters of *Missing 411: Eastern United States*.

Ontario

Eastern Ontario

Y ou will immediately notice that Algonquin Provincial Park dominates this region. Predominantly during the summer months, 300,000 visitors frequent the park. This park has many areas that are wild and remote. With eight rivers and 2,500 lakes, 10 percent of the park is underwater. The park was named after the Algonquin-speaking First Nations People of Canada.

The Algonquin Park is best known for its population of moose and its 2,000-plus black bear, a very large population for the size of the park. The most amazing thing about this region is that there is not one reported missing person inside the Algonquin Provincial Park, not one! Considering the remote nature of the park, ability to get lost, numerous rivers, lakes, and wildlife threats, this is an amazing statistic.

While there are no people reported missing inside Algonquin Park, there are seven reported missing people on the perimeter. It does seem odd that people are missing on the perimeter of the park, yet nobody is missing inside. It sounds like the national park service of Canada is utilizing the same policy as the U.S. National Park Service.

I usually conduct an Internet search of the regions I'm researching to understand any unusual events and current trends. There are two highly unusual events that occurred in Algonquin Park that received long-term media coverage.

In May of 1978 George Halfkenny (16 years) and his brother Mark (12 years) and their friend William Rhindress (15) entered the park to go fishing. The boys didn't return from the trip and a search ensued. The boys were found mauled and deceased. A May 17, 1978 article in the *Windsor Star* stated, "there was quite a bit of mauling and the bodies were partially eaten." The killing of the boys was blamed on an angry male black bear. The article later states that the only known attack in the area occurred in 1881 when John Dennison was killed by a wounded bear. There was one puzzling statement made by Sergeant Tom Parker of the Pembroke RCMP. In an *Associated Press* Article on May 18, 1978 Parker stated that Dr. R.G. Tasker a pathologist at

Pembroke Civil Hospital stated the following, "the youths all bore marks indicating that they had been mauled by an animal." Readers need to carefully understand statements made by officials, "mauled by an animal", not mauled by a bear. Dr. Tasker chose his words carefully and doctors usually are precise about their diagnosis and descriptions, I don't think this was an oversight.

The second incident in Algonquin Park occurred on October 11, 1991, Raymond Jakubaukas (32) and Carola Frehe (48) were camping on Opeongo Lake in the south-central area of the park. This is one of the largest lakes in the park. They had set up their campsite on Bates Island and were in the process of securing the camp and getting dinner ready when a black bear attacked and killed both people. Articles in the *Toronto Star* state that law enforcement officials claim the bear broke each person's neck and consumed their remains. Officials arrived at the site five days after the people were killed and claimed the bear was still on the scene consuming the bodies. A park official called the killings "off the scale" of normal bear behavior.

I have spent thousands of hours in the outdoors and an equal number researching wildlife issues. The killing of a human by a black bear is extremely rare, and I have never heard of a black bear killing two people in one incident let alone three. It's probably occurred before; I just don't know of it. It's equally mind-boggling that the bear was able to break the neck of each person, not an easy injury to inflict. It seems highly unusual that the bear could withstand the fight of one individual while the other was under attack. Maybe a grizzly would maintain the fight, but it's hard to believe a black bear would stay and fight while exposing itself to injury. I have no doubt that both incidents occurred, but this is very, very unusual.

Missing People in Eastern Ontario by Date

Missing Person	Date Missing•Age•Sex
Diane Prevost	09/17/66•2•F
Brian Henry	05/05/74•21•M
Jane Smith	08/09/75•20•F

Michael McIntyre 04/07/94•37•M
William Reed 08/01/95•69•M
Joan Lawrence 09/23/98•77•F
Michael Hinsperger 05/13/10•57•M

Diane Prevost
Missing: 09/17/66, Grundy Lake Provincial Park, Ontario
Age at disappearance: 2

On Saturday, September 17, 1966, Diane Prevost was camping with her parents, three siblings, and her grandparents. On this day Diane's dad was fishing at the dock, and she was playing on the beach nearby. Her mom was initially with her but decided to go back to the campsite. She notified Diane's dad, Bernard, that she was leaving and to watch Diane. He said he would. Bernard turned to fish and a few minutes later turned back around and Diane was gone.

Diane had expressed sincere fear of the water in the days before the disappearance. While her siblings routinely went in and around the water, Diane would not. The family never believed that Diane went near the water or possibly drown.

Police were notified and a lengthy search of the park took place. As nightfall started to hit, Bernard asked the police to close the gates of the park to ensure that no cars would leave without being searched. The police refused. Bernard insisted that the police search the woods, not the lake, because he feared his daughter had gone into the forest. Police concentrated on the lake. On Sunday, divers were brought in and searched the lake. Diane was not found in the water.

Two years after Diane disappeared, bones were found near a bathroom in the park. It was feared this was Diane. The bones turned out to belong to a dog.

This was the first recorded case of a child's disappearance in the Sudbury Police District. To the compliment of the police, the search for Diane lasted four weeks and covered thousands of acres of forest; but no evidence of Diane was ever found.

In August 2008 Diane's sister, Lise Nastuk, sought the assistance of a psychic to see if Diane could be located. The psychic stated that she would be located, but Diane has not been found.

Brian Henry
Missing: 05/05/74, Canadore College, Ontario
Age at disappearance: 21
5'6", 130 lb.

On May 5, 1974, at approximately 3:00 p.m., Brian Henry got a ride from his father to Canadore College in North Bay, Ontario, to walk the nature trails. The area around the college can be quite remote. The college is located in the southwestern portion of the city near several rivers and lakes. Brian's dad arrived to pick the young man up, he never arrived. There were searches of the area, but nothing was ever found of Brian Henry.

Jane Smith
Missing: 08/09/75, Laurentian University, Sudbury, Ontario
Age at disappearance: 20
5'4", 114 lb.

In August 1975 Jane Smith was a student at Laurentian University in Sudbury, Ontario. She lived in a rural portion of southern Sudbury on Charlotte Street. Approximately a half mile to the southwest of Jane's residence is the Fielding Bird Sanctuary, and one mile to the southeast is the Lake Laurentian Conservation Area. There are many forests in the area around Charlotte Street.

At 2:00 a.m. on the day she disappeared, she was seen going to bed. At 7:30 a.m. the same morning, Jane was gone. She left behind all of her personal belongings. Police now say they "cannot rule out the possibility that Jane has been a victim of foul play due to the duration of time since she went missing."

Jane's disappearance is hauntingly familiar to three other students missing in the United States, also from rural locations. Ruth Baumgartner disappeared on May 4, 1937, from Wesleyan University in Delaware, Ohio. She was twenty-one when she disappeared in the middle of the night from her dorm room. Ron Tammen was attending Miami University in Oxford, Ohio. On April 19, 1953, he disappeared from his dorm room in the middle of the night. Ron was nineteen years old when he went missing. Richard Cox was a cadet at the U.S. Military Academy at West Point, New York. On January 14, 1950, Richard disappeared in the middle of the night with no clues as to where he went. Richard was twenty-two years old.

Agnes May Appleyard
Missing: 04/27/86, Emsdale, Ontario
Age at disappearance: 59
5'1", 130 lb.

Emsdale, Ontario, is located just west of Algonquin Provincial Park in a rural area of Northern Ontario. Agnes Appleyard was last seen by neighbors in her front yard. The roads in the area don't get significant vehicular traffic and the details about what happened to Agnes are not clear. Agnes has never been found.

Michael James McIntyre
Missing: 04/07/94, Round Lake, Ontario
Age at disappearance: 37
6'2", 189 lb.

In April of 1994, Michael McIntyre was living with his father at Round Lake, approximately six miles northwest of Killaloe. Michael was known as an outdoorsman who regularly walked the woods. He knew the area and was comfortable by himself in the forests of Ontario. On April 7, 1994, Michael disappeared somewhere in the area around his father's residence. Law enforcement officers believe it is highly unlikely that Michael became lost anywhere in the area surrounding his dad's house. There are no clues as to where he is now.

William Reed
Missing: 08/01/95, Redbridge, Ontario
Age at disappearance: 69
5'6", 185 lb.

William Reed lived in Redbridge, Ontario, and a note found in his residence indicated that he had gone fishing. It was unusual for William to leave unannounced, so this caused concern for his friends and family. The note stated that William was going to Phelps Township. A search of the Phelps area found William's truck, with his wallet and keys inside, on Gibson Mill Road. Nobody knew where William went. His truck was found near a river, an empty lot, and a light industrial area. An extensive search of the area produced no conclusive results.

Joan Dorothy Lawrence
Missing: 09/23/98, Huntsville, Ontario
Age at disappearance: 77
5'4", 116 lb.

Joan Lawrence lived in a rural part of Huntsville, Ontario, on North Lancellot Road. Skeleton, Siding, and dozens of other lakes dot the landscape in this area. The region has heavy timber cover with few roads.

Joan lived approximately two or three miles outside of Huntsville. The last confirmed sighting of Joan was on September 23, 1998, but because of the rural location where she lived, she was not seen on a regular basis. There have been allegations in press articles that she was victimized by a family who owned a business that catered to older adults in the Huntsville area, but murder charges have never been filed.

Michael Hinsperger
Missing: 05/13/10, Carson Lake, Ontario
Age at disappearance: 57
5', 130 lb.

In May of 2010, Michael Hinsperger was in a canoe on Carson Lake in the Carson Lake Provincial Park west of Algonquin Provincial Park. This lake sits adjacent to Trout, Otter, and Kulas lakes. Highway 60 bisects the park and runs on the western perimeter of Carson Lake. There are residences on the lake and a road that follows the perimeter. The area around the lake has heavy timber and brush.

Michael's canoe was located, but he was never found. The lake is approximately two-thirds of a mile long and not deep. The lake was extensively searched, and Michael's body never surfaced.

Northern Ontario

There is one case listed in the Northern Ontario section, the case of Geraldine Huggan. The reader needs to digest all aspects of this case and carefully understand the statements of the First Nations searchers that participated in the SAR. Geraldine's case is quite unique for this region of North America and if not for the persistence of searchers, this would never have been solved.

Missing Person	Date Missing•Age•Sex
Geraldine Huggan	07/05/53•5•F

Geraldine Huggan
Missing: 07/05/53, 10:00 a.m., six miles west of Minaki, Ontario
Age at disappearance: 5

Mr. and Mrs. Jared Huggan left their home in Winnipeg for a six-week summer vacation. They brought their three daughters to visit the girls' grandparents at their summer cottage in Wade, Ontario, six miles west of Minaki. The area around the cottage is swampy and has many lakes. There is also a Canadian Railroad line that ran through the territory. This was an extremely remote and wild part of Northern Ontario.

On July 5, 1953, the families were getting their supplies together to spend the day at Fox Lake. Two of the girls were in the front yard of the cabin and Geraldine was in the side yard. At 10:00 a.m. the families were ready to leave but couldn't find Geraldine. She had been left alone for less than ten minutes. The families did an extensive search but couldn't find the girl. A call was made for police in Minaki and they responded.

Once RCMP from Minaki arrived, they also made a call to First Nations trackers who lived in the region. A call was also made to federal army personnel in Winnipeg for assistance.

As the search was starting, heavy rains hit the Wade area and greatly affected the searchers and their ability to follow footprints. Geraldine's father was one of the leaders of the search party. He informed all searchers that Geraldine didn't like the dark and if lost would sit and cry. She didn't wander. This was good news for the searchers as they felt that the search efforts would be brief and she'd be found quickly.

Nobody thought the search would last for three days, but the third day searchers found what they believed were Geraldine's footprints high on a rock ledge above Fox Lake. The search numbers now reached two hundred and included aircraft, First Nations People, and RCMP.

The search started to drag into the seventh day and still searchers had not found the girl or further evidence of where she was located. At this point Kenora prospector Harry Hawes joined the search for Geraldine. He had been credited with finding two lost boys from Kenora two years earlier. He had found the boys very near Long Lake, and Harry thought the girl would be found there too. He never explained why he felt Geraldine would be found at that lake (of the twelve lakes in the area), but he clearly made that statement.

A July 15 article in the *Winnipeg Free Press* stated: "Ontario Police said Wednesday that a newly discovered print was not too old and pointed out that bushes in the area are laden with berries and that the water in the lake is fit for human consumption." The point of the article is that there was food and water in the area to help a person survive.

Nine days into the search, First Nation searchers found a fleck of what they believed was Geraldine's shirt on the eastern shore of Long Lake. The cloth was shown to Geraldine's parents, who confirmed it was from her shirt. The thread from the cloth appeared to have been pulled off the shirt as if someone had walked by and pulled it away.

On the tenth day of the search, Indians (the term used in articles) were at the far northeastern corner of Long Lake. Six hundred feet south of the railroad tracks, they found what they believed were Geraldine's remains. The searchers found the girl's plaid shirt and her blue jeans. In the area near the clothes, searchers also located a small meadow where the ground had been matted down, indicating something large had been dragged there. Near the meadow searchers found Geraldine's blue jeans had one leg turned inside out, an unusual find that was noted. The exact location of the scene was between Catastrophe Lake and Long Lake, at their northern ends. The area was swampy and had the appearance of a brutal scene. There was blood in the area. A July 16 article in the *Calgary Herald* included the following: "'There was not enough left for either a proper burial or an inquest,' said Dr. D. J. Mason, coroner." Further clarity was given in a July 16 article in the *Sarasota Herald*: "There was no indication immediately as to the cause of the child's death. The body had been mauled, apparently by wild animals, but Indian searchers said there was no blood on the clothing." Trackers also stated that they found wolf hair and tracks in the area of the remains, but believed the wolf arrived after Geraldine died.

Several articles made insinuations that the girl may have died from a wolf attack. The Indians (First Nation) apparently heard about this statement and came back making the statement that there was no blood on her clothing. If a wolf had attacked Geraldine, it is generally believed that the clothes would have been torn to shreds and there would have been blood and bite marks on all the clothing. Also, Geraldine's pant leg was turned inside out; this happens when someone removes the pants. Again, the pants weren't torn.

There was other controversy about this case. Seven days into the search, Indian trackers had found what they believed to be an adult-sized track in the moss in the search area. A July 15, 1953, article in the *Winnipeg Free Press* titled "Controversy" included the following narrative: "After discovery of the Sunday clue [footprint] there had been some controversy among searchers as to whether they could have been animal tracks or prints of an adult shrunken in the moss." Indian trackers tend to know the land better than others—period. If the Indian trackers stated that the way the moss reacted indicates the track may have come from an adult, I would tend to believe them.

Case Summary

This case is near the top of my list for complexity and intrigue. No, I do not believe that a wolf killed Geraldine—no way. The scene would have been much more gruesome; blood would be all over the clothing; and the clothing would be shredded. I also believe Geraldine's skull would have been found (it wasn't). The teams didn't even find enough bones to give the girl a burial (per newspaper articles).

I've been in the bush in the far north, and I understand the terrain. It is very quiet up north when the wind is not blowing. If you yell for someone, your voice can easily travel up to hundreds of yards. When Geraldine disappeared, she was only missing ten minutes before her parents started to search. The bush area in the north can be extremely thick, swampy, and movement can be very slow. The idea that a five-year-old girl could be out of voice range in just ten minutes is very hard to believe.

It was never clarified why prospector Harry Hawes believed Geraldine would be found at Long Lake. It is also not known if the boys he found two years earlier were found alive. The circumstances behind how and when they were found are not available.

I believe geographical landmarks are named for a specific reason. Whether it is a mountain, lake, or stream, names associated with those locations usually have historical significance. I'd like to know how Catastrophe Lake got its name.

One of the most revealing newspaper articles included an interesting quote: "The body had been mauled, apparently by wild animals, but Indian searchers said there was no blood on the clothing." The portion, "apparently by wild animals," doesn't sound like a very firm statement. I don't believe this statement was framed the way it was by accident. I don't think the evidence that an animal devoured the girl was very strong, and this is supported by the Indians' statements.

What happened to Geraldine Huggan? There are many opinions of what might have happened to Geraldine, but the answers with the most credibility would probably come from the Indians who were searching because they know their land and its history best.

There are many similarities between the deaths of Geraldine Huggan and Bart Schleyer from the Yukon Territory (see the "Yukon" chapter for details).

Western Ontario Missing Person List by Date

Missing Person	Date Missing•Age•Sex
Fernand Martin	04/24/60•36•M
Sander Lingman	11/01/60•35•M
Raymond Juranitich	10/08/75•48•M
Toivo Reinikanen	09/26/84•36•M
Nicolas Hibbert	07/08/88•66•M
William Caswell	07/21/91•52•M
Kenneth Churney	03/15/97•36•M
Zbigniew Gajda	01/04/01•42•M
Michael Bailey	04/20/07•38•M
Christine Calayca	08/06/07•20•F

Fernand Martin
Missing: 04/24/64, north side of Pakashkan Lake, Ontario
Age at disappearance: 36
5'10", 180 lb.

Pakashkan Lake is northwest of Thunder Bay in an isolated area near Brightsand River Provincial Park. A portion of the lake borders the park on the western edge. Pakashkan Lake has a remote outpost at the northern end of the lake that isn't visited often and rarely visited in April. Fernand Martin was a trapper and had lines set in early April. He went back into the area to check his traps and never returned. No evidence was ever found.

Sander Lingman
Missing: 11/01/60, Gripp Lake, northwest of Nakina, Ontario
Age at disappearance: 35

Gripp Lake is approximately forty-five miles northwest of Nakina and ten miles south of the Sedgman Lake Provincial Nature Reserve. This is a desolate area of Northern Ontario with few roads or people.

Sander was with a group of people who were staking claims in the area. The men left at the beginning of the day and were supposed to return at night. Sander never returned. A search of the area found no evidence of Sander Lingman. A rural detachment of the RCMP in Greenstone is handling the investigation.

Raymond Juranitch
Missing: 10/08/75, Ogoki Reservoir, Timiskaming, Ontario
Age at disappearance: 48
6', 198 lb.

The Ogoki Reservoir is fifty miles northeast of Armstrong,
Ontario. It is a large body of fresh
water with several small islands.
Raymond Juranitch went hunting
and fishing in the area and set his
camp on one of the small islands.

Something tragic happened
and he disappeared. His belongings were found strewn around
the island as though someone got
upset and destroyed them. It's interesting that his camp was destroyed as this is a very isolated region with few visitors at this time of the year.

Raymond was last seen alone in a fifteen-foot aluminum canoe powered by a 9.8-horsepower outboard motor. Raymond was a rug-ged outdoorsman who knew the outdoors well. Raymond has never been found.

Toivo Reinikainen
Missing: 09/26/84, Walsh Township, Ontario
Age at disappearance: 36
5'8", 189 lb.

In September 1984 Toivo Reinikainen was working at a remote timber camp north of Marathon, Ontario. He worked for the Great West Timber Company and stayed at a company facility.

Toivo was last seen at the camp in the early morning hours of September 26. Deadhorse Road is a public-access road that goes to the facility, but it is very rough and remote.

Approximately one hundred miles east from where Toivo disappeared, another individual disappeared from another timber camp. The disappearance of Aju Chukwudiebere Iroaga is chronicled in the Calayca case.

Nicholas Hibbert a.k.a. Nicholas Hibbart
Missing: 07/08/88, Gravel River, Nipigon, ON
Age at disappearance: 66
On July 8, 1988, police officers patrolling along the Gravel River observed Nicolas Hibbert prospecting the area. His camp was nearby. Police returned on July 25 and found the camp burned to the ground and no evidence of Nicholas anywhere in the area. An extensive archival search on Nicholas did not produce any additional information.

William George Caswell
Missing: 07/21/91, Panache Lake, Ontario
Age at disappearance: 52
6'1", 240 lb.
On July 21, 1991, William Caswell and his daughter were boating on Panache Lake northwest of Thunder Bay. William's daughter later explained to investigators that they were traveling on smooth water when they were both suddenly thrown into the water for some unknown reason. The daughter was able to swim to shore, but her dad was never found. Law enforcement searched the area and dragged the lake without finding a body.

Kenneth James Churney
Missing: 03/15/97, Terrace Bay, Ontario
Age at disappearance: 36
6'1", 200 lb.
Kenneth Churney took a trail off Pine Crescent Road and went into the bush on his snowmobile. This road is on the northern perimeter of the city and leads into a very remote area. Kenneth disappeared in proximity to Christina Calayca's disappearance (see below), although he disappeared in a different season.

It is odd that searchers were not able to at least find the snow-mobile that Kenneth was operating. There are few facts available on this case.

Zbigniew Gajda
Missing: 01/04/01, Caribou Island Point, Thunder Bay, Ontario
Age at disappearance: 42
5'10", 163 lb.

Zbigniew Gajda left the Thunder Bay area on his snowmobile to go ice fishing on Lake Superior. Some reports indicate he was last sighted near Caribou Island Point. Many of the facts surrounding this case and the Kenneth Churney case (above) are very similar.

Michael Norman Bailey
Missing: 04/20/07, Thunder Bay, Ontario
Age at disappearance: 38
6', 200 lb.

On April 20, 2007, Thunder Bay police responded to a report that an individual was camping on private property. That individual was Michael Bailey. Upon contact Michael stated that he didn't realize he was on private property and would gladly camp elsewhere. He packed his belongings and was observed by police walking on Bowkler Road. The police had offered him a ride but he refused.

Michael was on the southwestern perimeter of Thunder Bay, a somewhat remote location. A large river runs near the private property and several farms are just to the southwest. Michael was never seen again after this incident.

Christina Calayca
Missing: 08/06/07, Terrace Bay, Ontario
Age at disappearance: 20
5'2", 125 lb.

In August 2007 Christina Calayca was camping with her cousin and two of his friends at Rainbow Falls Provincial Park.

The park is on the Trans-Canada Highway (Hwy. 17) between Schreiber and Rossport and occupies a remote area of the coast. Christina was a Toronto teacher and not someone who camps or visits the woods regularly. On the day of her disappearance, Christina went jogging with one of her cousin's friends. Somewhere during the run, the two went different directions and Christina was never seen again. She has not contacted family or friends since.

Thunder Bay police conducted a massive search consisting of eighty police officers, volunteers, helicopters, canines, and airplanes. The seventeen days of searching didn't produce one clue. Law enforcement officials stated that there were no aggressive bears in the area, and they believed Christine could have survived in the wild because of the relatively warm nights and the abundance of fresh water. They have ruled out any involvement of her cousin or his friends, and they have stated that they do not believe she was abducted.

It is hard to believe that Christina was disoriented or lost while running in the park. The trails are well defined and many of the roads are paved and easy to follow.

Approximately 120 miles east of where Christine disappeared, another individual went missing on May 16, 2006. Aju Chukwudiebere Iroaga was a forestry worker planting saplings in a remote region fifty miles north of White River, Ontario. This is a desolate area along the White River. The twenty-six-year-old tree planter had quit his job and was assigned to meet a helicopter to be lifted out of the area. He never arrived for the trip. There are hundreds of lakes, streams, and creeks in this area and an abundance of wildlife. Aju was described to be in very good shape and able to survive in the wild. Police conducted an extensive weeklong air and ground search but found nothing. Aju's case and Christina's case are similar, as they were both alone in the wild and in relative proximity when they disappeared.

Manitoba Missing Person List by Date

Missing Person	Date Missing•Age•Sex
Betty Wolfrum	05/15/34•4•F
George Wanke*	07/27/35•58•M
Jack Pike*	09/05/35•5•M
Mr. Bell*	08/31/36•62•M
Simon Skogan*	07/02/40•9•M

*Details on the disappearances of the following individuals can be found in the corresponding chapters of *Book#2, Missing 411: Eastern United States*:
George Wanke, "Berry Pickers"
Jack Pike, "Berry Pickers"
Mr. Bell, "Farmers"
Simon Skogan, "Berry Pickers"

Betty Wolfrum
Missing: 05/15/34, Moosehorn, Manitoba
Age at disappearance: 4

When considering the thousands of missing person cases I've researched over the years, the Betty Wolfrum disappearance has a special place on my list as one of the most unusual.

Moosehorn, Manitoba, is approximately 160 miles north of the United States border and 120 miles northwest of Winnipeg. The town is located on Highway 6 just north of Dog Lake and just south of Lake Saint Martin in an area surrounded by large bodies of water and wetlands. A large farming community predominantly supports the region.

The Wolfrum family owned a small farm on the outskirts of Moosehorn just southwest of Spearhill. On May 15, 1934, Carl Wolfrum put sleeping four-year-old Betty in a small carriage in front of the farmhouse and went into the field to do spring seeding. Betty Wolfrum disappeared.

The Wolfrum farm is in a very remote area of Manitoba that is dotted by small family farms. It has very few visitors, and it's rare to see a neighbor traveling the roadway. Where there is not farmland, there is significant tundra and wetlands with swamps. The day Betty disappeared, Carl did not see anyone near his home or hear anyone driving on the roadway. He also didn't see any dust clouds on the roads near his farm, which appear when someone is traveling the roads.

Carl discovered his daughter was missing and promptly searched the yard and farm before he contacted neighbors for assistance. After a lengthy search, a neighbor left to contact the RCMP. The searchers were aware that Betty was young, and she didn't speak English. Mrs. Wolfrum was from Germany and had only taught Betty basic words in German.

The first five days of searching were very uneventful. Over one hundred police officers, farmers, and other volunteers scoured the farms and swamps surrounding the Wolfrum farm without finding any trace of Betty. On Saturday morning the clouds dumped heavy rain in the area, and this convinced the RCMP that Betty would not survive. The nights had been brisk, and the general feeling was that searchers had covered every possible area where Betty could be and they hadn't found anything.

On Sunday at approximately 2:00 p.m., Spearhill farmer Roy Rosin left his farmhouse and took a walk, hoping to find Betty. Approximately two miles from the Wolfrum residence, Roy found Betty walking in a swampy area. She was semi-conscious and calling for her dad. Roy picked the girl up and carried her home. A doctor was summoned and examined Betty.

A May 21, 1934, article in the *Saskatoon Star* had the following interview with the doctor who examined Betty, Physician Frank Walkin:

This is to certify that today I examined Betty Wolfrum. The history of the case is that this child has been lost 110-120 hours. Examination of the child reveals very little loss of flesh and no evidence of dehydration. Furthermore, in view of the fact there have been so many mosquitoes present, it is significant that there are no bites or scratches present. In my opinion this child has had food, water and some shelter for the past 3 to 4 days as I do not believe that a child who has always been delicate could have withstood this long exposure and show so little trace.

It was also noted in many papers that Betty was found completely dry (even though it had rained heavily the previous day and night), and that her clothing and shoes were fairly clean considering the time she spent in the bush.

A May 22, 1934, article in the *Montreal Gazette* had the following headline: "Girl is Terrified." The article states that Betty had hardly spoken once she arrived home. The family stated that Betty was "whimpering softly" and sleeping a lot.

Another interesting and intriguing part of this case was brought forward by a neighboring farmer, George Romein. He told authorities that the last three days prior to Betty being found, one of his cows had returned from deep in the bush milked on each of those days. He stated that this had never happened before but that it was obvious to him that someone had been milking the cow.

The RCMP interviewed Roy Rosin at length about his ability to find Betty when everyone else had failed. A May 23, 1934, article in the *Winnipeg Free Press* understood the importance of Roy's actions and covered it in their story. Roy did admit that he went almost straight to the exact spot where he found Betty. You can read a lot into some styles of writing, and you could tell that the reporters believed that Roy knew more than he was telling. It wasn't a belief that Roy knew the kidnappers, but he did know more facts of the story. Here is the last paragraph in the article: "Furthermore, when queried by the newspapermen on the scene Monday, he [Rosin] admitted that he had not told all. He did say that when he went on his successful quest for Betty, 'I did not expect to come back alive, or if I did come back I would be all broken up.'"

Roy's statement is one of the most baffling I have ever read from a searcher. It's understood that the RCMP debriefed Roy at length; however, they refused to clarify what they learned from their interview. Why? What could he have known that was so sensitive that he couldn't tell the family, the press or public? The only other clue that was given to the family was that Roy left the Wolfrum farm Sunday afternoon at 1:00 p.m. and found the girl two miles away at approximately 2:00 p.m. The RCMP did state that the area where he found Betty was searched several times during the five days she was missing.

The RCMP went back into the bush and swamps to the area where Betty was found. When she was found, Betty was missing her coat, hat, and one shoe, items that were never found by the RCMP or searchers who continued to scour the area.

Three days after Betty was found, she started to talk with her mother in German. She told her mom that she had met a mother and daughter while she was gone, and that she had seen a cat that had scratched her. She explained that on the morning she was found, a man had pointed for her to walk in the direction that would lead to her farm, which she was doing when she was found.

After hearing Mrs. Wolfrum retell Betty's statement, the RCMP again scoured the area for shelter and evidence of food consumption and sleeping areas. Nothing was found. Remember, the night before Betty was found, it rained extremely heavily, yet Betty was found dry and clean. How can that be?

There is no feasible way that anyone could have gotten in or out of the Moosehorn region without other farmers noticing a vehicle or coach. The RCMP were completely stumped by this case. They were reluctant to speak with the press about all the facts surrounding the incident, and their reasons were never fully disclosed. The police did confirm that they believed Betty had been kidnapped.

Conclusions

This is another case where a small child goes missing under highly unusual conditions. It does not appear that international borders mean anything in these cases; the similarities between Canadian and U.S. cases are obvious.

Somehow and somewhere Betty Wolfrum was sheltered while she was missing. The RCMP could not find a shelter, and they didn't believe that anyone traveled in or out of the area while Betty was missing. This area isn't like a metropolitan area; it is a remote area where everyone knows their neighbors, their vehicles, and their wagons. The million-dollar question is, where did Betty obtain food and shelter?

Betty was fed and hydrated while she was missing. How was this happening? The answer to part of this question is the milking of George Romein's cow. Betty was too small to milk the cow, and her parents confirmed she didn't know how. Someone milked the cow and probably supplied Betty with the fluid. If someone was milking the cow daily, that means that someone stayed in that immediate area and didn't leave the region with Betty. How were they able to avoid searchers? Remember, it wasn't just one person avoiding searchers; there were four people avoiding the search parties—Betty, the girl and mother, and what was probably a father.

It would be inappropriate not to acknowledge the efforts of Dr. Walkin and the RCMP working the Wolfrum case. Even though this incident occurred miles from a major metropolitan area and there resources were limited, the professionals investigating this disappearance were able to recognize factors that many jurisdictions working the cases in this book were unable to comprehend. The indicators of suspicious circumstances are present in many of the abductions. Sometimes, though, local law enforcement officers are too occupied with the fact that they found the victim to properly examine the circumstances surrounding the disappearance. It should also be noted that without spending years researching missing people events, the chances of recognizing recurring factors are slim.

The person who could probably answer almost every question about this disappearance—Roy Rosin—is reluctant to talk. Roy knew exactly where to look, when to look, and to go alone. Why would he say he knew there was danger associated with going to the location where he found Betty, and state that he knew he might come back battered? If Roy had these feelings, why not take a battalion of RCMP to defend you and ensure the release of Betty? It was Roy's knowledge of his property and the region that gave him the knowledge that led to Betty's discovery.

Farmers know their land like you and I know the insides of our homes. The farmer is on his land every day of his life; it's his job to know what's on it and when there are threats to his livestock and crops. I believe that Roy was a very, very smart man. He knew that taking other people to get Betty would cause further harm and disruption than going alone. Roy was probably seen daily by the person or people who had Betty. Anyone seeing Roy on the land wouldn't be surprised or shocked, and if Roy had an agreement with whomever occupied that location, he probably knew he was either going to easily retrieve Betty or die trying.

I believe that Roy was a good man, a man who probably told the RCMP an incredible story. The reluctance of the RCMP to share a witness/hero's story is not just unusual but something I had never seen or read.

In the articles I found, there is no mention of whether or not the Wolfrums stayed on their property and continued to farm.

Chapter Summary

The province of Manitoba is huge. The fact that all the missing persons in Manitoba who meet the criteria of this book disappeared in a six-year window—three of those in a twenty-seven-month period—is truly astonishing. What was happening in this region from 1934 to 1940 and then suddenly stopped?

Saskatchewan

Saskatchewan Missing Person List by Date

Missing Person	Date Missing•Age•Sex
Eddie Hamilton*	07/06/28•2•M
Richard Spyglass	08/05/64•5•M
Ashley Krestianson	07/14/94•8•F
Raymond Tunnicliffe*	08/26/02•79•M

*Details on the disappearances of Eddie Hamilton and Raymond Tunnicliffe can be found in the "Berry Pickers" chapter of *Book#2, Missing 411: Eastern United States.*

Richard Spyglass
Missing: 08/05/64, 7:00 p.m., Mosquito Indian Reserve, Saskatchewan, Ontario
Age at disappearance: 5
Mute child

On August 5, 1964, Richard Spyglass was with a group of family members who were bailing hay on the Mosquito Indian Reserve approximately seventy miles northwest of Saskatoon. It was early evening when the group realized that Richard had disappeared. The men searched the fields and then expanded into the bogs and sloughs of the area. After a short time, local law enforcement was notified and they responded with twenty officers and search dogs.

The exact area of the search is twenty miles south of North Battleford. The area is swampy, with many lakes and dams. This area is one of the last in the region that hasn't been fully developed into a farming area. Searchers didn't believe Richard could have traveled far because of the thick brush and his young age.

Dozens of people searched for Richard and knew he couldn't speak; he was mute since birth. The searchers decided that since the boy could hear, they would constantly blasted a message calling for him. Unfortunately, this didn't work.

Almost twenty-four hours after Richard disappeared, Ted Menssa was working his farm 8½ miles to the north. Ted stated that there was a very old street near where he was working, and he saw the boy standing in the road, not saying anything. The boy was carrying a bottle of freshly picked berries. The farmer offered the boy some food but he refused it. Ted said the boy had a few scratches on his face, and he didn't say anything. Ted was later informed that the boy was a mute. Richard was found far outside the confines of the search area, and this shocked many of the searchers.

Case Summary

The first puzzling aspect of this case is that Richard was found carrying a bottle of freshly picked berries. The area where he went missing is extremely wild (without many residents). Where did he get the bottle and the berries? There isn't one SAR book anywhere that states that a five-year-old boy could wander 8½ miles through swamps and bush in a twenty-four-hour period. How did Richard manage to accomplish this? In the book *Lost Person Behavior* by Robert Koester, he states that a child between the ages of four and six will be found 95 percent of the time in less than a 5.1 mile radius from the point last seen.

In my humble opinion, there appears to be an inordinate amount of young children who go missing under the circumstances described in this book in which the children are suffering from some type of disability and cannot speak or are too young to describe what happened to them. Is this merely a coincidence?

Ashley Krestianson
Missing: 07/14/94, Tisdale, Saskatchewan, Ontario
Age at disappearance: 8
Blonde hair

Kelly Krestianson had taken her twin eight-year-old girls, Lindsay and Ashley, to the Barrier Chaparrel Vacation Ranch on the outskirts of Tisdale, Saskatchewan. Here is the description that the vacation ranch had on their Web site: "At Barrier Chaparral, a prairie ranch vacation combines wide open spaces with great natural beauty and physical activities that range from challenging to exhilarating. Guests enjoy the pristine prairie air and tranquil rural lifestyle as they join in trail rides, canoeing, fishing and trapshooting, plus rodeos and paw wows."

The ranch leverages the area history in regards to First Nations People.

On July 14, 1994, Kelly had to leave the ranch for a few hours to deliver Avon products to local farmers' and ranchers' wives. Lindsay and Ashley stayed at the ranch and visited with a local friend. The girls decided they would go horseback riding and would have a footrace back to the stables. Ashley told the girls that she knew a shortcut and raced off down another trail. Lindsay and their friend took the main trail and arrived at the stables. Ashley never arrived.

Lindsay quickly became worried and notified the ranch authorities. The ranch started a quick search and then notified local authorities and Ashley's dad, Buddy. Buddy worked for the Canadian Highway Authority in Tisdale and was quickly on the scene.

The RCMP responded immediately and in force. Within hours after arriving, RCMP officials had called for four additional cities to respond with their detachments. Within three days there were four airplanes, four canine teams, one army helicopter equipped with FLIR, and over five hundred searchers scouring the ranch for the young girl. The helicopter pilot conducted low flyovers through the area looking for a heat signature on the ground, but nothing was found after several days in the air.

The area around the ranch is very swampy, grassy, and at points, extremely thick with vegetation. It would be hard to imagine any young person making great progress through such a diverse and tough environment. One of the main issues hampering search efforts the first three days was that the area was hit by heavy rains, which obliterated tracks and reduced the scent in the air. The shortcut that Ashley had taken was a clear path, and a person would not be confused about which direction to take, this was a baffling point to investigators.

After two weeks of not finding any evidence of Ashley, the government called off their search. The termination of the search angered many residents, and a few continued with the SAR despite the government pulling all resources. The government's theory was that Ashley could not have survived in the elements for over two weeks.

It was during the second week in September, more than two months after Ashley disappeared, that a hunter stumbled upon the young girl's skeleton 3.125 miles east and 4.375 miles south of the guest ranch. The bones were found in a very rugged area of high grass and swamps.

The RCMP reported to the press that at the scene of the skeleton they found a pair of girl's shorts and one shoe. No shirt or other shoe was found, even though the RCMP did an extensive search of the area for evidence.

The RCMP also made a statement about the location of Ashley's remains. They hadn't searched the area on the ground because they never believed that Ashley could have gotten that far in those rugged conditions.

The search for Ashley Krestianson was described as the largest at the time in the history of Alberta. The province threw every available resource into this effort and still couldn't find the girl before it was too late. The province utilized the best search information and still didn't search far enough out to find Ashley.

The location of Ashley's body and the rationale behind why it was found there does not make sense. The circumstances are similar to the Kory Kelly case in Minnesota (See Missing-411 Eastern United States).

CONCLUSIONS

Significant Cases

All of the missing people in this book are significant and import-ant, and there have been many times when I've stopped reading and writing and paused to think about the many missing I've researched. It's troubling. Here I highlight a few cases that seem to have com-mon elements.

Bodies

The cases of Schleyer (Yukon), Huggan (Ontario), Atadero (Colorado), McCullar (Crater Lake), and Winters (Crater Lake, OR) seem to have similarities. In each of the five cases, the pants of the victim were found near the remains, yet major amounts of blood were not present on any clothing found. When you review each of these cases, there was controversy and questions about how they met their demise and the circumstances of their disappearance.

The other case that has similarities to the list above is the disap-pearance of Robert Springfield from Montana. The only body parts of Robert's that were found were a partial skull and femur. There is no rational explanation for what happened in any of these incidents. The local jurisdiction in the Robert Springfield case was suspicious of the find and called the FBI. It's also important to note that the specifics about each of these cases wouldn't have been revealed (excluding Huggan) without interviewing people directly related to the investigation or litigation paperwork filed with the courts (Springfield). It almost appears as though news services sometimes temper the story or don't ask specific questions in regards to the scene.

Scary Events

The cases listed below represent an incident where the children screamed or yelled and then disappeared. Think through this clearly: children do not disappear and they do not run off and vanish—period. If there is a child's scream in conjunction with a disappearance, I think it's a rational assumption that they were confronted with something they could not overcome and they were deathly afraid. There were witnesses nearby in each of these incidents which did hear the scream. If a bear or mountain lion attacked these individuals there would be a bloody scene with torn clothing and evidence of a struggle, this wasn't the case. In each of these incidents the victim was somehow quickly taken from the scene.

08/04/32, Wesley Piatote (7), Nespelem, Washington

Picking huckleberries with his mother when they became separated. The mom hears Wesley scream two times and then he disappears. Wesley is never found. This story is found in the second book of this series, *Missing 411: Eastern United States.*

09/05/35, Jack Pike (5), Saint Norbert, Manitoba

Boy was with his family picking blueberries when his parents hear a scream and the boy disappears. Jack is found days later semiconscious and later dies.

This story can be found in the second book of this series, *Missing 411: Eastern United States.*

09/07/36, Harold King (3), Washburn, Wisconsin

The boy went missing from his rural home in Wisconsin. The third day of searching for the boy, searchers heard "wailing" coming from a swampy area three miles from the boy's home. He was later found in that same swamp, barely alive. This story can be found in the second book of this series, *Missing 411: Eastern United States.*

05/21/41, Eldridge Albright (3), Woodstock, Maryland

The boy was playing in a creek behind his rural home. His grandmother was on the back porch and heard a series of screams getting further and further away. The boy disappeared. Almost two days after the boy vanished, he was found. Eldridge either couldn't remember or wouldn't say what happened to him. This story can be found in the second book of this series, *Missing 411: Eastern United States.*

12/01/46, Paula Welden (18), Bennington, Vermont
Paula went hiking in an area that was rural and rugged but known for hiking. At about the time the girl went missing, other hikers heard a female scream in an area near swamps next to the mountains. This story can be found in the second book of this series, *Missing 411: Eastern United States.*

05/05/50, Anna Thorpe (2), Dunbar, Pennsylvania
Anna was playing in the backyard of her rural home when her mom heard a sharp scream. She ran to the backyard but the girl was gone. An extensive search found the girl three miles from her residence in the middle of a blackberry bush. This story can be found in the second book of this series, *Missing 411: Eastern United States.*

10/19/73, Jimmy Duffy (2), Wenatchee Lake, Washington
Sleeping in a camper shell, parents hear a scream and run to the truck. The boy is never found.

Proximity to Parents
There are eleven cases of missing children from Washington under the age of ten listed in this book. The Piatote (7), Duffy (2), Goodwin (8), and Panknin (4) cases from Washington all have eerily strange similarities. Each of these represents a boy who went missing in the woods in proximity to his parents. The Goodwin and Panknin cases were only three months apart. The Goodwin and Piatote cases both occurred in August. Are these coincidences? If you look at the entire United States, there are many cases in which a small boy disappeared while in proximity to a parent and was never found.

Elevation and Distance

Some of the stories I found defy common sense and logic with regards to elevation and distance. When we normally think of a missing child, we tend to believe they wander a short distance away and are found sitting on a rock around the next bend of the trail.

07/02/38, Albert Beilhartz (4), Rocky Mountain National Park, Colorado

Albert disappeared during a holiday trip with his parents. The boy was walking with family when he somehow went missing. NPS officials diverted and drained a river but didn't find the boy. A witness reported seeing a young boy high up a mountain, miles from where Albert disappeared. The witness stated that the boy could not have arrived in the area without assistance. Searchers scoured the mountain but never found Albert. Who took the child to the location where the witness saw him?

11/10/38, Jerry Hayes (5), Rucker Canyon, Arizona

The boy supposedly wandered away from a hunting camp occupied by his parents. Nine days after he went missing, Jerry was found 4½ miles from camp and one thousand feet uphill on a mountain. The boy's shoes and socks had disappeared and were never found. He had died of exposure.

02/07/42, Ronald McGee (2), Congress, Arizona

Ronald disappeared from an area behind his home. Four days after the boy vanished, searchers tracked him up a mountain four hundred feet in elevation and twelve miles away. The boy was found deceased with many scratches and horrible tears on his body.

10/30/45, Mike McDonald (2), Sulphur Springs, Arizona

Mike left his yard with his dog and disappeared. Twenty-four hours later and an amazing fifteen miles away, two cowboys saw the boy's dog sitting on a dirt mound. Under the mound in a small cave, they found Mike alive. Nobody understands how he found the cave or how he arrived at that location.

04/10/52, Keith Parkins (2), Ritter, Oregon

Keith was visiting his grandparents farm in the hills of Oregon when he somehow managed to disappear. Nineteen hours later, a searcher found the boy in a creek bed twelve miles from the farm. The boy was unconscious and lying on dry rocks. He had climbed two mountains and over numerous fences to reach the location where he was found. Newspaper articles stated that the boy must have ran nonstop for twelve hours to get there. How is this possible?

07/13/57, David Allen Scott (2), Mono Village, California

David was camping with his parents on the eastern slopes of the Sierra Nevada when he wandered away. Searchers combed the area, exhausted all leads, and started to search up hills. Four days after David disappeared, searchers climbed three thousand feet uphill from the campsite, over a mountain, then slightly uphill on another mountain where, amongst boulders, they found David's body. The boy was wearing one sock and a t-shirt. No pants and no shoes were found. David had allegedly died of exposure. How is this possible for a two-year-old?

08/22/63, Donald Griffen (4), Huntington Lake, California

Donald was camping near a lake with his family when he vanished. Four days later, searchers found the boy deceased on a freshly fallen pine tree limb. He was six miles from the campsite and three thousand feet higher in elevation. Searchers were shocked the boy could have gotten that far. It's interesting to note the similarities between the Griffen and Scott cases: both in California, both in the Sierras, both found over three thousand feet uphill from the point last seen.

06/24/93, Kenny Miller (12), Meiss Meadows, north of Yosemite, California

Kenny was hiking with his parents when they got separated and he went missing. He was found deceased ten days later 2½ miles from the point he was last seen and 1,400 feet higher in elevation. The boy was found without shoes or socks in an area where it had been snowing.

10/02/99, Jaryd Atadero (3), Comanche Peak Wilderness, Colorado
    Jaryd disappeared while hiking a well-known and easily iden-
tified trail with a group of adults. The boy asked two fishermen if
there are bear in the area—the last time anyone saw him. Four years
later, Jaryd's skull and one tooth are found high off the trail in an
area investigators don't believe he could have reached alone.

    I've raised two children and been around many kids during my
life. Some of the distances and elevations allegedly covered by the
young kids listed above are hard to believe. Two-year-olds have
just learned to walk, yet we are led to believe they can walk fifteen
mountain miles in twenty-four hours.

High Elevation Disappearances
    There are several cases highlighted in this book involving
climbers that are above ten thousand feet and seem to vanish. If the
reader is not familiar with fauna and landscape, then it's important
to understand that once a hiker reaches the Alpine region (generally
above eight thousand feet elevation in North America), trees are no
longer present. If there are no more trees, then there are far few-
er places to hide. If someone disappears above eight thousand feet,
then they should be fairly easy to locate.
    In recent times the disappearances of Carl Landers (Mount Shas-
ta, 1999) and Michelle Vanek (Colorado, 2005) are truly puzzling.
Canines couldn't pick up their scents, there were no witnesses (even
though other climbers were on the mountain at the same time), and
nobody saw them descend. Both of the mountains they were on were
over fourteen thousand feet in elevation and both individuals disappeared above timberline. In each case there were extensive searches
but nothing was ever found that belonged to either climber. How is
this possible?

National Park Service

From the onset of this project, I looked to the National Park Service for missing person statistics, numbers, copies of case files, and general assistance on information in their system. They were the only U.S. organization I targeted that was required by FOIA law to release data when requested (cities and states are not covered by this federal law). The NPS has a large law enforcement branch that has experience in SAR and criminal investigations. The NPS actually has special agents assigned as investigators at many of their parks. It would be incorrect to state that the NPS had not cooperated with my efforts to acquire information; however, in some cases they were evasive.

Early in my FOIA process, I requested a list of all missing people inside the NPS system. I asked for the location, date, and a short paragraph of the circumstances of each disappearance. Since I was a published author of two books, I requested an author's exemption for the costs associated with the FOIA. I had felt that this FOIA would be fairly easy because it was a straightforward request for data that every state and local law enforcement department keeps.

I was told that my books were not in enough libraries to qualify for the author's exemption. I spent a week looking for this qualification in any FOIA literature and found none. This was an arbitrary act on the part of an NPS attorney to force me to pay for all FOIA inquiries, and an obvious move to dissuade me from asking for missing person information.

The NPS responded by stating that they *do not* track missing people. They do not keep missing people lists at any location (including individual parks); thus any list would have to be developed from scratch. They confirmed multiple times that they *did not* maintain a master list of all missing people in their system.

The attorney-advisor for NPS said they do not have a computer system that would allow them to query for "missing persons" and the NPS would need to hand-search each of their files in the 392 National Park Service units in order to develop a master list. The letter estimated that it would take 47,000 hours to accommodate my request. Some of the searching could be done by a GS-5 clerical staff at the rate of $24 per hour, but the majority of the work would need to be done by a GS-9 professional at $42 per hour. If I take a midpoint between $24 and $42, this would be $33. Multiply $33 by 47,000 hours and you get the cost for the NPS to produce a list of missing people in their jurisdiction: $1,551,000. No, this starving author could not afford that figure for the NPS to do their own job. To serve as a gauge as to how long 47,000 hours actually is, there are 2,080 working hours in a year (tabulating eight hours per day and five days per week).

The NPS says they do not have the functional capability to query any computer system in their organization and find out who went missing at their properties. How is this possible? They have stated that they do not keep lists of missing people at each of the parks where the incidents occurred. If a body turns up twenty years after someone goes missing in a specific valley, how would anyone know who this person might be?

I then focused my energy in obtaining a list of missing people from Yosemite National Park. The NPS again confirmed that there was no national repository in their system that contained missing people information. They stated that they had had discussions with their national headquarters and confirmed that this information was not maintained or tracked.

On October 29, 2010, I received an e-mail from Charis Wilson, the NPS FOIA director for the western United States. She confirmed that Yosemite did not have any lists of missing people. Charis communicated that Yosemite staff would have to hand-search documents starting with the inception of the park, October 1, 1890. The park estimated it would take 352 hours of work by a GS-5 and 700 hours by a GS-9 to develop a list of missing people in Yosemite. The grand total would be $37,848.

It took three years to complete this book, and during that time I had many conversations with law enforcement friends, and several were top administrators in their departments. None of my friends believed the NPS wasn't tracking missing people. Each of these top administrators stated that this information is something that all law enforcement agencies must track and monitor to understand and evaluate—the public would demand this. Many of my friends encouraged me to visit my local member of Congress and start legislative action against the NPS to initiate the tracking process on missing people and make the data available to the public. Imagine if it were your son or daughter who went missing in a national park and they had no list of the missing people where your child disappeared.

Some of you may be wondering why the NPS is claiming they don't have this data. I believe they do have the data, and that the data they possess would shock the average American citizen. I wasn't able to gather every missing person report in the parks I wrote about, but even without every case, the number of missing I discovered was staggering. I believe it's a matter of dollars and cents. The NPS is concerned about releasing their data because it could cause negative press, and concerned citizens may choose not to visit national parks, meaning less revenue.

Michael Ghiglieri and Butch Farabee authored a book titled *Off the Wall: Death in Yosemite*. Their book contains 608 pages about deaths, missing people, and murders inside Yosemite National Park. It offers the reader an insider's look at the multitude of serious incidents that have occurred at Yosemite. It's staggering. Butch Farabee had an inside track to the information because he was a long-term employee in Yosemite. I had a conversation with him about the NPS's refusal to supply reports on the Stacy Arras case. He couldn't understand why they were refusing.

Advisory: Don't ever hold the rank and file employees at the NPS accountable for what you have learned through this book. The employees of the park service who have contact with the public are outstanding individuals and love their jobs. It is the NPS administrators—those you never see—who make public policy. It is those public policy officials that should be held accountable by every citizen in the United States as to why missing people are not tracked inside their parks.

In my book on missing people for the eastern United States, *Missing 411: Eastern United States*, I provide an extensive list of children missing from the Great Smoky Mountains National Park and discuss their disappearances. There are many other children from other national parks, but one missing girl from Yosemite National Park still haunts me: Stacy Arras, 14, missing July 17, 1981.

I sent an e-mail to Charis Wilson asking why Stacy Arras was not listed in the National Center for Missing and Exploited Children. The response was shocking. I was informed that the NPS does not list children if they disappeared before the federally mandated date of required reporting—1984. There are many, many, many children listed in the national center database who went missing before 1984. Every family of every missing child should demand that there son or daughter be listed in that database.

After hearing stories of adults who suspected they may have been abducted as a child, many of those same people checked the database and discovered they were under another name. The National Center for Missing Children is a valuable resource that needs to be utilized to its maximum potential. The exclusion of these children by the NPS is a calculated decision to keep these cases from public view. Remember, the NPS refused to disclose any case reports on Stacy Arras, another prime example of their resolve to keep this information away from the public. But why? What is in the Arras file that the NPS feels we should not see?

Next Steps

I hope this book has raised your awareness of missing people in the western United States and Canada. The second book in this series, *Missing 411: Eastern United States*, is equally compelling and enlightening as it puts the frame around the window to this story. The eastern United States edition also includes the following lists, with each group of missing people itemized and extensively analyzed:

Missing Children Under Ten Years of Age, The Master List
Missing Adults: The Master List

The two books were originally one very large manuscript, but it had to be split. The issues that I have highlighted in this edition are again brought to the reader with different geographical circumstances, in different states, and with different clusters, but under equally suspicious circumstances. One state in the eastern United States has more children missing than any other state I have researched, and no other state comes close. That's Pennsylvania, and you can read about those incidents in the eastern United States edition.

Before you arrive at any conclusions about the missing person issue, please read the eastern United States edition of this book to fully understand how different geography can impact these highly unusual disappearances.

Always walk in pairs when you are hiking, and please carry a personal transponder.

You can contact me anytime at Missing411@yahoo.com.

INDEX